BABY
WARS

ALSO BY DR. ROBIN BAKER

Sperm Wars: The Science of Sex

BABY WARS

The Dynamics of Family Conflict

*by Dr. Robin Baker
and Elizabeth Oram*

THE ECCO PRESS

First published in Great Britain in 1998 by Fourth Estate Limited
Copyright 1998 © by Dr. Robin Baker and Elizabeth Oram

THE ECCO PRESS
100 West Broad Street
Hopewell, New Jersey 08525

Printed in the United States of America

Library of Congress Cataloging-in-Publication Data
Baker, Robin, 1944–
Baby wars : the dynamics of family conflict / Robin
Baker and Elizabeth Oram. — 1st ed.
p.   cm.
Originally published : London : Fourth Estate, 1998.
Includes bibliographical references.
ISBN 0-88001-658-2
1. Family. 2. Parenthood. 3. Interpersonal
conflict. 4. Evolution (Biology)—Social aspects.
5. Human reproduction—Social aspects. I. Oram,
Elizabeth. II. Title.
HQ728.B35   1999
306.85—dc21   98-35619
CIP
9 8 7 6 5 4 3 2 1

FIRST EDITION 1999

To Nat and Mimi

Contents

Acknowledgements

This book is a collection of scenes illustrating different aspects of parenthood and family life, each followed by a discussion of the behaviour of the scene's main characters. The aim is to highlight the many interesting and new ideas that have recently been generated by evolutionary biology, but to do so in a way that will be intelligible to a lay audience. Such a book could not have been written without the ground-breaking research carried out by huge numbers of scientists. We have opted, though, not to load the pages with footnotes and references, so our major acknowledgement must go to all of those unnamed people whose research or insight has contributed in any way, large or small, to the ideas and stories presented in these pages. For the sake of those readers who might wish to pursue matters further, there is a list of further reading at the end of the book. Wherever possible, we have limited the list to books that are readily accessible, rather than to research papers and the like.

We gratefully acknowledge the support we have received from our publishers from the earliest stages of planning and writing. Christopher Potter of Fourth Estate, UK publisher of the year in 1996, believed in the project from the start, and gave us the encouragement that we needed to see us through the long months of research and writing. Laura Susijn, also, played a key role in winding up our motivation and getting us started; now working for our agents, Sheil Land Associates, she has continued to provide helpful insight, advice and encouragement.

Finally, I, RRB, would like to thank the School of Biological Sciences at the University of Manchester, who in late September 1996 accepted at what must be record short notice my request for early retirement on 1 October that same year, so that I could concentrate on a career in writing. It took a great deal of effort and organisation on the part of several people, Dr Ron Butler in particular, to make my departure possible. Special mention should also go to Chris Bainbridge and Charlie Nicholls who have the dubious distinction of being my last ever research students. Not only did they accept with magnanimity my sudden disappearance and hence reduced supervision, they also volunteered to shoulder the main burden of supervising those undergraduate research projects for which I continued to be responsible.

We thank them all. Without their help this book would have taken many months longer to write.

Introduction

Parenthood and family life affect everybody. Moreover, most people, first as children and then twenty or thirty years later as parents themselves, undergo both sides of the experience. Many will have fond memories of family life, and many will have memories that they prefer to forget. Neither childhood nor parenthood is easy, and from time to time even in the most tranquil of families the stresses and strains of everyday life rise to the surface. In fact, for some people, family life is nothing short of a running battle. To a greater or lesser extent, *babies* mean *wars* in all families.

When family strife surfaces, many people are tempted to blame themselves – or their partner, parents or grandparents – suspecting an element of inadequacy. But as this book will show, internal conflicts are a normal, inevitable and important feature of parenthood and family life: without conflict, most people would gain less from the experience. This paradox is one of the major themes of the book.

In *Baby Wars*, as in the earlier *Sperm Wars* which dealt with human sexual behaviour, each topic to be discussed is first illustrated by a short scene in the style of a fictionalised case-study. Each scene shows people experiencing a phase of childhood or adulthood in which a particular aspect is highlighted, and is then followed by an interpretation of the behaviour shown by the scene's main characters. The subjects we cover range from the commonplace, such as conception campaigns, pregnancy sickness, pain during labour and sleepless nights, to the illegal, such as incest and child abuse.

As in *Sperm Wars*, the theoretical and philosophical perspective of the discussions is that of the evolutionary biologist. Such a perspective is the most basic, for it seeks to explain the evolutionary origin of all facets of the human condition, of which parental behaviour and family life are just two. Other scientific disciplines

xi

– biology, medicine, psychology, sociology and anthropology, for example – accept that humans have a particular anatomy, body chemistry and behaviour, then seek causal links and connections from there upwards. In contrast, evolutionary biology is interested in the shaping of the genetic programming that produces that anatomy, that body chemistry and that behaviour in the first place.

The technique of evolutionary biology is very simple. Whatever aspect of human behaviour is being discussed, the evolutionary biologist looks first to see what repercussions the behaviour has for a person's reproductive output, sometimes termed reproductive success. The expectation is that any behaviour that occurs widely will be found to enhance a person's reproductive success. This sounds straightforward enough but, as will be revealed in the course of this book, the way that behaviour might enhance reproduction is not always obvious. The challenge facing the evolutionary biologist is to explain it. Having done so, he or she appraises the explanation in the context of ancestral human environments – which is where and when the modern human condition evolved – and then in the context of other animals. If the same behaviour is found in a wide range of human cultures and in other animals, and if in all situations the way it enhances reproductive success is the same, then the evolutionary biologist can usually rest assured that the explanation is justified. And he or she can usually assume, too, that the chemical, neural and cerebral basis for the behaviour has been programmed into the human genetic makeup by the evolutionary process.

It became evident from the media and popular response to *Sperm Wars* that for many people the major revelation in the book was the suggestion that even as complex a behaviour as sexual activity could be programmed by natural selection. We suspect that readers' response to *Baby Wars* may well be similar. But important though that point is, it would be a pity if the book's contribution to people's way of thinking about parenthood ended there. Much of the fascination of the evolutionary biologist's analysis of parental behaviour derives from the completely new light it throws on the behaviour and situations that are within everybody's experience. Why do women suffer pregnancy sickness? Why is a baby's cry such a stressful sound? Why do brothers and sisters disagree so often? Why do adolescents rebel and suffer wanderlust? The answers to such questions are fascinating in themselves, as well as being part of the overall picture of the evolution of human parental behaviour.

Not surprisingly, the thinking that underpins the approach of the evolutionary biologist is the Darwinian theory of evolution by natural selection. We do not mean here evolution in the sense that has been the focus of innumerable philosophical treatises on the meaning of life. The natural selection at the heart of this book is not open to such philosophical argument. In fact, it is scarcely even biological: it is simple mathematics, and as such it is closed to argument.

The principle is this. *If* some instance of behaviour has a genetic element *and if* individuals possessing one form of the gene in question have on average a greater reproductive success than those possessing other forms, then *with the certainty of mathematics* the population will eventually come to be dominated by individuals possessing the most successful form of the gene. Most of us are the descendants of the people who reproduced most successfully in their generation. Few of us are the descendants of those who reproduced less successfully. And, obviously, none of us are the descendants of those who did not reproduce at all. As parental behaviour is such an important part of reproductive success in humans, then the vast majority in our generation are bound to be the descendants of past generations' best parents.

This principle is irrefutable and should be widely embraced as part of popular culture, yet it is not. And the main reason seems to be emotional rather than cerebral. Whereas more and more people are beginning to realise that their anatomy and various medical conditions are the product of their genes, most find it very difficult to accept that the way they *behave* might have anything to do with genes. They have no difficulty in believing that the colour of their eyes, their hair and their skin is determined for them at conception by the genes they inherit from their parents, and many are also familiar with the fact that many diseases – breast cancer and cystic fibrosis, for example – can be inherited from their parents. So why is it that most of us continue to be resistant to the idea that our behaviour might also be dependent on the genes we inherit from our ancestors?

Research is increasingly showing that behaviour is under genetic influence, even control. For example, a man's sexual appetite, predisposition to promiscuity and so on, as well as his level of aggression, are a function of how much testosterone and other androgens his body produces. This, in part, depends on the size of his testes, and testis size is under genetic control. Take, as another example, bisexuality. The evidence that it is genetically inherited is now so overwhelming that prejudice can be the only reason for objecting to the idea. Many mental conditions are now thought to be genetic – schizophrenia, for example. So, too, is a predisposition to alcoholism. Tens of millions of Americans, particularly those of American Indian or Japanese ancestry but some of European as well, have a genetic inability to deal with alcohol. And geneticists are now concluding that there are even genes for violent and antisocial behaviour.

One of the obstacles to the acceptance of a genetic basis for behaviour is that we often don't appreciate how much of our behaviour is driven chemically rather than cerebrally. We tend to assume that our brains are in control, simply because that is how it feels. But research is making it increasingly obvious that this is not the case. Ask someone suffering from the depths of clinical depression how much mental control he has over his thoughts and behaviour. Ask the same of someone suffering from SAD (seasonally affective disorder – depression due to low exposure to sunlight). The answer will be very clear – none. And the fact is that both owe their despair to a low level of one chemical or another (serotonin, for example) in the brain. The precise nature of their feelings depends on which chemical and which part of the brain is most affected. Or ask a woman how much control she has over her mood at different stages of her menstrual cycle. Similar answer. And the reason is that all of her changes in mood and behaviour are chemically induced, by hormones, the production of which is genetically controlled.

Even those who do accept that their anatomy, body chemistry and behaviour have a genetic basis still often find it difficult to accept that they have no control over their genes. They feel uneasy with any suggestion that they are simply a chassis for their genetic engine. Or even if they don't mind being a chassis, they at least want to think that they are also the driver. Of course, in one sense people *are* the vehicle for their genes: they carry them from place to place and drop off copies of them – in sperm or eggs – at various stops through life's journey. But it is the genes themselves that are their own drivers. It is they that orchestrate a person's development from fertilised egg to adult. It is they that determine what sex a person should be, what he, if male, should look like, how he should be put together, how his brain should be wired up, which hormones he should have and in what quantities – and, consequently, how he should behave. It is the genes, even, that construct the chassis that carries them around. Like it or not, there is no escaping the conclusion that *behaviour is orchestrated by genes*.

This does not mean, of course, that environment and experience do not also play a part. The brain is wired up and programmed by genes to remember past experiences and, when placed in a novel situation, to make use of those past experiences in order to decide on a suitable course of action. If this course of action works out badly, then the brain is programmed to remember and not to make the same mistake next time. Genes even programme the brain, early on in life, to make fine adjustments to its 'wiring' in response to its early experiences.

Most of the time, the human body goes about the business of organising its life without bothering the brain, leaving it free to do what it does best, monitoring and remembering what can be seen, smelt, and so on. The brain is also programmed to remember where we are, where we put things, who we are with, and how to get from one place to another. It does its best to make sure we don't get eaten by a tiger or walk under a bus. These tasks are the brain's forte, and the less it is bothered by bodily matters, the better it performs. Occasionally, however, the body has no option but to consult the brain.

Take as an example the fact that the body needs refuelling from time to time. What happens is that it generates a feeling of hunger, and often, after checking its current chemistry and working out what proteins, vitamins or whatever are in short supply, it generates a *specific* hunger. It produces a thought in the conscious mind that, say, maybe a banana would be a good idea. No, not an apple – a banana. At its best with tasks like this, the brain now tries to remember – or, failing that, work out – where it might find the nearest banana, given the body's location, the time of day and so on. Of course, the brain thinks the whole business of wanting a banana is its own idea, but it isn't. The urge for a banana is the consequence of the body carrying out millions of chemical checks, following a set of instructions laid down in the first instance by the genes. It was the genes, also, that fixed how low banana chemicals could get in the body before it should tell the brain to find one. The only time the process works slightly differently is when opportunism comes into play. The eyes spot a banana nearby, the brain tells the body, the body does a quick check of its chemical reserves and says, 'Yes, we'll soon be low on banana chemicals – eat the banana,' or 'No, we've got plenty. Leave it, but if you see an apple . . .'

Sex, parenthood and all other aspects of behaviour work in the same way as hunger. The genes provide the instructions, the body carries them out and, when necessary, calls on the brain to remember or calculate how best to do what has to be done. In their turn, our genes have been fashioned by the way natural selection has treated our ancestors, whether it's a question of the way we behave as parents, lovers, scholars, warriors or competitors, or any other aspect of life. And it is because our genes and body chemistry, rather than our brains, control our behaviour that most of this book is concerned with behaviour that is driven *subconsciously*. We pay very little attention to people's conscious rationalisation of *why* they do what they do. Evolutionary biology is concerned with *what people actually do*, rather than with what they think, say, or feel. And in particular, in this book, we are concerned with the way people's behaviour influences their reproductive success.

People are subconsciously programmed for parenthood. More-over, as we noted earlier, they are programmed to be good and successful parents. Why? Because over the past few millennia, those who were not good parents, or who never became parents, left few or no descendants to inherit their characteristics. And as the product of generations of successful parents, we all carry around with us the genes that push us into becoming parents in our turn. These genes prepare us for parenthood when we are young, lead us through the parental maze in our middle years, and predispose us to reflect on our parental successes and failures when we are old. Of course, many who read this book will not – or not yet – be parents. Many of these will say, perhaps adamantly, that it is not a role they seek, while others will desperately want to become parents but, at least for the moment, be unable to do so. And all of them may say that their example contradicts the suggestion that people are programmed for parenthood. But as we shall see, people who avoid or miss out on parenthood are as much a part of the story as those 'earth mothers' and fathers with children running into double figures.

People vary in their programming, in their genetic *strategies*, for parenthood. This variation is not only fascinating, it is also the raw material on which natural selection continues to act in the modern generation. Some genetic programmes work better than others, so some people are more successful parents than others.

To the evolutionary biologist parenthood is a contest – a contest between genes. Of course, we do not see the genes competing. What we see instead is a competition between people, between individuals – but its the same thing. In each generation, genes get packaged together in different combinations, each bundle being an individual person. Each gene's quest is to become packaged together with other genes to produce a person who is reproductively so successful that every gene in the bundle receives a major boost in its attempt to multiply – and to multiply down the generations. From this perspective, each package – each individual person – is a genetic experiment. In every generation, some of these experiments are very successful, some moderately so, and some are downright failures.

Before we go any further, we need to look at this question of difference. How is it that if natural selection has been rigorously favouring the most successful behaviour in each generation, people do not all behave in the same way – and perfectly? There are, in fact, many reasons why evolution does *not* work in this way, but first it is important to separate out two completely different aspects of the process. The first concerns an evolutionary mechanism: under some circumstances, natural selection predisposes different people to behave differently, but in such a way that they all reproduce equally well. The second is a feature of the evolutionary process: natural selection finds it very difficult to shape a perfect response, with the result that people behave differently, and some are more successful than others.

First, let's consider the fact that natural selection shapes people to behave differently in order to succeed equally well. For example, *Sperm Wars* discussed in detail why some people are heterosexual, some homosexual, some bisexual, while others are prostitutes, yet others rapists – and all of them are manifestations of different ways of pursuing reproductive success, with their own particular advantages and disadvantages. Very often, the success of any given course of action depends on what proportion of people pursue that course and it is evolution that fixes the proportions. Moreover, it fixes the proportions of people who behave in each different way at just those levels at which every strategy has the same average reproductive success. Indeed, the human population consists of myriads of individuals who, while all in subconscious pursuit of reproductive success, are each employing a strategy that may differ considerably from the strategies employed by those around them. As often as not, therefore, evolution generates *genetic differences*, rather than exact similarities, between individuals.

A second factor that accounts for people succeeding equally well by behaving differently is that natural selection shapes people to alter their behaviour to suit their circumstances – to employ *conditional strategies*. We are genetically programmed to check our situation, then behave accordingly. This means that different people behave differently because their circumstances differ, but all are behaving in the most appropriate way for their situation. An observer might easily be misled, of course, into thinking that conditional strategies are not genetic at all, that people's behaviour is determined entirely by their environment. But the fact is that the instructions first to check the situation and then to respond accordingly are programmed just as rigorously and genetically as any other strategy.

Now let's move on to the fact that natural selection finds it very difficult to design a perfect response. There are several reasons for this. The first is that it cannot easily get rid of genes that are only slightly less successful than their rivals. Such genes will, inevitably, slowly decline over the generations, but it can take many thousands of years for an only slightly inferior gene to disappear completely. Meanwhile, people inherit these less successful ones from their less successful ancestors – and behave less successfully than their more fortunate contemporaries.

New genes arise by mutation, and the mutation rate is low. But since we contain so many genes, it is not surprising that many of us harbour one, or even several, newly mutated genes that have arisen either in us or in our parents or grandparents. Most of these mutations probably make little difference to the way we function or behave, but occasionally a mutation will occur that causes us – and, therefore, our descendants – great problems. Perhaps even more occasionally a mutation may actually be an improvement on what existed before and may give us and our descendants an edge over our contemporaries. Natural selection will then propel that gene into an ever greater proportion of the population in future generations. But as far as a gene for the perfect strategy is concerned, unless it arises through mutation in the first place natural selection cannot produce later generations who have a perfect strategy. In the meantime, since it can only act on the best of the genes available to it, even the most successful people are not strategically perfect.

We have said that people's behaviour is not determined by their environment, but environment does have an important role to play. And another reason why we do not all behave perfectly is that environments differ, both geographically and historically. Genes and behaviour that were hugely successful at one place and time may struggle for survival at another. Half a million years ago, humans were largely naked hunters of animals and gatherers of fruit, nuts and roots. Many of the genes we possess today were carried down the ages high on the wave of their success at out-competing other genes in that particular environment. Since then, many human cultures have passed through tens of thousands of years of wearing at least some clothes, and ten to fifteen thousand years of herding animals and growing crops. Recently, many others have also passed through a few hundred years of industrialisation. Of course, some genes will have been successful in all of these situations, and it will be those that most of us possess today. Other genes will have had their heyday in hunter-gatherer or agriculturist times and will have struggled ever since and be on the decline. Those of us who still possess those genes don't find it as easy as others do to compete in the modern environment.

It may be that only a minority of us possess genes, some of them perhaps very recent mutations, that suit us to the modern industrial environment, and such genes may be widely scattered and diverse. One person, for example, may have a gene that empowers his lungs to cope with breathing polluted atmospheres but also one that makes him react badly to man-made chemicals. Another may have genes that make her resistant to modern sexually transmitted diseases, but another that gives her a drug-dependent psychology that prohibits her from reproducing. It will be a long time before the genes that are best for life in a modern environment become common enough for the majority of people to have them all – and by then the environment will probably have changed yet again. *Evolution may chase perfection, but rarely has time to achieve it.*

The final reason that we do not all function perfectly as a consequence of evolution is that it is not acting on us alone – it is also acting on our biological rivals. It is gradually being discovered that, to a surprising degree, our success at everything from simple survival to the intricacies of attracting a mate depends on our genetic resistance to disease. It depends on how well our genes cope during our childhood and adolescence with the myriad of disease organisms that are constantly attacking us. These organisms, ranging from viruses and bacteria to tapeworms and other parasites, are constantly trying to use our bodies for their own growth, survival and reproduction. Some of the diseases that they cause are obvious, such as measles. Others are less obvious, giving symptoms so subliminal we never even notice them. Yet all can reduce our vigour, make us more accident-prone, affect our fertility, and our attractiveness. People whose genes are particularly resistant to these diseases achieve greater reproductive success than the rest.

In each generation, the most successful diseases are those that can outmanoeuvre people's genes and physiology. No sooner does natural selection start to favour a human gene that conveys resistance to a particular disease, than it also favours a gene in that disease organism that is unaffected by human resistance. Occasionally, parasites become extinct, evolutionarily outmanoeuvred by their hosts; occasionally, hosts become extinct, outmanoeuvred by their parasites. Most of the time, however, host and parasite are locked in an evolutionary arms race, each trying to produce the perfect gene to finish off the other's resistance, but in the meantime coexisting in an uneasy balance in which each is suffering at the hands of the other. As a result, both organisms function imperfectly throughout life and throughout the generations.

The idea, sometimes encountered, that modern humans stand somehow outside of evolution, that natural selection is no longer acting on them, is a myth. Indeed, humans are as exposed to the forces of natural selection in the modern world as they have ever been – it is only the nature of those forces that has changed. Natural selection does not come to a stop for any species until the genetic contribution made to future generations by different individuals is numerically independent of the genes they themselves possess. This is far from being the case for modern humans. Those of us alive today will make a contribution to future generations that depends in large part on the genes we each carry. In just the same way that more of us today carry genes that were successful in past generations, so the most successful genes in *our* generation will numerically dominate the generations to come. This applies as much to parental behaviour as to anything else. There can be no argument over this, nor is there any room for sentiment – it is the harsh reality of basic mathematics.

CHAPTER ONE

Highs and Lows

SCENE 1
Real Soap

Even as he stood up to speak, there were tears in his eyes. Looking around at the people who had come to celebrate his son's coming of age, he knew that the emotion of the moment – and the lump in his throat – were in danger of ruining this, one of his proudest moments. He paused, then leaned forward to pick up his drink. The act of swallowing helped clear his throat, but even so, as he forced out his first words, his voice was unsteady.

He thanked the guests for coming to help him and his wife celebrate this special occasion. Half turning to her, smiling and radiant by his side, he told them what a wonderful partner and mother she had been. Moreover, beautiful as she had always been, never had she been more so than when pregnant with their son. Nor would he ever forget that magical moment when he held him in his arms for the first time.

His son had been a model child, he told the captivated audience. Always happy, always responsible, he had been a wonderful playmate, friend and helper to his younger sister. He turned to her, sitting by her brother's side. They were still inseparable friends.

In a final flurry of emotion, he praised his son's character yet again, drew attention to his good looks, then declared modestly that he didn't know what he had done to deserve two such wonderful children. He then asked the guests to join with him in drinking the health of his most cherished son.

There was scarcely a dry eye in the room as the son stood up to reply. More assured and marginally less emotional than his father, he too began by thanking the guests for coming to what for him too was a most special occasion. As he spoke, the eyes of many a young girl amongst his audience

1

betrayed their wish that he, or someone just like him, would sweep them off into a long and passionate relationship. He ended by turning to his parents and raising his glass. He thanked his father for being his friend and mentor, his mother for being always so serene and tolerant; he owed absolutely everything to them, their love and their constancy, he added. Echoing his father, he said that he too had no idea what he had done to deserve such wonderful parents, but he knew that in his life to come he wanted nothing more than to be just like them.

Scarcely had the credits begun to roll than the front door slammed to. The two viewers – a woman and her teenage daughter – just had time to exchange a look and laugh as they wiped away their tears, when a man's voice boomed out that there was mud all over the hall floor. Then the sitting-room door flew open and a large and very irate man stood framed in the doorway. There was mud all over the floor, he repeated, and what did they think they were doing, just sitting there *while there was mud all over the hall floor*? Suddenly recognising the theme music from the soap which was just ending, he ordered them to switch off 'that rubbish', but did it himself almost as he was speaking. Looming over the two women, he announced that they were idle and good for nothing, that they never did anything but sit in front of the box. Pointing in the direction of the muddy floor, he thundered on that their son was no better, that if he didn't start working soon he would never get anywhere, that only trouble could come from hanging around on street corners, and that he obviously got his character from his mother.

Emotionally charged by the programme she had just watched, the mother leaped to her feet. He was just as bad, she shouted back. He was lazier than any of them, and she knew damn well where their son got his laziness from. The daughter snapped at the pair of them not to start arguing yet again – she couldn't stand it, she screamed – and ran out of the room. The woman pointed out to her mate what his bad temper had done, said she wished she had never met him, then asked why he didn't go out and get drunk tonight, like he did every night. He stormed out of the room, muttering obscenities under his breath as he went.

As he opened the front door, his son brushed past him into the house without a word, ignoring his father's promise to murder him if he left any more mud on the floor. When his mother pointed out what trouble he had caused and yelled at him to clear up his mess, he swore at her and stamped upstairs, spreading yet more mud as he went.

As the mother threw herself on to the sofa, she heard her offspring quarrelling upstairs. She threw back her head and yelled – so loudly that it hurt her throat and chest – 'Will everybody just shut up, go away, and leave me in peace!'

The traditionally romantic view of parenthood is of a man and a woman in a long-term monogamous relationship working together to achieve a mutual aim, the producing and raising of a family. During pregnancy, the man is caring and attentive while the woman slowly swells, serenely waiting to give birth to the much longed-for baby. They then cherish and nurture each of their children, leading them happily and healthily through life and doing their best to encourage each child to realise his or her full potential. The children in their turn help each other and reward their parents' efforts with a continual show of gratitude and admiration for all that has been, and is being, done for them.

And of course, there are moments and situations when such romanticism is briefly realised. Every so often, even real people get a glimpse of the parental paradise portrayed on the television in the scene just depicted. But as all parents know, the day-to-day reality of parenthood and family life is very different. Pain and discomfort during pregnancy and labour, the difficulties of caring for babies and young children, arguments about and between children and the trials of adolescence are within every parent's experience. For some, parenthood may be a solitary affair and hence potentially even more difficult. For others, the nuclear family may give way to separation and step-parenthood. And for a few, potentially devastating problems such as incest, neglect, abuse or even murder may cloud their years as parents.

Most of the time, parenting does not involve extremes of emotions – it's more a pot-pourri of minor rewards and vexations. But almost any situation can escalate in a flash. It is as if family life is forever on a knife-edge. Those moments when parenthood is easy and rewarding can so readily metamorphose into nothing but conflict and worry.

Why should parenthood run along a knife-edge? Why should there be so many potential problems in something that is such an ancient and basic feature of human reproduction? Humans and their primate ancestors have been parenting now for so many millennia that we could perhaps be excused for expecting it all

3

to be plain sailing. But it is not – and the aim of this book is to explain, using the philosophical and scientific perspective of the evolutionary biologist, why it is not.

The short answer is that although both parents and children all stand to gain if everybody cooperates, they stand to gain even more if at the same time they can promote their own interests. As it turns out, almost every aspect of parenthood generates a biological conflict of interests, and it is this conflict that spawns the difficulties that all parents experience. The result is that babies mean wars – between mother and father, between parents and children, and between the children themselves.

Getting Started

SCENE 2
Conception Campaigns

It was late summer. The day had been hot, but as the couple left the bar to walk home, the air already had the damp chill of autumn. As long as they took the short cut across the park it was only half a mile – and walking instead of taking a taxi made them feel better about the fact that they had been drinking. They could even convince themselves that they were still taking their fitness regime seriously. It wasn't of the four-minute-mile, body-building type. In fact the woman, in particular, had been warned to avoid excessive exercise. It was more the anti-flab, 'wouldn't it be good to be able to run up the stairs and whistle at the same time?' type. Walking home from an evening at the local bar was just about right.

After a few hundred metres along poorly lit streets, they turned off the road through a gate and set off across the park that in daylight was a green oasis in a brick and concrete desert. Tonight, not only did the poor lighting turn the green to black, but the cool air had produced a narrow shroud of mist that hovered above the grass to about knee height.

The shortest route across the park took them through a children's playground. Fenced off, to keep children in and dogs out, access was through a badly hung gate that dragged over the ground as they opened it. The woman couldn't resist a few goes on the swing, and when they reached the roundabout she got on and asked him to push her. With the cool air brushing past, she felt exhilarated, and as he became bored and let it stop she asked for more. This time, once it was moving he jumped on, and held her as they spun round and round, one hand on the metal rail and the other around her waist.

It was probably the moment of closeness and contact that did it, but as the roundabout slowed to a halt the same thought occurred to them both. Registering the paraphernalia of children and childhood, they looked at each other; this would be a good place, they said almost simultaneously. Wouldn't it be brilliant – and a tale to tell – if it happened here!

But how? Especially if the roundabout was to be spinning – they agreed that for the experience to be perfect the roundabout had to be spinning. The woman tried kneeling, head down and bottom in the air, but when he started to turn the roundabout, she fell sideways. The only way was for her to lie on her back, arms above her head, holding on to the rails where they joined the central hub. She said it would probably be all right, as long as he was quick. With that, she stood up and began the difficult job of taking off her knickers without removing her shoes.

He had some doubts as to whether he could do it. Six months ago he could get an erection at any time and any place and, if he was naked and excited enough, it could last for half an hour. Recent events, though, had shaken his confidence. But as she shoved her knickers into her pocket, his partner expressed great faith in his ability.

He contemplated trying to do it while fully dressed but decided he couldn't, so, looking nervously around into the misty darkness of the park, he took off his trousers and underpants. When he stood in front of her in his long shirt, she could only laugh. His nervousness, the cold air, and perhaps the evening's alcohol as well had combined to produce a devastating effect on his penis. It seemed to be hiding, nestling for warmth and safety in his pubic hair, his groin like a bird's nest containing a single purple egg. He looked as though he needed a bit of help, she said, and pulled him towards her. Sitting legs apart, on the edge of the roundabout, she put her mouth over his penis. It was a while before she felt any response, but eventually the moist warmth did the trick. The impressive erection that she had once taken for granted was nowadays a relief to see. Once achieved, however, it could usually be relied upon. She settled back into position, pulled up her coat and skirt, raised her knees, opened her legs and reached back behind her head for the metal bars. It wasn't perfect, but it was as comfortable and accessible a position as she could manage.

He began to push the roundabout and, excited at last, enjoyed the feel of his erect penis slapping against his belly as he ran. Judging his moment, he clambered on board and, as they spun faster, scrambled on top of her. With even more difficulty – she wasn't very lubricated – he managed to push his penis inside her. Thrusting was difficult, and ejaculation didn't come easily. In truth, the roundabout had stopped for some time before he first spurted – though when they related the story to their friends over the weeks to come, they claimed he had managed it while still in motion.

Despite the discomfort of their position, he didn't withdraw until he was sure he had parted with every last drop of semen, by which time a thought was beginning to agitate her. If she started walking home immediately, she might lose some of the hard-earned sperm. When she told him the problem, he had a moment of inspiration: centrifugal force was the answer. If she lay with her head to the outside of the roundabout he suggested, and he spun her as fast as he could, centrifugal force would push the semen further up into her body.

And that's what they did, to the bemusement of two teenagers who had wandered into the park looking for somewhere to have their first kiss and grope. They hurried past, keeping their distance so as to avoid involvement in the bizarre ritual they were witnessing. Here was a woman, on her back on a roundabout, legs raised and feet on the central hub, arms reaching up and holding on to the metal bars. The man, still half-naked, his legs shrouded in mist, was running round and round pushing the roundabout, his shirt flattened over his shrunken penis and flapping against his bottom.

The couple had been together for eight years before deciding the time had come to start a family. Now they looked back in disbelief at all those years of contraception, at the weeks of worry that she might be pregnant if they took a chance, or she missed a pill, or if a condom misbehaved. For six months now, they had been having the most active of sex lives without a contraceptive in sight, and still she had not conceived. When they first began their conception campaign, the greater sensations of unprotected sex and the prospect of conception had fuelled their sexual excitement. The decision to conceive had revitalised what, if they were honest, had become a flagging and routine sexual relationship. But once they had made the decision, they had no trouble having sex more or less every day for weeks on end. For him, in particular, it was paradise. He had always wanted to ejaculate far more often than she had wanted intercourse, and had needed to masturbate whenever they missed a couple of days. But now that he had carte blanche to inseminate her whenever he wanted to, he felt no further need to masturbate. Moreover, it was coming inside her that was their mutual priority. He didn't even have to worry about whether or when she climaxed. At least at first, it really was a case of her lying back, opening her legs and him inseminating her.

But things began to change when her first period, then her second and third, came and went. They began to read books, seek the advice of fertile friends — and worry. They couldn't begin to question his fertility. With his high sex drive and voluminous, healthy-looking semen they took his potency for granted. So, they reasoned, it had to be her. They began to fret that it had been a mistake to wait until she was thirty before trying to start a family. Perhaps she wasn't producing eggs?

They tried using an ovulation-predictor kit bought from the chemist, but it was expensive and she produced positive results at all sorts of strange times in her cycle. So, after finding what looked like a useful graph in one of her books on pregnancy, she began taking her temperature first thing every morning. But the graph she produced looked nothing like the one in the book. Even so, she carried on taking her temperature. It didn't cost anything, and it made them feel they were at least doing *something* positive, other than the obvious, towards conception.

On friends' advice they tried having sex every other day, then every three days, instead of daily. At first the man automatically began masturbating again on the days in between, but then he forced himself to abstain in case the habit was lowering his fertility. Abstinence proved to be difficult, and sometimes he gave in to the urge, but he made a big effort and managed to restrain himself more often than not. After reading a newspaper article, he also stopped having hot baths and started to wear loose-fitting underpants.

Unlike her partner, the woman had never masturbated often, but she began to worry that her occasional habit might be part of their problem. Maybe it was important to climax *during intercourse*. Normally she would climax only about one-third of the time, and had been doing so even less during their intensive campaign, when insemination had taken priority. Following her hunch, she gave up masturbating completely and they began to make a special effort for her to have an orgasm during intercourse. But the more they tried, the more difficult she found it to respond, and they were reluctantly forced to let nature take its course over her orgasm. But what she did do was to lie motionless after sex with her feet raised and resting against the bedroom wall, so that the semen stayed inside her vagina for longer. However, none of their ploys worked, and her next four periods cast a gloom.

Reading that sperm might find it easier to enter the womb if she lay on her front rather than on her back, every intercourse during the eighth month of their program he entered her from behind. Sometimes she lay on the bed, legs apart; sometimes she knelt with her bottom in the air. Afterwards, she would carry on lying on her front for half an hour.

Throughout that month, he tried to concentrate hard when his climax approached, doing his best to spurt as far up inside her as possible. It was about now that he found his interest in sex with her beginning to wane. On three occasions, when she thought she felt a stirring of her libido that might mean the time was right, he was totally unable to respond. Whatever she did to help, nothing would give him an erection. So more and more, they found themselves needing to generate sexual excitement through novelty. One weekend they arranged not to have to go out at all and spent the entire time naked, so that whenever he felt interested he could take her. Up to a point it had worked. Once he found himself erect, watching her working at the kitchen sink, wearing rubber gloves. With her spreading her legs and bending her knees a little, he entered her, though with some difficulty, from behind as she leaned forward over the sink. They also had sex while watching a pornographic video. But the day they had earmarked to celebrate eight months of unprotected sex was marred by the onset of yet another period.

Having rung the changes on everything they could think of – frequency, clothes, position – in desperation they had decided to try changing the location. Although rational people, they had begun to blame the house for their failure. They reasoned that if they had sex in a more 'natural' place, maybe conception would be automatic.

Early on in the ninth month they had used the garden, sneaking out naked, blanket in hand, to have sex under the stars. While he was thrusting, she focused on the brightest star in the sky and thought cosmic thoughts. Two nights later, in a rush of madness, they ran out in the middle of a thunderstorm and did it in torrential rain on the grass. She convinced herself that lightning flashed across the night sky at the moment he began to ejaculate and that, as he gave his last spurt, thunder rumbled around the horizon. With increasing daring, they chose the middle of the lawn in broad daylight.

Both found the risk of being seen exciting, and began trying to think of alternatives to their garden. In part this stemmed from a need to generate sexual excitement where it no longer existed. But it was also, in part, to pander to their irrational superstition that the more daring the location the more likely her body was to be 'shocked' into conception.

The previous Sunday, they had driven into the country to a wood they knew and re-enacted a challenge that the man had once set himself as a frustrated and solitary adolescent. Carrying their clothes in a bag, they walked naked through the wood, hiding behind trees whenever anyone approached. Their task was to reach a river, nearly a mile away, without being seen – or, at least, without being arrested. They succeeded, apart from an excitable and inquisitive dog who found them and, out of sight of its owner, persisted in trying to lick their groins. The excitement of naked vulnerability and the thrill of success in their task meant that when eventually they slipped down the side of the river bank to lie in the tall grass, the sex they had was their most satisfying for months.

And now they had just done it in a playground, surrounded by the spirits of children. As they dressed to walk home, they both felt that if they hadn't succeeded this month, they never would.

This chapter takes a close look at the first step on the road to parenthood – conception. For many couples this is a very short step, quickly over, that they scarcely notice. For others, like the couple in the scene above, conception requires an intensive campaign and brings with it many questions and worries. We are about to follow the same couple through three scenes, covering about two years of their lives.

When it comes to conception, the world in general, and our couple in particular, could be excused for thinking that natural selection is a diabolically inefficient and mischievous force. How can it be that, after millions of years of evolution, with natural selection acting rigorously in each generation on something as fundamental as conception, a couple can still have such trouble producing a baby? There are many possible answers, and almost all derive from the basic fact that conception is a battle – either a battle between the couple and other (infectious) organisms or, cooperative though the man and woman in the scene might have appeared, a battle between the couple themselves.

On average, it takes four or five months for a *fertile* couple to conceive after they start having unprotected sex. One in three conceive in their first month, but after that the chances of conceiving in any one month fall quickly to about one in twenty. One in ten *fertile* couples take more than one year to conceive, and one in twenty take more than two. If we include infertile and sub-fertile couples in our figures, then, after a year of unprotected sex only about 60–75 per cent will have conceived. Such averages, however, hide a multitude of factors which generate perfectly normal variation. Some couples can have unprotected sex for years before suddenly conceiving. Yet others conceive in the first month every time they try.

Considering that sex and procreation are such important parts of most people's lives, the majority of us are surprisingly uninformed on the subject. The couple we have just watched are not unusual in the way they became increasingly confused and irrational about what was needed for conception to take place. However, we shouldn't be too critical of them, because even biomedical researchers are still uncertain about many aspects of the process.

The couple in the scene became more and more obsessed with practicalities. Had it been a mistake, waiting so long before trying to start a family? How could they tell the best stage in her cycle to have sex? How *often* should they have sex? What position should they adopt? What could they do to make sure his semen went as far up her vagina as possible? How could they keep it inside her for as long as possible after intercourse? Should he avoid masturbating? Should *she* avoid masturbating? How important was it that she had an orgasm during intercourse? Should he avoid hot baths and tight underpants?

The truth is that, as long as they are both fertile, none of these factors matter. All they really needed to do was have sex whenever, however, wherever and in whatever position appealed to them. Then, if the man and the moment were right for her body, the woman would have conceived. Natural selection has in fact been very efficient at shaping the path to conception. What people invariably fail to appreciate is that just because their conscious brains tell them it would be very convenient to conceive *now*, to do so is not always in their long-term reproductive interests. A person's body knows this and makes its own judgements; whatever his or her conscious wish, his or her body rules the day. The brain cannot force conception if the body has decided that conception is not in its long-term interests.

There are two factors that tend to generate confusion on the subject of failure to conceive. First, procreation is only *one* of the functions of intercourse. This is why, over a lifetime, a person has sex about three thousand times but, depending on where he or she lives, produces on average only between two and seven children.

The other functions of intercourse will emerge during the course of this chapter. Second, most of the time it is more important as far as a couple's long-term reproductive output is concerned for them *to avoid* conception rather than procreate. People's brains realise this, albeit dimly, as well as their bodies, which is one reason why the couple in the scene used contraception for eight years. But just because their brains decided the time had come to reproduce did not mean that their bodies would automatically concur.

Given these two factors, natural selection has actually performed a fantastic job in reconciling all the different requirements that humans and other species have of intercourse and reproduction. It seems to be inefficient only when, as for the couple in the scene, conception becomes the one and only *conscious* aim of intercourse. Their bodies may well be playing a different game – and, as usual, their bodies' wishes will prevail. What might be going on? Is it really possible that, desperate though their conscious minds are to have a baby, their bodies have a different plan? If so, how can that plan possibly be furthering each person's reproductive output if it is denying them the obvious path to that end?

These general questions will be more easily answered later; in discussing this scene, we shall concentrate on the practical questions with which our couple became so obsessed.

Had it been a mistake, waiting so long before trying to start a family? They were both thirty years old when they began their conception campaign, and could be excused for thinking that perhaps they were less fertile than they once had been. And at first sight, the evidence might seem to fuel their worries. Below the age of twenty-five, around 90 per cent of women conceive within six months of unprotected intercourse, whereas above the age of thirty-five, less than 20 per cent do. There are two main reasons for this change with age, both of which should be reassuring to our thirty-year-old couple.

Like most people, they will have heard the claim that a man's fertility peaks at age eighteen and declines from this point onwards. However, although it is true that an eighteen-year-old can maintain an erection for longer than an older man, there is no indication that his sperm are any more fertile. In fact, a man is actually at his peak of sperm production between the ages of twenty and thirty. We shall discuss male age and reproduction in more detail later. The man's age is most unlikely to have been a factor in this scene; here we concentrate on the age of the woman.

The number of eggs a woman produces each year changes as she goes through life. Most women realise that if they don't menstruate they are almost certainly not producing eggs and so are unlikely to conceive. What most women *do not* realise, however, is that even when they do menstruate, they haven't necessarily ovulated. Cycles without ovulation are termed *anovulatory* and are infertile, rendering conception impossible no matter how often a couple have sex. There is nothing unnatural about having some infertile cycles. Every normal, healthy, fertile woman has them. And far from being a threat to her fertility they are, in fact, an essential part of her reproductive life. They are one of the most important means by which a woman's body *avoids* conception when to conceive would be bad for her long-term reproductive output. In other words, without infertile cycles, a woman would conceive far more often than would be good for her.

Infertile cycles vary in frequency with a woman's age. Just after puberty when a girl first begins to have periods, over 90 per cent of her cycles will be infertile. Even by the age of twenty, 60 per cent of cycles are still infertile. It is between twenty-five and thirty-five that a woman is least likely to have infertile cycles, although even at this age one cycle in five is still infertile. Beyond thirty-five, the proportion begins to decrease, and by the age of fifty the majority of cycles are again infertile – but about then, of course, most women cease to have them anyway. The last cycle, as part of the menopause, usually happens between the ages of forty-eight and fifty-one. The woman in the scene, therefore, need not have worried about having delayed trying for a family until she was thirty. However, it is clear from the conception rate figures given earlier that the proportion of fertile cycles cannot be the only factor. Something other than female fertility must influence the chances of conception – which brings us to the next of the couple's worries.

The main reason that couples over thirty-five or so fail to conceive as quickly as younger couples is that they are less likely to have sex during the most fertile days in the woman's cycle. And this is because they tend to have sex less often than younger couples – a factor that didn't apply, however, to the couple in the scene, who at some stages in their campaign had sex every day. Even with infrequent sex, though, the problem of missing the fertile days can be avoided, if couples can tell precisely when in each cycle the woman is fertile. This was one of the questions that preoccupied our couple. How could they recognise the best stage in the woman's cycle to have sex? They knew, as most educated couples in modern industrialised societies know, that there are only certain days in each cycle that a woman can conceive – but which few days? And why should it have been so difficult for them to know when those days had arrived?

In ovulatory, as opposed to anovulatory, cycles there comes a day roughly in mid-cycle when one of the woman's two ovaries sheds an egg – ovulation. After the egg is released from her ovary, it spends a few brief moments floating freely in her body cavity. It is then sucked into the open end of the nearer of the two oviducts on the first leg of its eighty-hour journey to her womb, travelling at a speed of about one millimetre an hour. On its way the egg can be fertilised if it meets a sperm, but time and location are critical. There is only one zone in the oviduct, nearly a third of the way between ovary and womb, where fertilisation is likely. And on top of that, an unfertilised human egg lives only for twelve to thirty-six hours.

A surprising number of people think that women are most likely to conceive if they have sex in the days *after* ovulation. This is not true. Because the egg lives for such a short time and because there is only one zone in each of her oviducts where sperm can actually fertilise the egg, conception is more likely if the couple have sex *before* ovulation. Then sperm are ready and waiting when the egg arrives in the fertilisation zone. A woman is most likely to conceive if she has unprotected sex *two days before* she ovulates. Then she has a one-in-three chance of conceiving in that cycle – and this is as good as it gets. Intercourses before and after this two-day optimum are less and less likely to be successful. Six days before ovulation the chances are virtually zero, and five days before they are only one in ten. This is because, once inside a woman, sperm stay fertile for up to only five days. Intercourse on the actual day of ovulation also has only a one-in-ten chance of success. And on the day after that the chances are virtually zero, as it is highly unlikely that the egg is still alive. So what our couple needed was to be able to recognise when there were only two days to go to ovulation. Is there any way they could have?

Unfortunately, the answer is no – or at best, 'maybe'. Before modern medical research and modern technology the answer would have been a categorical no. Unlike some female primates – chimpanzees, for example – that develop red vaginas and crusty bottoms to advertise that they have entered the fertile phase of their cycle, women's bodies actually go out of their way to *hide* their most fertile phase. And our species is not unique in this. Many other female primates, such as marmosets and orang-utans, do the same. This hiding of the fertile phase, or *sexual crypsis*, has been so effectively shaped by natural selection that neither a woman's partner, nor even she herself, can tell when intercourse is most likely to lead to conception.

It is testimony to the efficiency of sexual crypsis that until the advent of biomedical research our ancestors had a very hazy picture of conception. Indeed, many could see no link at all between intercourse and pregnancy, mainly because people had intercourse so many times without becoming pregnant – on average about one pregnancy for every five hundred inseminations – that a link between the two seemed absurd. Until the 1920s, people entertained a wide range of beliefs concerning fertility and conception. Indigenous Australians, Brazilians and many Africans thought that babies entered the mother from the environment, such as while she was swimming. In other parts of Africa it was thought that babies were formed entirely from menstrual blood accumulating in the female. Various other societies realised that a man was involved in some way, but thought that he simply primed the female's body for conception, then played no further part.

In contrast, other cultures thought that only the man was involved. They thought that whole babies originated and were 'incubated' in the man, perhaps in his brain, then passed to his penis before being 'seeded' into the female in the seminal fluid. Aristotle was one of the major supporters of this seeding hypothesis. When sperm were first seen under a microscope about three hundred years ago, scientists really thought they could see tiny whole humans in human sperm, donkeys in donkey sperm, and so on. The entities were hence named spermatozoa, which means 'seed animals'.

The first European to suggest that the female might also play a role in conception was Hippocrates. He suggested that the menstrual blood, once it stopped flowing out of the vagina, accumulated in the mother to form the baby's flesh, the seminal fluid then forming the brain and bones. As a result, people thought the end of menstruation was the most fertile time. It was not until the late 1800s when sperm were first seen fertilising eggs (in starfish and sea urchins) that a role for the female – the production of eggs – was acknowledged. Even then, it was not until the 1920s that medical research demonstrated the most fertile phase of the menstrual cycle to be mid-cycle, not the end of menstruation.

Their bodies are so good at hiding their fertility that the conundrum of when in their cycle women conceive was only finally answered by biomedical research. And the mystery was not solved by people simply watching each other, because every aspect of a woman's chemistry and behaviour takes part in the cover-up. Women feel like sex – and don't feel like sex – on and off throughout their cycle. Similarly, they have good moods and bad moods on and off throughout their cycle. Undoubtedly women *do* experience high libido and seek or welcome intercourse during the fertile phase of their cycle, but these instances are so well hidden amongst decoy moments of libido that neither a woman nor the men around her can tell which ones signify fertility and which do not. The couple in the scene, therefore, did the right thing in having sex whenever her libido rose, but it didn't always mean what they hoped it meant.

Although a woman's libido fails to give a sure-fire indication of fertility, biomedical research has discovered three other methods that give as good an indication, if not a better one. All, though, are imperfect, and two require modern technology – an ovulation-detector kit or a thermometer – which we shall discuss in a moment. But the first method requires only the woman's fingers.

During her fertile phase, she might notice an increased wetness on her vaginal lips. And, if she puts her fingers in her vagina and pulls out some mucus, she will find that it is very stretchy. During infertile phases, this mucus is much less stretchy but much thicker. So what is it, where does it come from, and why, despite sexual crypsis, does it change in consistency during the fertile phase of her menstrual cycle?

This tell-tale mucus has its origin in the cervix, the narrow passage through which sperm have to pass on their way from vagina to womb. When a woman is lying flat on her back, her womb is a bit like an upside-down vase perched on top of her vagina. The cervix is the neck of this vase and protrudes through the 'roof' of the vagina by about an inch. The cervix is plugged with mucus which is secreted by the cervical walls themselves. The mucus flows slowly down the length of the cervix like a glacier. Little by little, the older end of the mucus glacier oozes out of the cervix and into the vagina. The main function of the cervical mucus is to make life difficult for any viruses and bacteria that try to get into the womb, so most of the time it is relatively thick and difficult to penetrate. The consequence, of course, is that sperm too find it difficult to get through – a bit like having to swim through treacle. So during the fertile phase the cervix has no choice but to make its mucus easier to penetrate – otherwise, sperm could not easily get through from the vagina into the womb. Nevertheless, even during the fertile phase a woman cannot afford to lose all of her protection against diseases.

The way the cervix solves this dual problem is first to make its mucus plug more liquid, so that sperm can swim through more easily, but at the same time to increase the 'glaciers' flow rate. This speeding-up has been judged to perfection by natural selection. Fast-swimming sperm can still make headway and get through – a bit like salmon swimming up stream – but the slower-moving bacteria and viruses get flushed out. It is these changes in mucus flow and consistency that might alert a woman, and her partner, to the fact that she is in her fertile phase.

It has also been suggested that cervical and vaginal secretions might smell more pleasant during her fertile phase. However, studies in which women wore tampons overnight at different stages of their cycle, then had them ranked for 'pleasantness' of odour by a panel who could smell but not see the tampons, found no evidence for this claim. The only change in smell during the cycle was that menstrual secretions were ranked as less pleasant than non-menstrual.

So why weren't the couple in our scene advised to keep a close eye on the woman's secretions and decide from those when it was best to have sex? Some people are advised to do just this – and it's certainly worth a try. Unfortunately, the method is no more reliable and no easier to use than anything else we have considered. This is because mucus can become stretchy quite a few days before peak fertility and remain so for quite a few days afterwards. Peak fertility does sometimes coincide with days of peak mucus condition, but by no means always. In addition there is a practical problem: the difficulty with waiting for a peak of anything is that identification of the peak is not possible until it has passed and the decline is obvious – and then it is too late.

Instead of watching for copious and stretchy cervical mucus, the couple in the scene opted for 'technological' substitutes. First, they tried commercial ovulation-predictor kits, then the woman began taking her temperature every morning. Both of these methods can help, but neither is foolproof. One problem is that, once again, both work by identifying either a peak or a trough. They therefore have the same problem as the cervical-mucus test: by the time the peak or trough is identified as such, it is too late.

In principle, ovulation-predictor kits should obviate this problem, and the most recent versions are as easy to use as pregnancy-testing kits. The woman simply puts the sampler into her urine stream, then waits a few minutes. If ovulation is imminent, a blue line appears. Although the system is testing for the presence of a hormone that is always present – it peaks two days before ovulation – the manufacturers have set the sensitivity of the test so that the kit should react positively only if the hormone is present at or above the level that indicates the all-important peak. And for most women it works.

Unfortunately, *actual* levels of this hormone differ from person to person. A few people never get a positive response because their peak level is below the threshold of the kit's sensitivity; a few others always get a positive response because even their basic level is above the threshold. Both types of women are having normal, fertile cycles but neither can predict, using this kind of kit, when they are going to ovulate. Admittedly such women are in the minority, but, unfortunately for the woman in the scene, she fell into one of these categories.

Similarly, taking her temperature was of little use to her in her campaign. The graph in the book will have shown a temperature curve that gradually fell during the days of menstruation, stayed low for about two weeks, then showed one day with a really low temperature before slowly rising, then levelling off at a high 'plateau'. If conception does not occur, the temperature begins to fall again at the beginning of the next menstruation. If conception *has* occurred, the temperature stays high. This is the classic 'biphasic' curve of a fertile menstrual cycle. Infertile anovulatory cycles have a temperature curve that stays low throughout.

For a couple trying to conceive, there are two important features of a fertile biphasic curve. If they count back fourteen days from the first day of bleeding, they can identify the day the woman ovulated in that cycle. The one-day dip in temperature, or 'nadir', is *usually* two days before that. What our couple should have been looking for in her temperature records, therefore, was the day of the nadir. Having sex on that day might have given the greatest chance of conception.

Unfortunately, there are problems even with this system. An infection, such as flu, will of course give a woman an unusually high temperature at any time in her cycle. Even more mischievously, her temperature does not stay *consistently* low in those critical two weeks or so before ovulation. It goes up and down considerably, depending on several factors. For example, it will be unusually high if she is a bit later than usual in taking her temperature, if she has moved around a lot, or if she has eaten. It will also be high if she has drunk a lot of alcohol the night before. And although it rarely reaches the high plateau that comes after ovulation and that tends to fluctuate far less, these inevitable ups and downs before ovulation nevertheless make it very difficult to spot when the nadir has occurred until the plateau is established several days later. But by then it's too late – the egg has been produced and has died.

Keeping a temperature record does have some uses, though. First, over a number of cycles, it allows a practised eye to judge whether the woman is ovulating at all and, if so, in what proportion of her cycles. Second, it is really useful for those who wish *to avoid* pregnancy but who also want as much as possible to avoid using contraceptives. Once the high plateau of the temperature curve has begun, the couple have about ten days – the remainder of that cycle – in which they can have unprotected sex with relative impunity.

As a tool for deciding when it is best to have sex in order to conceive, however, temperature records are fairly useless. So why look for signs of the fertile phase at all? Surely, if the menstrual cycle lasts twenty-eight days and ovulation occurs fourteen days before the start of the next period, it follows that ovulation will occur fourteen days after the start of the previous period? In which case, the day of peak fertility will be day 12. Surely, all our couple in the scene had to do was wait for a period to start, count the days, and then make sure they had sex on day 12.

Unfortunately, this doesn't work either. In fashioning a woman's body for sexual crypsis, natural selection has easily forestalled such simple arithmetic. Only rarely does a woman actually ovulate on day 14 of her cycle. While it *is* true that the length of time *from ovulation* to the beginning of the next period is a fairly reliable fourteen days, the length of time from the beginning of a period *to ovulation* is not. It is, in fact, incredibly variable, both from woman to woman and from cycle to cycle in the same woman – anything from 4–5 days to 40–50 – and this is why the time interval from one period to the next is also so variable. So sex on day 12 is no more likely to lead to conception than on any other day of the cycle.

Some women insist that they know when they ovulate because they feel a pain – the so-called 'mittelschmertz' (literally, middle pain') – in their lower abdomen round about mid-cycle. This pain *could* be caused by irritation of the lining of the body cavity due to blood or other fluid escaping from the ovary at ovulation. However, it is not known how often such a pain really does coincide with ovulation, nor is it known how reliably women can distinguish it from other, similar, pains in the abdomen. But even if they can, this ability is of little use for conception. As we have already seen, once a woman has ovulated the chances of conception are minimal, even if she manages to have intercourse immediately.

So, because of human sexual crypsis, our couple couldn't tell when the woman was most fertile. But why should that have mattered? As long as they had sex every day, surely they would be bound to hit the day of peak fertility, two days before ovulation? They tried this, but it didn't work, so they tried having sex every two or three days instead. Which strategy *should* have been best? How often should they have had sex? The fact is that there is actually no advantage, for conception, in having sex every day. The man doesn't inseminate any more sperm in total and the chances of missing the egg are no less, in principle, than if the couple have sex every two to three days. In fact, there may be some disadvantage in having sex every day. But how can this be?

When a man inseminates a woman, a few sperm go straight to the two oviducts, arriving there less than an hour after ejaculation.

Of these 'vanguard' sperm, some keep travelling until they reach the fertilisation zone, but some stop almost as soon as they enter the oviduct and settle down in a sort of rest area in its lower reaches. Most sperm, however, do not even try to go to the oviducts immediately. Instead, they travel a much shorter distance to alternative resting places – the multitudinous 'crypts' in the inner wall of the cervix. The entrances to these crypts make the cervical wall look in places like the top of a pepper-pot – perfect spots for sperm to rest a while. Over the next five days, the sperm leave the crypts one by one and complete their journey through the womb to their second rest area in one of the two oviducts. These rest areas have now been vacated by the earlier vanguard sperm which have already left to swim through the remainder of the oviduct, passing through the fertilisation zone on their way, and out into the woman's body cavity. Here they die. Only one sperm in about every 150 billion that are inseminated into a woman is lucky enough to meet and fertilise an egg while passing through the fertilisation zone.

The result of this clever sequencing of sperm behaviour is that from about an hour after every intercourse, and for the next five days, a steady trickle of sperm pass through the zone of fertilisation. The important point is that as long as couples have sex every two, or even three, days there will always be sperm passing through the zone. No egg should escape fertilisation.

So having sex every day does not increase the chances of conceiving. And it doesn't even increase the number of sperm passing through the oviduct. This is because a man's body carries out a very sophisticated calculation during intercourse: the number of sperm he ejaculates changes according to the length of time since he last inseminated his partner. The shorter the time, the fewer sperm he ejaculates. So precisely does a man's body make this adjustment that the total number of sperm that passes through her oviducts will be the same whether he inseminates her twice a day or twice a week.

It is even possible that, if a couple have sex *too* often, the number of sperm passing through the woman's oviducts will be smaller, not greater. This is because the sperm begin to get in each other's way. Any sperm from a previous insemination that are still in the cervical mucus at the next insemination block the channels, which are very narrow, thus making it more difficult for the later sperm to get through. Sex every other day is probably about optimal, but as long as couples never leave more than a three- to four-day gap between intercourses they are most unlikely to miss having a sperm meet the egg while the latter is alive and well and in the fertilisation zone. The couple in the scene met this requirement, but still didn't succeed. So what else could have gone wrong?

Their worries focused on whether or not his sperm were 'getting through' to her eggs. They wondered if changing their position during sex would make a difference. In addition, he tried to spurt his semen as far inside her as he could, and she tried to make sure that she lost as little of it after intercourse as possible. If they had only known what really happens inside a woman's body after ejaculation, they would have realised there was little value in doing anything other than follow their natural inclinations.

Many people imagine that the vagina, cervix and womb are more or less one straight tube, so that if the man exerts enough force and accuracy he can squirt his sperm right up near the egg. We have already seen that this isn't the case. When the woman lies on her back, the womb sits *on top* of the vagina with the cervix poking through the vaginal roof by about an inch. Not only that, but the channel through the cervix is filled with mucus. Finally, to make accurate and forceful delivery impossible, the cervix grows bigger during intercourse and stretches down to reach the floor of the vagina, so that the tip of the penis is presented not with the womb's entrance but with a wall – the front of the cervix. Whether the man dribbles or spurts, his sperm end up forming a pool on the floor of the vagina and get into the cervix and womb by their own efforts, not because of any action of his. With the cervix dangling in the seminal pool and its mucus mixing with the semen, the sperm simply swim into the mucus.

With this image in mind, we can see that the couple were, of course, correct in thinking that her position during and after intercourse must have *some* bearing. The seminal pool at the top of the vagina stays there as the penis is withdrawn, no matter what position is adopted. This is partly because the pool coagulates, becoming more jelly-like almost immediately it is formed, and partly because the vagina closes behind the shrinking penis, holding the pool in place. Only in the woman-on-top position is there a danger that part of the pool may be lost before sperm have had time to escape safely into the cervix. Even then, such loss is only really a danger if the man withdraws too quickly after insemination, while he is still partly erect.

Not only does sexual position have little influence on the retention of the seminal pool, it also has little if any influence on the ability of sperm to escape from the pool. This is because of the neat design of the cervix. In the missionary position, for instance, the pool is deposited on the floor of the vagina with the cervix dipping into it. In the rear-entry position, either the cervix is underneath the seminal pool, like a plug-hole in a sink, or it sticks up and hangs back down, like a coiled spring 'walking' downstairs. In the woman-on-top position, the vagina is nearly vertical. The cervix protrudes through the front wall of the vagina, curving to hang down into the seminal pool left behind by the retreating penis after ejaculation. Moreover, no matter how she changes her position after insemination, gravity will ensure that even a coagulated pool of semen will slide into a new position. Gravity will also ensure that her cervix continues to dangle into the pool, maintaining contact between mucus and semen.

It might at first seem that the couple were eventually correct – that rear-entry intercourse followed by the woman lying on her front was the best. A 'plug-hole' arrangement might, after all, seem the best for maximum contact between seminal pool and cervical opening. But even this isn't so. In its resting state, after the excitement of intercourse, the cervix protrudes nearly an inch into the vagina. Few seminal pools will be so deep that, even if she lies on her front, the woman can force contact between cervical opening and seminal pool any longer than the cervix itself dictates. Once it has withdrawn from the pool, there is probably nothing she can do to make it go back in.

This apparent perversity in the design and behaviour of the cervix is no accident. The truth is that more often than not a woman neither wants nor needs all the sperm that a man injects into her. *Most* of the sperm in the seminal pool are geriatric or otherwise redundant, at least as far as she is concerned. Her cervix dips into the semen pool simply to sip the best and discard the rest. She doesn't want the pool inside her any longer than is necessary to collect the required number of fit and fertile sperm. The seminal fluid is there to protect the sperm from the acidic secretions in her vagina, not for the woman's benefit. In fact, not only does seminal fluid harbour diseases but, if it ever got into her womb, it could be dangerous. In laboratory experiments, seminal fluid dropped on to womb muscles makes them contract violently, producing spasms and cramps. Had the couple known all of this, they wouldn't have tried so hard to prevent her from 'leaking' after intercourse.

The material a woman loses in the hour or two after sex is known as the 'flowback' and, despite the worries of the couple on the roundabout, it is a normal and important consequence of intercourse. Flowback is simply unwanted material, a mixture of cervical mucus (which is harmless), seminal fluid (which is not) and those sperm which were too old or lame to escape from the seminal pool and penetrate the cervical mucus. The woman is better off without them all, so she ejects them. Within minutes of the male ejaculating, her cervix dips, sips, selects and eventually rejects. The best thing she can do is to let her cervix make all of the decisions – not that she has any real choice. Her cervix has been programmed to have total control over the situation, and to be immune to anything that she does or that happens to her – such as being chased by a tiger – after intercourse. In any conception campaign, the cervix and its mucus are a woman's best ally.

The woman in the scene would never have made the link, but it is precisely because her cervix and mucus are so important to her that from time to time she experienced the urge to masturbate. Masturbation is a form of 'cervical housekeeping'. Cervical mucus is forever getting cluttered up with debris. Menstrual remnants, old sperm from previous inseminations, cells from her womb, and, most dangerous of all, occasional colonies of invading viruses or bacteria all accumulate, particularly in the older mucus plugging the cervix where it protrudes into the vagina. Much of the time, the slow glacier-like flow of the mucus is enough to keep the cervix clean and healthy, but occasionally something more dynamic is called for. It's a bit like the way the nose keeps itself healthy via a slow secretion of mucus, then, occasionally, when it needs to speed up, produces a runny nose, or a more forceful sneeze or nose-blow.

Even once the cervical mucus has oozed from the cervix into the vagina, its job isn't finished. As it runs down, it forms a thin coating on the vaginal walls. When a woman gets excited during sex, her vaginal walls sweat. This liquid itself isn't slippery, but when combined with the coating of old cervical mucus the mixture becomes very slippery indeed. It is this that provides a woman with her main lubrication during intercourse. Again, most of the time the steady flow and drip of mucus is enough, but whenever the coating becomes too thin, a sudden influx of mucus is needed.

An orgasm via masturbation solves a dual problem. In the absence of the complicating, if not spoiling, effects of semen, the orgasm rids her cervix of the older mucus, thus relining the vaginal walls, ready to lubricate her next intercourse. And orgasm in the absence of semen probably also makes the remaining cervical mucus more acidic, and hence more resistant to invasion by infectious organisms. Since these effects are beneficial to a woman in the midst of a conception campaign, when the urge to masturbate strikes it shouldn't be suppressed. She can rest assured that her body is continuously monitoring the state of her cervix and vagina. If they ever need the tidying-up effects of an orgasm, she will feel the urge to masturbate. Of course, she doesn't have to do the deed by herself. An orgasm stimulated by a partner will do exactly the same job, as long as it is before intercourse, not afterwards.

The same benefits to the cervix are also achieved via nocturnal orgasms – orgasms experienced while asleep, usually but not always in association with sexual dreams. Relatively few women experience, or at least remember, such episodes compared with those who get the urge to masturbate. By the age of twenty, about 10 per cent of women have experienced a nocturnal orgasm and even by the time they are forty only about 40 per cent have done so. In contrast, about 80 per cent from time to time want to masturbate. Those who never experience or feel the urge to orgasm in the absence of a man clearly have no need for cervical housekeeping beyond the routine flow and drip of their mucus glacier.

The woman in our scene worried not only about *having* orgasms in the absence of her partner, but also about *not having* them during intercourse. Again, she need not have worried. It has been known for decades that an orgasm during intercourse is not necessary for conception. It is true that an orgasm simultaneously with her partner's climax, or at any time afterwards up until she loses her flowback, will increase the number of sperm she retains in her cervix from that intercourse. This difference in numbers, however, will make no difference to her chances of conceiving, for reasons we shall discuss later in this chapter.

What about the man's masturbation habits? He, too, worried that he was prejudicing their chances and had phases when he did his very best not to succumb to his urges. Was it important that he tried? Once again, the answer is no. When a man masturbates, he sheds the oldest of his sperm from their storage tubes. The result is that when he next inseminates a woman, he does indeed ejaculate fewer sperm – but they are younger and more active. A greater proportion of them manage to escape the seminal pool and enter the cervical mucus, and because they are younger they will stay alive longer. Just as with a woman and her cervical mucus, a man's body keeps an eye on the health and vigour of the sperm he has in storage, and when it decides that some need to be shed it triggers in him an urge to masturbate. Or, as with women, he may instead shed them at night, while asleep. Either way, the shedding of sperm can be a positive step for a man intent on his partner conceiving.

In addition, our man worried that hot baths and tight underpants might be reducing his fertility. Again, he had no need to. It is true that sperm prefer to be kept relatively cool while they are being stored. This is why the main storage tube, the epididymis, is positioned on the surface of the testes, just under the skin of the scrotal sac, and why the testes dangle instead of being tucked safely away inside the body. When a man is naked his sperm experience a temperature six degrees centigrade lower than the rest of his body, whereas when he is clothed the difference is three degrees. The tighter his clothes and the more hot baths he has, the higher the average temperature to which his sperm are exposed. A higher testicular temperature does indeed make him produce slightly fewer sperm – and slightly more geriatric sperm. The difference, however, is statistical rather than dramatic, and is most unlikely to make any difference to the chances of conception, particularly after the combined effects of his masturbations and the woman's cervical selection.

One factor not consciously considered by the couple but which in principle might have influenced the success of their campaign was the time of year. We don't usually think of humans as seasonal breeders, but women *are* more likely to ovulate and hence conceive in some months than others. It is this seasonal pattern to ovulation that leads to birth peaks some nine months later. In northern temperate latitudes, for example, more people are born in February/March, with a secondary peak in September, reflecting peaks of ovulation and conception in May/June and December. It was late summer when we first met the couple in the scene, and they had already been trying to conceive for nine months, spanning both of the peak times.

We can now see that most of our couple's worries and 'remedies' during their conception campaign were unnecessary. Clearly, something had stopped them from conceiving, but it probably wasn't any of the factors they had consciously considered. In any case, after their exploits in the garden, in the wood and on the roundabout, they were quite optimistic.

SCENE 3
Barren Times

A fortnight or so after their escapade on the roundabout, the couple held a dinner party, a get-together with the womans' ex-college friends and their partners. Ten years earlier, the four women had shared a flat together in their final year before graduation. Three still lived in the city, within easy travelling distance of each other, but the fourth had moved quite far away. When she made the twice-yearly visit – usually with her partner and her two children – they would all meet at one or other of their homes to eat, drink and talk over old times. Except for the couple who were tonight's hosts, they all had children.

The first hour or so had been rather uncomfortable for the hostess and her partner as the three mothers swapped stories about their children's behaviour, misbehaviour, excretions and other habits. With the smugness of proven fertility, the three romanticised the days before parenthood when they could do what they wanted and come and go as they pleased. But they were considerate enough to draw short of saying how lucky their childless friend was, for they all knew that she had been trying to conceive for months. So confident had she been in their fertility and so excited that the contraceptive barriers were about to drop that she had broadcast the start of their conception campaign to them all.

Despite these tense moments, she had managed to enjoy the evening – not least because deep inside she was nurturing the belief that at last she might be joining the club. Her period was *three days* late! As her guests grew increasingly drunk the conversation became more and more bawdy and personal. The hostess had even, from time to time, managed to forget or at least be less preoccupied with the stresses of the last few months.

As the alcohol did its work, she and her partner related some of their recent adventures, scoring a few points by emphasising how often they were having sex. The *pièce de résistance* was undoubtedly the roundabout tale. They knew it would be a winner. At one point they even thought there was going to be a demand for an excursion to the site and a demonstration of how they had managed it. Then, as she savoured the moment, the woman leaned forward to pour herself another glass of wine – and froze. There it was, that unmistakable warm, wet sensation between her legs. For a second she thought – she hoped – that it was just from the excitement of talking about their sexual exploits. But in her heart she knew. Her period was starting.

She paused for a second, hand on bottle. Suddenly she was alone in the room, isolated by her thoughts, the noise and conversation around her just background. Then she sat back, every fibre concentrating on the feeling in her vagina, registering and analysing every nuance of sensation. Somebody asked if she was all right. Forcing a smile, she replied that she was fine but stood up and excused herself, saying she had to go to the toilet. Once inside the bathroom, as she scrambled to pull down and examine her knickers, she saw the sight she had come to hate, the brown stain that heralded the red flood to come, destroying her hopes for yet another month – and this month, of all months. After the river bank and the roundabout, she had convinced herself that finding stains in her knickers was a thing of the past, to be forgotten until she, too, would be complaining of the deprivations of parenthood.

Bursting into tears, she turned sideways and looked at her reflection in the mirrored wall of the bathroom. Knickers around her knees, wet-eyed, she despaired of herself and hated her body. Why her? Everybody else found it so easy. What was wrong with her? All she wanted was a baby. It wasn't fair. It really wasn't fair.

She had been sobbing for quite a while when one of her friends, the out-of-town one, knocked on the bathroom door to see if she was all right. She let her in and the pair of them sat, perched uncomfortably on the edge of the bath, the visitor's arm around the distraught woman's shoulders. Her friend tried to console her. When told the flow was so far only a stain, she said she could still be pregnant. When she had conceived *her* second child, her period had actually been quite noticeable. Not as heavy as usual, but enough for her to think she hadn't conceived that month, until she began to get the other signs – so she shouldn't give up hope yet.

The other wanted to believe her, but she just knew her period was coming, she said. Her friend asked how long they had been trying, even though she knew, really, that it was nine months. It had been mentioned often enough that evening. Nine months was nothing, she said reassuringly. She knew people who had tried for years before they succeeded. When asked, though, she had to admit that both of hers had been conceived straight away.

She had read enough about conception over the past few months, the tear-stained woman said, to know that sometimes it could take a while. She also knew that if she went to the doctor's he would probably only tell her to go away and keep trying for several more months before taking her seriously. But the thought of yet more trying and of having their hopes dashed at the end of each month that passed, seemed like purgatory. She didn't think she could stand it. She would crack up. All she wanted was a baby – why couldn't she have a baby? She was a woman – what was wrong with her? Eventually, she calmed down, thanks mainly to her friend and to her drunken partner who joined them, somewhat belatedly, in the bathroom. On hearing the news, he responded at first with disbelief – then briefly raged at the universe before collecting himself and sharing her sadness.

Her return to the dining-room and her explanation for her absence dampened everybody's spirits and curtailed the after-dinner conversation. The two local couples phoned politely early for taxis and the visitors from afar made their excuses and went to bed early, looking in first on their two children, who were sleeping peacefully in the room the hosts had been waiting to turn into a nursery.

The childless couple had a miserable night, especially when an early-hours visit to the bathroom confirmed that her period was in full flow. On first getting into bed they had spent an hour going over the events of the previous month, examining every last detail, trying to find a reason for their failure. The escapades they had so much enjoyed recounting that evening, so recently the source of their hopes, now seemed silly and counter-productive, maybe even the *cause* of their failure. Next month, they agreed, they would just have sex in bed.

The following morning, while the other two were showering or dealing with the children, the woman had a long conversation over coffee with her friend's partner. He couldn't reassure her, but she found it cathartic to talk in detail and at length about her hopes and fears with someone she didn't know that well but who was genuinely sympathetic. She felt similarly encouraged a week later when, without telling her partner, she went to the doctor's. It was less rewarding when they returned as a couple, and the doctor told them all the things they had already read, gave them all the reassurances they had already heard, and sent them away to try for a few months more, telling her to take her temperature every morning, which she was already doing.

Their relationship nearly didn't survive the next few months as they ran through a gamut of problems, some of which they had anticipated and many of which they hadn't. Sex, which had once been such a pleasure to them, gradually became a chore. Despite themselves, fears for their personal fertility drove each to hope that the fault was with the other. Everything became tainted, even the way they felt about each other's body. Arousal for either of them now seemed to take an eternity. They desperately wanted reassurance which neither could give, and they began to shy away from situations in which sex was inevitable but avoidance an indictment.

The tension, sexual and otherwise, led to more and more arguments. Momentary disagreements were fanned into day-long silences. Occasionally, one or the other would storm out of the house and drive around town for hours at a time, trying to make sense of his or her life and emotions. Even watching television together became a strain. Every programme seemed to contain something to remind them of their situation. As well as a plethora of programmes dealing with sex, childbirth and parenthood, even apparently innocent moments left just as deep a mark. Whether brief shots of cute children or advertisements with nuclear families having fun flying kites and eating just the right brand of cereal, it all hurt. In the end, even film sequences of couples having sex made them feel uncomfortable.

The woman, in particular, found the outside world an assault on her emotions. Every pregnant woman, every pram, every sweet toddler made her ache with longing, until she found some relief in looking for reasons to dislike other people's children. She would watch out for runny noses and faces with rashes, listen for the tantrums and detect evidence of dirty nappies, then try to feel grateful that she was being spared all of that. But the ploy rarely worked for long. The next minute or the next day, the sight of a perfect baby would bring back her longing, her sadness, her angry despair. By the time they went back to see the doctor, they were suffering the emotional fall-out of four failed attempts at intercourse – not even the hint of an erection – and their relationship was at an all-time low. What the woman didn't know, because her partner hadn't told her, was that even on the two previous occasions when he had at least managed to penetrate, absolutely nothing had stirred in his groin and he had only pretended to ejaculate.

The doctor examined her temperature charts, said he couldn't see any obvious problem, and sent the pair of them for a series of tests. While they waited for the results, the hopes of each that the problem lay with the other were reignited. Paradoxically, though, these same thoughts made them feel an anticipatory sympathy for each other – as if the news they hoped for in secret had already been given. Also they were both relieved that at last something positive was happening. They were no longer alone – someone else, even if he or she was just an anonymous figure in a distant laboratory, was working on their problem. As the day of judgement grew nearer, they grew more philosophical, and began to give each other the support and reassurance that each had needed for months. The day they went to get the decision on their fertility prospects, they felt closer than at any time since the dinner-party.

A worldwide study of human fertility carried out by the World Health Organisation, published in 1990, concluded that about 15 per cent of humans are infertile. (In industrial countries the figure is nearer 10 per cent and roughly equal for men and women.) This means that about one in six couples worldwide find it impossible, or at least extremely difficult, to conceive. In a third of such couples, the problem lies with the man, in a third with the woman, and in the remaining third with both. Moreover, if any couple have not conceived after two years of unprotected sex, without medical assistance they have only a one in four chance of conceiving thereafter. It is quite likely, therefore, that the couple in the scene above will not be able to solve their problem simply by continuing to have sex. On the other hand, there is a good chance that medical tests will identify the cause of their problem.

A study coordinated by the World Health Organisation in twenty-five countries and involving more than ten thousand infertile couples showed that blocked oviducts in women and problems in sperm production or passage in men were the main causes of infertility. So if either one of our couple has problems of this type, he or she will soon be diagnosed.

It might seem surprising that such a high level of infertility exists, given that for generations natural selection has favoured only the most fertile of men and women. Why hasn't it rid the human population of such a basic problem, thereby giving humankind victory in the battle for fertility? The answer, which will surprise many people, is that over half of the cases of human infertility are due not to a failure of the body, but to disease – infections of the urinogenital system that find their way into oviducts or sperm storage tubules, causing inflammation and blockages. The result is that eggs and sperm are unable to reach the destinations necessary for fertilisation. Sometimes such infections cause only temporary bouts of infertility, with normal fertility returning once the infection subsides. Others, however, can cause enduring blockages and hence permanent infertility. Such diseases include what might appear to be the most innocuous childhood infections, passing irritations that are scarcely noticed. If a person is unlucky, however, a single bout of a urinogenital infection early on can cause a lifetime of infertility.

The fact that most cases of infertility are caused by disease explains natural selection's failure to rid humans of the problem. The point is that disease organisms have their own way to make in the world, and natural selection has no allegiances. If any of these organisms produce a mechanism to further their own reproduction at the expense of ours, natural selection will favour them; if we can do the same, it will favour us. The consequence is an evolutionary arms race between diseases and ourselves which neither side has yet won. The uneasy balance in which they and us coexist means that, in any generation, some people escape the ravages of disease and infertility, and some don't.

Maybe one or other of the two main characters in our scene, having fallen prey to what seemed a mild urinogenital infection earlier in life, is one of the unfortunate 10 per cent or so who are either infertile or sub-fertile. If so, they will soon know – the tests will tell them. They will also soon know if the woman has hormonal problems. These could result in her never ovulating, or, even if she does ovulate and an egg is fertilised, a hormonal imbalance could result in her body never allowing the egg to implant in her womb. As already noted, an examination of her temperature charts will give the practised eye a fairly good indication of whether her cycles are fertile or not. But the tests she has undergone will have measured actual hormone levels and will give a much more definitive indication of whether she has problems in this area.

If the couple do have any problems of this sort, there will almost certainly be an appropriate form of medical assistance for them. Surgery, hormone therapy or in-vitro fertilisation (IVF) – or a combination of these – or nowadays even surrogacy, can in principle bypass most such problems. IVF allows the woman's egg to be fertilised by the man's sperm, in a dish, thus circumventing obstacles such as blocked oviducts. IVF also offers a solution if the man has difficulties with sperm production or insemination. Techniques have now been developed which allow a single sperm, even an immature one without a tail, to achieve fertilisation by being injected right into the egg. Usually, in most IVF treatments, the fertilised egg is re-implanted in the mother's womb, and then pregnancy and birth proceed as normal. Nowadays, however, if the mother is unable to implant an egg or carry a baby in her womb, her fertilised egg can be introduced into the womb of a surrogate mother, who hands the baby to the genetic parents when it is born.

Wonderful though such treatments seem in principle, their success rate isn't always very high, most methods failing more often than they succeed. Nevertheless, they do bring hope to couples who would otherwise find no solution to their childlessness. The couple in the scene have not yet reached this stage. Not all lengthy conception campaigns are due to infertility or sub-fertility. Many are set in motion by temporary conditions that eventually clear, enabling a couple suddenly and seemingly inexplicably to achieve conception.

One of the most important factors in these temporary phases of infertility is stress, and it can come from any source. Financial hardship, cramped living conditions, accident, illness or death within the family, worries about a partner's fidelity can all produce stress, and stress is a powerful contraceptive. Just about every aspect of a conception campaign can be affected – loss of libido, erection difficulties, failure to ovulate, failure to implant and miscarriage are all more likely if people are under strain. Men are also more likely to produce infertile ejaculates. The net result is that the more stressed a couple are, the less likely they are to conceive. And, as our couple discovered, failure to conceive can itself generate even more stress. Nor is it any accident that stress promotes temporary infertility. Natural selection has linked the two with a vengeance.

In a later chapter we shall see how important it is, biologically, for a couple to have just the right number of children. For the moment, the critical point is that the fewer children they have, the more important it is for them to have them at the best possible times. Above all, they should avoid conception when times are bad – and by linking stress with natural contraception, natural selection has done just that. It has shaped their bodies' chemistry to try to make sure that, for the time being, they do not embark on something as demanding as parenthood – for their own *long-term* reproductive good.

Maybe, then, the couple in the scene were under strain before they began their attempts to conceive. Perhaps their finances were not yet stable, their careers not sufficiently advanced, their home not spacious enough. There could have been problems with their parents, or perhaps neither was totally convinced that he or she could rely on the other.

As we consider this possibility, it is important to realise that it is not the couple's *absolute* situation that matters, but rather how that situation matches up to their expectations. Circumstances that might stress the couple in the scene would certainly not bother a couple living in a drainpipe in the Third World, because their expectations are different. Nevertheless, just because our couple have a relatively comfortable life does not mean that stress cannot influence their chances of conception. Whatever might have put them under pressure before they started trying to conceive, one thing is certain. Once they had begun their campaign and failed to conceive, they became even more stressed. In particular, each began to question the other's fertility. If stress was the cause of their problems, they were unlikely to succeed until they sorted things out.

The couple's relationship foundered as, month after month, failure followed failure. By the time we left them, their relationship was still intact, but they would not be unusual if it had not been.

Infertile couples have a significantly higher separation rate than couples with children, and from an evolutionary perspective this is not surprising. If each one of a pair is doing the best he or she can to enhance his or her personal reproductive output, staying with an infertile partner is obviously disadvantageous. In the hope, which even their conscious minds registered, that the problem lay with the other one, not with him- or herself, both the man and the woman were secretly acknowledging to themselves that they might do better to part company and find another mate.

Time was not on their side, whatever the eventual solution. Although there is no other problem in waiting until thirty or even later before trying to start a family – as long as success comes relatively quickly – for women, in particular, failure to conceive at thirty can impose pressures of its own. At this age, though criteria vary from country to country, it is often difficult to get accepted on to in-vitro fertilisation programmes, not least because the chances of success rapidly decrease after thirty. There is a decline, too, in the chances of finding, settling down and conceiving with a new partner. As time went on, therefore, the woman in the scene would have become increasingly anxious.

When women who are fighting infertility are interviewed, they often feel the need to justify logically why they want to conceive. This should not be necessary. In the Introduction we pointed out the inevitability of the drive to have children: genes that programme people *not* to do so are ruthlessly weeded out by natural selection. As long as a person produces at least one child, there is still the chance of long-term reproductive success; in fact, for some, one may be the optimal family size. But *no children* can never be the optimum, and people's bodies should yearn to reproduce at least once, even if they wait a long time for the right moment. We should not be surprised if some find it difficult to justify their yearning for parenthood: the yearning is of the body, and does not always reach the brain in any logical form. Only evolutionary biology makes it obvious why the vast majority of people are programmed to want children.

Natural selection is impressed not by what people say, only by what they do. Many a woman who maintains she will never have children ends her life with as many children and grandchildren as her contemporaries. Her early stand is simply part of a subconscious strategy for family planning, her brain belying the subtle underlying

35

plans of her body. The couple in our scene, who consciously wanted children, were doing everything they could to conceive. Any month that she ovulated, her egg would almost certainly have been fertilised. There are, therefore, only two possible explanations for their failure. One, of course, is that they are infertile or sub-fertile and thus will need medical assistance at some point. The other is that either or both are subconsciously avoiding conception. For all they know, one or other of their bodies, in order to enhance its lifetime's reproductive output, may have a powerful reason *not* to conceive just yet. If so, personal stress has done its contraceptive job.

Which possibility is most likely is not yet clear. All is about to be revealed, however, as we rejoin them in the doctor's surgery, as they wait to hear the medical judgement.

SCENE 4
Success?

According to the doctor, it was good news. As they sat, watching him riffle through various test reports, peering at some for longer than others, they felt a mixture of relief and disbelief. Evidently her tubes were clear, her womb looked healthy, she was ovulating, and her hormone profile was as it should be. He had perhaps slightly fewer sperm than would be expected – unless he ejaculated particularly often, the doctor commented, without looking up – and perhaps slightly more with strange-shaped heads, but nothing that wasn't within the normal range for a fertile man. He couldn't see any advantage, or indeed reason, to refer them for in-vitro fertilisation or any other form of assisted conception. He might as well spare them the stress, pain and expense.

In short, he summarised, as far as he could see there was nothing to stop them having a baby in the normal way and all he could recommend was that they should just keep on trying. 'Throw away the temperature charts,' he advised. 'Try and forget about it – just do what comes naturally.'

'... and why not take a holiday?' was his parting shot. 'Go and enjoy yourselves – get rid of some of that stress.'

They were very quiet on the way home, relief and confusion mingling in their minds. Both were relieved that they appeared to be fertile. But they were puzzled as to why, therefore, eighteen months after they had stopped using any kind of contraception, she wasn't pregnant. And, though they exchanged not a word about it, both felt an irrational tinge of disappointment that the other hadn't been found to have a problem. The prospect of simply carrying on trying, with no explanation of what they might be doing wrong, filled them with dismay – and boredom.

After they had returned home and downed a bottle of wine, they 'celebrated', if somewhat half-heartedly, by having sex. Then, starting on their second bottle while still in bed, they discussed the earliest date they could take a holiday. Despite the doctor's advice, and despite their better judgement, they found themselves trying to work out when her next two periods were due so that they could time it for when she would be most fertile. But after booking their holiday for six weeks' time, her next period came a week earlier than expected and ruined all their calculations.

The weekend before their holiday, they had a visit from their out-of-town friends and their two children. They were just passing through and would stay overnight. The woman's other two college friends and their partners were busy, so they couldn't have their usual get-together.

Invariably, whenever the two couples met and the children were finally in bed, the women would get slightly drunk, and their partners a lot more so. As was also usual, conversation would range from nostalgic reminiscences of college days, to future job prospects, sex – and conception problems. To the disappointment of their visitors, there were no racy stories this time – just the report from the doctor. When the men were slumped in their chairs, asleep, the two women fell to talking about former lovers.

The hostess woke the next morning with a clear head, sound stomach and, to her surprise – for it was a rare feeling these days – an overwhelming desire for a penis inside her. Congratulating herself on having judged to perfection the amount she had drunk the night before, she set about waking her sleeping partner by playing with his genitals. He moaned, not with pleasure or excitement but because of the pain in his right temple and a feeling of nausea. Even so, as if with a mind of its own – it had been three days since he ejaculated, which was a long time for him – his penis responded to the challenge. During intercourse, and in the moments after ejaculation, his hangover cleared, only to return as coital excitement faded.

After briefly drifting off to sleep, the woman got out of bed, showered, pulled on a bath-robe and went downstairs to start on the messy kitchen they had abandoned the night before. Hardly had she begun than she heard her visitors' children leaping around upstairs. Whenever they stayed, the children had the habit of coming into their bedroom and wanting to play games with her partner. He was very good, very patient with children — he would make a wonderful father, if he ever had chance. As she listened to the revelry upstairs, sadness threatened to overwhelm her.

Fifteen minutes later, showered and dressed but still pale and dishevelled, her partner appeared, herded noisily along by the children. They were urging him to take them to the local shop, as he often did when they visited. On such occasions, he invariably had a hangover and found the walk therapeutic. Usually, he would buy his newspaper and something for them — something that almost always stopped them from wanting breakfast when they returned. Today, though, although agreeing to go, he insisted on having a cup of coffee first. As he drank, the children's mother entered the kitchen and apologised profusely for her offspring. She too felt like a walk, so she'd go along with them, to protect him from their worst demands.

Scarcely had they closed the door when the children's father, in a hastily donned track-suit, joined the hostess in the kitchen. He had heard the door close and had guessed — since the trip to the shop was a ritual event — what was happening. As the woman pulled on her rubber gloves to deal with the mess in the sink, he — moving cautiously so as to nurse his head — set about making them both some coffee.

They spoke little, relaxed in each other's company after so many years' acquaintance. After a few minutes, he asked where she wanted her coffee. Still busy at the sink, she indicated the window ledge in front of her. He came up behind her and reached forward to put it where she had asked, but as he moved to go away, she drew his attention to something in the garden. To get a better view, he had to stand close behind her and peer over her shoulder through the window. Losing his balance slightly, he steadied himself by resting his hands on her waist and hips. The unexpected contact and proximity sent an immediate surge of sexual chemistry through both their bodies. Normally, such contact would have been momentary and he would have apologised. He apologised now, but left his hands in place moments longer than either would have expected. Despite themselves, both moved just enough for her bottom, as she leaned slightly forward over the sink, a dirty plate in her gloved hand, to nestle against his groin. Even through her dressing-gown and his track-suit, she could feel his penis stiffening.

They both froze, utterly confused by the events of the last few seconds. Changing his grip slightly, he eased her back against him and made the tiniest of movements with his groin – enough to send her a signal, but little enough for them both to pretend it hadn't happened, if necessary. After a moment, it was the woman who broke the silence.

'Do it,' she said, without moving her body an inch. 'Just do it.' There was more anger than passion in her quiet but determined voice. Then, when he didn't respond immediately, she repeated, 'Do it. Just do it.'

In a daze – on automatic, but shaking with the urgency of it – he pulled up her dressing-gown to expose her naked buttocks. Plate still in her hand, she didn't move except to bend further forward over the sink. He reached between her legs to locate her vagina, parting the lips with his fingers. She was very wet, he assumed from excitement, unaware that less than an hour previously she had been inseminated by her partner. Pulling down the front of his track-suit, he released his taut penis which now sprang free, harder and more erect than it had been for months. With his hand, he pushed it between her legs and rubbed its tip up and down between her lips, then tried to push it in. The tip went in, but the angle was wrong, and even standing on tip-toe he could enter no further. Feeling an ejaculation already on its way, he told her with urgency in his voice to lower herself a bit, and to open her legs a bit more. She obeyed – and immediately he was deep inside her. She stood still as a statue. Only the tiniest of sounds came from her throat as, after very few thrusts, he began to ejaculate, and a gentle ripple passed through her body. The whole process, from his hands first touching her waist to the first spurt of ejaculation, had taken just under three minutes.

Scarcely had the second spurt been delivered into her vagina than young voices were heard at the front door on the other side of the house, and only seconds later the still coupled pair heard the distant sound of keys in the lock. He was still inside her and not yet spent. Panicking, and with some discomfort, he pulled out his penis, still erect and spurting. Frantically, he pulled down her dressing-gown to cover her buttocks, and hoicked up his track-suit bottoms over his still hard penis. As he did so, the last dribble of semen wet his underpants.

They were just decent and moving apart when the children ran into the kitchen, and by the time their partners entered, the pair were on opposite sides of the room, he drinking coffee and complaining to his children about his hangover, she busying herself with the last of the washing-up. He spent a nervous few minutes until his penis shrank back to normal, afraid his partner would notice its size through his track-suit. The hostess had a bad moment too when, minutes after she had taken off her gloves and the adults were discussing what to have for breakfast, she noticed a drop of semen on the kitchen floor by the sink. With a deft movement of her bare foot she did away with the evidence.

Thanks largely to the children's boisterousness, the unease of the unfaithful pair went unnoticed. After lunch, the visitors set off on their journey and the other two returned to their normal routine. A few days later they went on their week's vacation, spending their days relaxing on hot, sunny beaches and their nights eating and drinking and watching the local children playing around the tables as they dined. They had sex at least every day and felt happier and more positive about their relationship than they had for over a year.

And this time, her period never came. Two weeks after returning home he woke to the sound of her being sick in the toilet, and that same day a test confirmed she was pregnant. The doctor accepted an accolade for suggesting that a holiday might do the trick, and before long she was feeling so ill she wondered if she really wanted to be pregnant after all. They waited three months, until the pregnancy felt secure, before breaking the news to their friends. And by the time they all next gathered together, there was no longer any need for talk about conception campaigns. They were all parents now – or so they thought.

So what happened? Why should a couple with no apparent medical problems suddenly conceive after nearly two years of failure?

There are, of course, many possibilities, and one of the most interesting but least obvious is that from the very beginning their conception campaign, far from being a cooperative venture, had in fact been a war of attrition; that deep down, only one of them had really wanted to conceive – until the month of their holiday.

Of course, couples often *openly* disagree about the best time to start a family, and such differences of opinion can cause bitter strife. Both the man and the woman will have good reasons for their respective stances, and invariably both will be trying to do what is best for their personal reproductive output. Natural selection will have shaped most people's ability to judge what really is best for them, and if that doesn't coincide with what is best for their partner, open conflict is inevitable. *Overt* disagreement, however, was not a feature of the situation for our couple. On the surface, they were cooperating as much as they possibly could. Any disagreement, therefore, had to be subconscious – and when we look at the way things turned out, there is more than a hint that the woman's body was actually playing a different and more covert game than the man's. Without doubt he, both consciously and subconsciously, had been doing his best to get his partner to conceive; and *consciously* the woman had been doing her best to cooperate. Unknown to either of them, however, her body may well have been delaying conception, waiting for the right moment, and perhaps even the right man. It is more than likely that the genetic father of the child born at the end of *her* conception campaign was not her partner, but her friend's partner – he with whom she had had a three-minute intercourse one Sunday morning while washing the dishes. And the reason is as follows.

There is a feature of a woman's menstrual cycle that we have not so far described and that has evolved specifically to allow her to take advantage of situations such as that illustrated in the scene above. What seems to happen in every menstrual cycle is this. In the days after the beginning of a period, a woman's body goes through a series of hormonal changes that prepare it to produce an egg but, about two days before ovulation can occur, her body effectively goes 'on hold'. Whether she eventually produces an egg or not depends on what happens in the days, or even weeks, that follow.

This holding period is an opportunity to collect sperm, perhaps just from her partner, perhaps not; perhaps just from one man, perhaps from two or more. In part, whether or not she ovulates will depend on how her body feels about the man or men from whom she has collected sperm. But most of all it will depend on how it feels about trying to produce a baby in the current circumstances, reflected in her level of stress. If the man and the moment seem absolutely right, ovulation and hence conception can actually be triggered by intercourse. If the man and the moment are not right, the intercourse may not influence, or may even inhibit, ovulation.

What is the evidence for this? Between days 14 and 35 of her cycle (taking the first day of bleeding as day 1) a woman is much more likely to conceive from a *one-off* intercourse than she is from a *routine* intercourse with her long-term partner. A one-off intercourse with a lover or a rapist, or even a one-off intercourse with a long-term partner who returns home briefly (on weekend leave, perhaps), are all more likely than routine intercourse to lead to conception *on these days of the cycle*. This doesn't mean that a woman's long-term partner cannot also trigger her to ovulate through routine intercourse. It is just that she is less likely to respond so positively to him under routine circumstances than she is to him, or to other men, in one-off circumstances.

The occasional triggering of ovulation by intercourse probably explains why a woman is most likely to conceive from intercourse *two days* before ovulation, despite the fact that from within about an hour of intercourse there is a steady trickle of sperm through her oviducts for up to five days. The reason is probably that if the man and the moment are right for her body, sex while she is 'on hold' actually triggers ovulation, but the process from trigger to ovulation takes two days. So rather than trying to judge when the woman is going to ovulate, a couple may as well simply have sex as and when they, and particularly she, feel like it.

In addition to this apparent ability to ovulate in response to opportunity, a woman's hormones lead her to be much more receptive to a lover, as opposed to her regular partner, while her body is on hold. We saw earlier that a woman will have sex with her long-term partner at any stage of her menstrual cycle, as part of sexual crypsis. As well as being much more likely to have sex with a lover during the holding period, a woman is programmed by her hormones to change her behaviour while on hold. Studies of the amount of time women spend on their own reveal that whereas those who have no long-term partner show little change during the menstrual cycle, those who do have long-term partners tend to spend less time with them and more time exploring new places during their most fertile phase. And, *while out of sight of their partner*, they dress and behave more provocatively.

Researchers in a Viennese discotheque photographed women and measured both the amount of bare skin they were revealing and how tight-fitting and transparent were their clothes. The women then had their saliva tested for oestrogen level. Those who had long-term partners but had left them at home for a night out 'with the girls' were much more likely to dress provocatively during the fertile phase of their cycle, when oestrogen levels were high, than at other times. Women without long-term partners at home showed no such variation.

The implication is that until a woman has a long-term partner to support her, she does not seek one-off intercourse during the 'on hold' phase of her cycle. A woman supported by a partner is much more likely to be driven by her body chemistry to try to attract the attention of other men during her 'on hold' phase. Moreover, given the chance, she is more likely to collect sperm from those men, and to conceive. The fact that the woman in the scene awoke that morning with an urge for a penis in her vagina suggests that she was on hold. Her body was waiting for yet another month to see what transpired before making a decision about ovulation. Moreover, the fact that, taking advantage of the briefest of opportunities, she allowed her friend's partner to inseminate her – maybe even unknowingly engineered it – also suggests her body was in the holding phase.

Why might this woman have been so much more keen to ovulate and conceive once she had collected sperm from another man? Ten years or so earlier, she and her partner had chosen to live together and share their lives, and since then they had been through so much together in the name of conception. Why renege on him now?

Sadly, for those who would wish things were different, natural selection has predisposed people's bodies to be selfish and single-minded; it has no mechanism for evolving true altruism. We are the descendants of people whose bodies put their own reproduction first, and we have inherited our ancestor's selfishness. True, our bodies cooperate with other bodies at many times in our lives – and often for long periods – but only when such cooperation enhances our personal reproductive success. The moment that such cooperation begins to threaten that reproductive success, our bodies do what is best for themselves, not what is best for the other person. Natural selection has favoured those bodies which, even while cooperating with a long-term partner, are continuously alert for the opportunity to enhance their reproductive success just that bit more than they can with that partner. If such an opportunity ever arises, the body does its best to take advantage, whatever the reproductive consequences for the partner – and that's precisely what the woman in our scene did.

It should not be surprising that a woman from time to time

encounters a situation in which infidelity might enhance her reproductive success. It is, in fact, an almost inevitable result of men
showing long-term parental care. We shall discuss the criteria by
which a woman selects her partner(s) in a later chapter, but there
is an important duality at issue here. On the one hand she has a
need for a man who can help her raise children. On the other, she
has a need for genes that in combination with her own will produce
attractive, fertile and successful children. Some of her difficulties
arise from having a much wider choice of gene-providers than of
long-term partners. It takes only a few minutes, as we have just
witnessed, to collect a man's genes, but many years of cooperation
from him to raise children.

In the scene, the woman with the conception problem seemed
quite content with her partner as a provider and as someone to
look after any children she might have. They were moderately
affluent, able to afford their own house, car and holidays. And her
partner, in the way he acted with her friend's offspring, showed
every indication that he would make a very good father, in terms
of caring for children. But maybe her body was unconvinced that
he was the best she could do in terms of genes for her children.
This may have been the reason her body didn't allow conception
in the first place – and once the seeds of fear over his fertility had
been sown, maybe her body's reluctance was reinforced.

Women seek different attributes in short-term than in long-term
partners. And the much greater choice of short-term gene-providers
opens up two main options. One is to find a man who, although
neither the best provider of genes nor the best partner, is at least the
best available compromise she can attract. The other is to choose
the best available long-term partner and then rely on infidelity to
obtain the best genes. The woman in the scene probably started
out, ten years earlier, following the first option. As we have just
seen, however, she ended up resorting to the second – and she is
not alone.

About 10 per cent of children are not sired by their supposed
fathers. Some men have a higher chance of being cuckolded
than others, and it is those of low wealth and status who fare
worst. Actual figures range from 1 per cent in high-status areas of
Switzerland and the USA, through 5–6 per cent for moderate-status
males in Britain and the USA, to 10–30 per cent for lower-status

males in Britain, France and the USA. Moreover, the men most likely to cuckold the lower-status males are those of higher status. Anthropological studies have shown precisely the same pattern. In society after society, men of higher wealth and status obtain partners earlier, maybe obtain more partners, start to reproduce earlier, are less likely to be cuckolded, and are more likely to cuckold other males. In all ways, therefore, men of wealth and status have the potential to be reproductively more successful than their lower-status contemporaries.

That there is a similar status-dependent pattern for female infidelity should not be surprising, and it goes like this. Women paired to wealthier, higher-status men have little to gain from infidelity and much to lose. Those paired to poor, lower-status men, on the other hand, have little to lose and potentially much to gain – especially if they can be unfaithful with men from higher up the social scale. For the woman in the scene, though, wealth- and status-seeking are unlikely to have been the motivation for her infidelity. She had no intention of leaving her own partner for her friend's, who in any case was no higher up any social scale than she was. Her body's interest in him can only have been genetic. She wanted his sperm and his genes, and she took advantage of an opportunity to get them. But her strategy would only really have paid off, reproductively, if any genetic gain was greater than the disadvantages she could have suffered from her infidelity – for there were potential dangers in her behaviour, as well as potential benefits.

First, there was the risk of contracting one or more sexually transmitted diseases. The more sexual partners a person has, the greater that risk. It isn't particularly high, but it is real, and every act of infidelity increases it and could be a threat to a person's future health and fertility. The other dangers would only materialise if her act of infidelity was discovered. At worst, she might have risked violence from her partner, or even from her friend. She might even have risked her partner leaving, particularly if she became pregnant soon enough after her infidelity for him to suspect that the child might not be his. And there were other dangers associated with lone and step-parenthood, which will be discussed in later chapters. Apart from the risk of disease, however, none of the dangers of infidelity was particularly great *as long as she could avoid discovery*.

The man, too, ran risks from his infidelity. He, too, was risking disease, desertion and perhaps even violence if his infidelity was discovered – violence from the woman's partner, and perhaps even from his own. Again, however, none of the dangers was particularly great *as long as he could avoid discovery*.

It is because of the importance of maintaining secrecy that the man and the woman instinctively reacted with urgency and guile when they heard their partners returning from the shop with the children. It is unlikely that either will have thought in advance about what they would do in such a situation, but when the moment came both went into automatic deception mode. Adrenaline flowed just as instantaneously and forcefully as if a tiger had burst into the room. And as it turned out, their deception was successful. Their partners remained ignorant of the events that had taken place during their ten-minute absence.

Humans are not the only species to use guile and deception to allow them to avoid the costs of infidelity while reaping its benefits. Given the driving force of a body chemically programmed to avoid discovery, suitable strategies can be invented without recourse to the human brain. Many people will have seen the film showing a female monkey foraging on the ground for food while being watched attentively from a high branch by her consort. Alongside her comes another male. He sits down, innocently picking at himself, hiding his erection from the first male. Every time the latter's attention is distracted, the other male taps the female on the shoulder. In an instant she stands and presents and he inseminates her, in an act not very different from the one we have just witnessed. So quick is their intercourse that by the time her consort looks back in their direction, they have resumed their previous activities, innocence personified.

The events that befell our man and woman in this scene clear up another conundrum from the early stages of the couple's conception campaign: the enigma of sexual crypsis. Once sex every day has become a duty rather than a pleasure, many a couple have cursed their inability to know when the woman is most fertile. To many, sexual crypsis seems at first to be one of natural selection's most mischievous tricks. But, on the contrary, in shaping sexual crypsis it has handed women one of their most powerful weapons in the control of their reproductive destinies.

The scene illustrates just why it is so important to a woman that her body betrays nothing about the stage she is at in her menstrual cycle. Crypsis gives her much greater freedom to choose the genetic father of her next child than if she advertised her fertility.

The females of those primates, such as baboons and chimpanzees, that do advertise their fertility have a hectic time during their fertile phase. Males fight over sexual access and the females are often pestered. Even worse, in many ways, the strongest male does his very best to make sure he is the only one to inseminate her. Of course, the female gains from all this the reproductive advantage of being inseminated primarily by the male who is fit and strong enough to win access and guard her. The price she pays for this, though, is a reduction in her freedom to select her own mate. There may be males she prefers to the dominant male, but he tries to prevent her from mating with them. For instance, there may be in the troop a younger male who, in a few years' time, is clearly going to be the most successful male, and whom she would prefer to father her child rather than the current dominant. Occasionally, such a female manages to 'be unfaithful' to the dominant male, as the example described above illustrates, but she won't find it as easy as a human female does. This is because the male who guards her, unlike his human counterpart, *knows* when she is fertile. Consequently he may even give up eating and sleeping for those few critical days, so that he can watch her continuously and make it very difficult for her to stray.

If the woman's partner in the scene had *known* what a critical day in his life it was, maybe he wouldn't have taken the other couple's children to the shops, leaving his partner alone with the other man. But to him, it seemed like any other day. Similarly, most men would have no objection to their partner going out to a discotheque with other women. But if a man *knew* it was a critical night, one on which his partner was chemically primed to attract, flirt, respond and conceive to another man, he might well not want her to go.

This, then, is why natural selection has designed a woman's body to hide its fertile phases from men. But why has it hidden the information even from *her* conscious mind? The answer is that for a woman to be able to conceal her fertility from men most convincingly, she needs also to conceal it from herself. That way, she is less likely to give off signals inadvertently.

There is one element of the scene that we have not yet considered. If, as we are supposing, the woman did conceive after her morning at the sink, she did so while she had sperm from two different men inside her. On waking, she had cajoled her partner into sex and within an hour she was having sex with her friend's partner. For at least the next five days, her body will have contained sperm from both, and there will have been a steady trickle from both passing through her oviducts. Approximately 4 per cent of children are conceived under such circumstances. Whenever a woman has sex with two different men within the space of a few days, the two lots of sperm compete for the prize of fertilising any egg she may produce. This competition is both a lottery and a race, but more than anything it is a war. Within the ejaculate of every normal, healthy, fertile man there are sperm of many different shapes and sizes. Some have large heads, some have small – some even have heads so small that there is no room for chromosomes and genes. Some sperm have short tails, while others have two, three or even four. Each of these types have different roles to play in sperm warfare. Fewer than 1 per cent of sperm are programmed to seek and fertilise the egg, the remainder being programmed for a variety of offensive and defensive actions: in their different ways, their job is to try to stop any other man's sperm from fertilising the egg.

Women sometimes gain from promoting sperm warfare. The woman in the scene will certainly have done so. During the previous two years her growing doubts about her partner's fertility will have made his standing as a suitable genetic father less certain. One way her body could put her partner and his ejaculates to the ultimate test would be to place his sperm in direct competition with the sperm of another man of proven fertility, and let them fight it out. And this is what she did.

The chances are that her partner's sperm would not have won the battle. Not least, this is because the sperm war she promoted was unequal, in that she actually biased the odds *against* her partner. How? On the morning in question she had no orgasm with her partner, but did with her lover. So, despite the last spurt of her lover's ejaculate ending up on the floor, she will almost certainly have retained more sperm in total from his early ejaculations than she did from all of her partner's. In which case, having the larger of the two sperm armies, her lover was the more likely to win the sperm war. As we have said before, her orgasm will have made no difference to her *chances* of conception, but if she did conceive while containing both men's sperm it will have made a difference to *which man* fertilised her egg.

So far we have assumed that the medical judgement on the woman's partner was correct and that he really was fertile. All the same, we cannot take it for granted that he *was* fertile just because medical tests failed to reveal any problem. Unfortunately, the study of male infertility is still a long way from allowing definitive statements to be made about any one man's fertility. Statistical correlations can be found between levels of fertility and all sorts of characteristics of ejaculates – the number of sperm, the proportion of normal-looking sperm and sperm motility, for example – but that is all they are, statistical correlations. Their implications cannot be applied with certainty to any one man. Men with poor-looking ejaculates are sometimes fertile, and men with magnificent-looking ones are sometimes infertile.

One of the commonest misconceptions is that men need to inseminate huge numbers of sperm for the intercourse to stand any chance of leading to pregnancy. The origin of this misconception is twofold. First, men normally *do* inseminate huge numbers of sperm: the average ejaculate contains about three hundred million of them. Second, medical studies show that men who ejaculate fewer than twenty million (via masturbation after three days' abstinence) are more likely to be sub-fertile than men who ejaculate the standard three hundred million.

What this means, though, is that low sperm numbers are some-times symptomatic of an underlying medical problem. It *does not* mean that if a man without such a problem inseminates only twenty million sperm, his partner will not conceive. If the sperm are healthy and fertile, very few are needed for conception. If a man ejaculates via masturbation, or from oral sex, less than an hour before having penetrative sex with his partner, he will inseminate her with only about twenty million sperm, or even fewer. There is a case on record of a vasectomised man who inseminated no more than a few tens of sperm at each insemination, yet his partner still became pregnant. Neither he nor the medical profession could believe that his sprinkling of sperm could have achieved fertilisation, and suspected that the man's partner had been unfaithful to him. She fiercely denied this, and asked for a paternity test using DNA fingerprinting. Sure enough, she was vindicated. Her partner was indeed the father of the child. Returning to our scene, whatever the medical judgement on the man's ejaculate, it was only *an opinion* on his fertility at a particular point, not a verdict on a permanent state.

So far, this discussion has assumed that the genetic father of the child was the man of proven fertility, not the woman's partner, because the fact that she conceived in the cycle in which she happened to be unfaithful suggests too much of a coincidence. But is it really not feasible that the man who actually got her pregnant was her partner?

One possibility is that the woman did not in fact conceive from either of the intercourses on the day of her infidelity. It could be that conception occurred in the week that followed, when the couple were on holiday – in which case their doctor will have deserved the accolade he received. From the first few months of their conception campaign, the couple had been under strain. Worries about their fertility had locked them into a self-perpetuating cycle, and the stress had quite possibly caused both of their bodies to switch into family-planning mode, as we have already discussed. Then, as each month went by, their relationship deteriorated and stress did its contraceptive work with even greater vigour. Possibly, therefore, despite the couple's conscious wishes, what both their bodies had decided was that, until conditions improved and until their relationship was more secure, conception might actually prejudice their long-term reproductive output. Then, relaxing on holiday and with the relief of having the medical tests behind them, their bodies may have decided the time was at last ripe. The man may have started to produce more fertile ejaculates; the woman may have become receptive to the whole process of sperm transport, fertilisation, implantation and pregnancy.

A second possibility is that there had been a medical problem all the time they had been trying to conceive which coincidentally cleared up at about the time they started having tests. Minor but recurrent bouts of infection of both male and female tracts can cause temporary blockages which clear without treatment, thus restoring fertility. Perhaps their bodies were actually delaying conception until the problem had cleared, at which point the couple conceived.

For the morally inclined, either of these scenarios may be the preferred explanation. However, it is still most likely that the woman conceived from her act of infidelity. If so, there is a huge but instructive irony surrounding that intercourse. For nearly two years, the woman and her partner had done their utmost to conceive, carefully choosing their moments and their positions, taking their time, and on every occasion doing their best to keep as much semen inside her for as long as possible. Yet here was a spontaneous coupling that lasted only three minutes, that took place while she was standing up, and in which part of the ejaculate ended up not in her vagina but on the kitchen floor.

The episode serves to illustrate the reality of conception. For a fertile woman, if the man and the moment are right, the process of fertilisation can be highly efficient. When a woman's body – as opposed to her mind – wants to conceive, it can do so easily.

CHAPTER THREE

Pregnancy, Labour and Serenity

SCENE 5
Sex during Pregnancy

He awoke from his dream at the moment of ejaculation. The relief was incredible — his unconscious mind had convinced him that circumstances would find ever more ingenious ways of thwarting his urge. He carefully got out of bed, anxious not to wake his partner, sleeping soundly beside him.

A glance at the clock on the bedside cabinet told him it had just turned midnight. She had been asleep for almost four hours already; she seemed to need so much sleep now that she was pregnant. A few months earlier she would never have gone to bed before ten, and if she had it would have been with him and to have sex. How long was it since they last had sex? Three months, at least.

While he was cleaning himself up in the bathroom, he thought back to the first few weeks of her pregnancy before they had actually known she was pregnant. Then they had had sex often, even more than usual, and more often than not she had initiated it. There was no doubt that her libido had suddenly increased at that time. And she had also wanted more orgasms, frequently asking him to masturbate her until she came. If the ultrasound scan hadn't told them otherwise, they would both have assumed she had conceived during this sudden rush of sexual activity.

He had enjoyed those first few weeks, but everything had changed with the onset of pregnancy sickness, and the headaches and the tiredness. Suddenly sex was the last thing on her mind. She started going to bed earlier and earlier. Physical contact went no further than cuddling and stroking. He didn't want to pressurise her and had carefully hidden his frustration — but frustrated he had certainly been. She had lost a bit of weight on account of her lack of appetite and her breasts had begun to swell. He was actually finding her more of a turn-on than usual, which seemed oddly inappropriate.

As time went on, though, she had begun to look more and more pregnant. Her waist thickened and she began to walk with a slight waddle. Subtly inviting him to disagree with her, she began saying how unattractive she felt. He reacted by finding other ways of complimenting her, but in truth he *was* finding her shape less and less attractive. Not that he felt any less for her. In fact, if anything, he felt more tender and affectionate towards her than ever. It was just that his urges towards her were no longer particularly sexual, a fact that made him feel guilty whenever they discussed their feelings for each other. What made things worse was that his feelings were changing just at a time when she was going through a period of insecurity. Once or twice she had even accused him of eyeing up other women. Things had come to a head one night when they had gone to a party together. It had started badly. Complaining she had nothing suitable to wear, she hadn't really wanted to go and would have much preferred to stay at home, watch television and have an early night.

He had been in good spirits and looking forward to a bit of socialising. Also, although he didn't tell her, he was looking forward to the opportunity to show off his pregnant partner. About halfway through the party the pair found themselves in separate groups, talking. He was having an intense discussion with a woman he knew vaguely from work, and although he had never taken much notice of her before, tonight he was finding her strangely attractive. Before he knew it he had been talking to her for over half an hour, at which point his partner came over, took a firm hold of his arm and suggested that it was time to leave. He could see something was wrong. Was she feeling ill, or had something upset her?

Having said a few awkward goodbyes they walked in silence to the car. She stared doggedly ahead; he snatched a few sideways glances at her. Once in the car she came right out with it: he had been flirting with the woman from his workplace. He tried to defend himself, but it was useless. She was determined not to listen. Just as they arrived home, she accused him of not liking her pregnant shape. Then, knowing it was ridiculous and regretting it almost as she spoke, she challenged him to prove that he still found her attractive by making love to her.

By now, sex with her was the last thing on his mind. He also knew that in his half-inebriated state the chances of his managing to get and maintain an erection weren't good, particularly given that he wasn't very interested anyway. All he really wanted to do was sleep. However, he simply said that he felt uneasy about having intercourse when she was this far on in her pregnancy. What if it started something? Couldn't they just go to bed and cuddle instead? In the end she agreed, and at first cuddle was what they did, she on her side with her legs bent and he with his arm round her and his hand resting gently on her bulge. He was asleep within minutes. She lay awake, her eyes glistening in the dark with unshed tears. It was over an hour before she finally fell asleep.

At same point in the early hours, each had become aware that the other was awake. They began to kiss in a lazy, sensuous way. He felt himself getting aroused – maybe the alcohol was wearing off. Neither of them said anything – they just continued kissing and stroking each other. He wasn't at all sure what she wanted him to do, bearing in mind their earlier agreement to take no chances. It wasn't long, though, before she left him in no doubt of her wishes. In a well practised if ungainly movement she slid on top of him, gently took hold of his penis and guided it into her vagina.

Their activity ended when he withdrew rather abruptly after ejaculation, worried that he might be doing some damage inside her. Except for one moment when her vagina had seemed unusually short, for him their intercourse hadn't felt much different from normal. Even so, he was reluctant to thrust, and was surprised when she seemed to climax.

Once she had inveigled him into her, she too had felt uneasy about what they were doing. Yes, she had reached orgasm – but quickly wished she hadn't. Immediately afterwards she had felt the baby turn completely over in her womb, just as if her orgasm had disturbed it in some way. She hadn't much enjoyed the feeling, and it had seemed ages before the agitation in her womb finally settled enough for her to drift back to sleep.

After cleaning himself up in the bathroom, the man stood staring into the cabinet mirror. Remembering his dream, he thought of the baby soon to be born and wondered if it would resemble him. Walking back into the bedroom, he looked at the dark shape of his sleeping partner. There was only a week or so to go before he would find out what he was letting himself in for. Presumably he would soon be pacing the room again in the early hours, but for a quite different reason.

At first sight, it seems strange for natural selection to have evolved the habit of continuing sex into, and sometimes throughout, pregnancy. Neither the man nor the woman would seem to enhance their reproductive output by it. The woman is already pregnant, so she cannot conceive further. It all seems even more peculiar in the light of the fact that virtually every sperm the male inseminates is ejected in the woman's flowback. So why should humans, and many other mammals, continue to have intercourse once the female has conceived?

The answer is that pregnancy is not the time of serene cooperation that many would expect or wish it to be. It is a time of conflict, both inside and outside the woman, as the three scenes in this chapter illustrate. Some of the battles take place inside the developing child and inside the mother's womb – these will be discussed in the next two scenes. Other battles, taking place between the man and the woman, are more conspicuous – we have just witnessed examples of these in the scene above. Some of these male/female conflicts are obvious and appreciated by all. Others are subtle and easily missed. But all involve sex.

One of the most subtle forms of conflict between a man and a woman is the sexual activity that occurs during the first few weeks of pregnancy. In fact, it is so subtle that few people would guess that the behaviour is driven by major differences in interest on the part of the participants. Less subtle are disagreements over how far into pregnancy the couple should continue having sex. And the least subtle of all are arguments over the man's heightened interest in other women at a time when his partner is at her most vulnerable.

None of these conflicts are perverse accidents. All flow inevitably from the fact that natural selection has predisposed men and women to give priority to their own reproductive performance, even at the expense of their partner's. Later, we shall consider the question that was uppermost in the conscious minds of the couple in the scene: how dangerous is sex during pregnancy? For if, as we shall argue, sex during pregnancy is a battle, is there a risk of casualties? First, though, if we are to understand any of these conflicts, we need to consider why the pressures on men and women are different.

Pregnancy is one of the most critical and *ambivalent* phases of life as far as the reproductive output of both the woman and her partner are concerned. On the one hand, an obvious major reproductive step has been accomplished by the woman and the child's genetic father. On the other, though it is intuitively less obvious, pregnancy can also be *a threat* to the long-term reproduction of both the woman and her partner. The nature of this threat needs elaborating.

As far as she is concerned, if anything goes wrong during the pregnancy her body may suffer to such an extent that her future reproduction may be compromised. In fact, damage could be so severe that it might actually prevent her from having further children (we discuss the physical damage a woman may suffer as a result of pregnancy towards the end of this chapter). On top of the physical dangers, there is also the risk that her partner may desert her or decide that he is going to offer her and the baby little in the way of future support. Often a woman is so dependent on her partner's support that if he does either of these things her child's survival and future success are jeopardised.

As far as the man is concerned, his partner's pregnancy *is* a major step towards his reproductive output – but only so long as he is the genetic father. If he is not, then her pregnancy is actually a threat to his long-term reproductive output. Not only may he be committing himself to many years of effort in order to enhance some other man's reproductive success at the expense of his own, but the next year or so will be a barren period during which *he* cannot make his partner pregnant. If he ever has strong reason to doubt his paternity of the child she is carrying, it may be in his long-term reproductive interests to leave her, particularly if he can find himself another woman.

Because of the potential threat to his long-term reproduction, a man's confidence in his paternity is one of the most important factors in how good a father he will be to the forthcoming child. Nearly every chapter in the rest of this book will have cause to interpret a man's paternal behaviour in this context. Sometimes his behaviour is consciously influenced by his confidence in his paternity. More often than not, though, it is influenced subconsciously, just as the paternal behaviour of other species is. Studies of animals as diverse as sparrows, lions and monkeys have shown that the quality of a male's paternal behaviour is strongly governed by the probability of his being the genetic father.

If a woman, just like the females of all these other species, is going to get maximum help from a man in the raising of her offspring, it is of vital importance to her that she does everything she can to convince him of his paternity. At the same time, it is vitally important for him to try to determine the real likelihood of his being the genetic father.

In the scene above, the man pondered over whether the baby would look like him. In doing so, he was showing the widespread human preoccupation with finding physical similarities between children and their parents. This preoccupation should not surprise us. If a man could tell whether a child was his simply by looking at it, he could also tell whether extended paternal care was in his long-term reproductive interests. The evidence is, however, that he cannot tell – or at least, not well enough to be certain. Studies vary in their results, but the overall conclusion is that a third party, comparing a child with a range of possible fathers, can identify the genetic father only slightly more often than if he or she simply guesses. This is not surprising, either – the child's appearance, after all, is determined by genes only half of which came from its father. Although similarities can be spotted even during the child's first year of babyhood, identification is very imprecise, and there is plenty of room for error. No surprises here, either. If a woman's genes allowed her child to look unmistakably like its father, she would lose her freedom to choose the best genetic father for that child just as surely as if she advertised the fertile phase of her cycle and allowed her partner to keep a twenty-four-hour watch on her. If women are to reap the genetic advantages of infidelity, therefore, it is vital that their genes compete with the father's to produce a child with as nondescript a face as possible. In fact, the more nondescript her baby's face, the more *any* man can find apparent similarities with his own. The chances are that at least one of the baby's features will resemble his, whether he is the father or not. Women seem to have won this genetic battle. Since no man can ever be absolutely certain that a child is his simply because he and others think they can see a similarity, if he is to judge the real likelihood he needs more information than he can gain from a simple comparison of appearances. If a woman can convince her partner that he is the father when he isn't – as we witnessed in the previous chapter when the woman probably conceived during an act of infidelity while working at the kitchen sink – then she gains reproductively (as does the genetic father) and her partner loses. If she fails to convince a man that he is the father when in fact he is, then they both lose reproductively, because the child will not receive the high-quality parental care that it otherwise would. So the pressure is on the man to judge the situation correctly and on the woman to convince her partner that he is the genetic father, whether he is or not. And it is never too soon for them both to respond to this pressure. The events leading up to and surrounding conception are especially critical.

In the months, or even years, during which a woman is waiting for the right moment to commit herself to pregnancy, it is important that she retains as many options as possible. Sexual crypsis, as we have already seen, gives her the upper hand. The man is vulnerable: all he can do is be on his guard and try to ensure that when the moment comes, he is the genetic father. Circumstances change, however, immediately the woman commits herself to carrying a given man's baby. Now it is she who is vulnerable, particularly if she has failed to convince her long-term partner that he is the father.

One way to increase his confidence would be to engage in a great deal of sexual activity with him *before* conception. More often than not, though, a woman continues on her cautious, sexually cryptic path right up until that moment. Then, once she has conceived, her body generates the urge for more frequent sex with him. Again, thanks largely to her sexual crypsis, a man's body can never exactly compute the date of his partner's conception, so that the tendency will always be for him to assume that conception occurred at around the time of her greatest libido and sexual activity. This is precisely how the woman behaved in the scene we have just witnessed: we can assume there was no subterfuge here and that, as in 90 per cent of conceptions, her long-term partner was also the genetic father of the child. But then, this is also precisely how the woman in the previous chapter behaved – the one who probably conceived to somebody else's partner, while bending over the kitchen sink. Her long-suffering partner assumed that after two years of trying it was their sexually active holiday that led to his becoming a father.

In a sense, continuing to have sex during pregnancy is the ultimate weapon in a woman's sexual crypsis. If she lost interest in sex as soon as she conceived, she would be giving a clear signal of her condition to the men around her. This would allow them all, but particularly her long-term partner, to make a much better assessment of who could and who could not be the genetic father. Offering extra sexual attention and access during pregnancy avoids giving any indication that she has conceived, and affords her the opportunity to give the man she has targeted, usually her long-term partner, a boost to his paternity confidence.

Women's bodies have evolved another ploy by which to hide the precise date of conception. They often menstruate two weeks after the event, and sometimes even the month or two after that. This pseudo-menstrual flow may be lighter than usual, but it is nonetheless heavy enough to cause confusion. Again, she can boost her partner's confidence in his paternity by showing him extra sexual attention when, in fact, she is already pregnant. Many a couple, and their doctors, have miscalculated the likely date of conception because of such decoy menstruations. Not until the advent in the past decade or so of routine ultrasonic scans of the baby at fourteen to eighteen weeks of pregnancy did it become possible to identify the date of conception, at least to within about a week.

Heightened libido in the early weeks of pregnancy is not confined to the Western industrialist world. !Kung bush-women, for example, show the same pattern, as do some other primates. Whether a species is monogamous, like gibbons, or whether the females openly have sex with many males, like chimpanzees, the females of many species benefit from boosting the paternity confidence of particular males by continuing sex into pregnancy. However, by no means all primate species show this type of behaviour: it seems to have evolved more often in species, like humans, with female sexual crypsis.

But why should a couple continue to have sex even after it is obvious to everybody that the woman *really is* pregnant? There are several possible explanations. Some are more likely than others – and, unfortunately, some are more sinister than others. All, however, hinge on the sexual acts still being part of an ongoing battle, because the pressures on men and women continue to differ throughout pregnancy.

Men do desert pregnant women. They are also unfaithful to them. This is because the nine months of pregnancy are a period which a man's body will see as unprofitable – and relatively secure. It is a time when his partner cannot aid him in what natural selection has dictated will be his overriding, albeit subconscious, sexual goal: the fertilisation of eggs. For at least those nine months, the only way he can pursue that goal is via other women. It should be no surprise, therefore, that men *are* more likely to be unfaithful while their partner is pregnant than at any other time. Nor should it be surprising to find that women, like the woman in the scene above, become very protective, possessive and jealous of their partner's attention during pregnancy. A woman has as great a need to guard against her partner's infidelity during this phase as *he* had to prevent her from being unfaithful in the phase leading up to conception. If he succeeds in infidelity, she can only lose. He might pick up a sexually transmitted disease which he might then pass on to her, or he might desert her for the other woman. Possessiveness is her strongest defence.

Matters are made worse for a woman by the fact that her pregnancy, as far as her partner is concerned, represents the very best time to be unfaithful. Although his primary subconscious goal in being unfaithful – the chance of siring an extra child by another woman – is always there, whether she is pregnant or not, several of the major costs of infidelity that would have restrained his philandering when she was not pregnant are now much reduced. Most importantly, the chances of his partner deserting him on discovering his infidelity diminish, because she cannot really afford to be without him after she has given birth. Also reduced is the likelihood that she will retaliate by being unfaithful herself.

There is, though, a new potential danger for a man contemplating infidelity while his partner is pregnant: that his actions will trigger a miscarriage. So miscarriage is another defence against desertion available to her. Discovering a partner's infidelity is a common trigger for a woman to abort or miscarry, as is a partner's death. The reason natural selection has designed such a drastic response is obvious: rather than carry to full term a child that has a diminished chance of paternal support, a woman's body opts instead to start again, perhaps with another man.

In the scene above, the woman continued to allow, and even instigated, sex until she was six months pregnant. Other women may do so right through their pregnancy. How does such sexual activity help a woman to guard against her partner's infidelity or desertion? One commonly voiced explanation, in relation to the females of other species as well as to humans, is that by having her partner ejaculate inside her, she reduces his desire to ejaculate inside any other female. This is optimistic – and unlikely. Even though men, on average, ejaculate only two to three times a week (depending on age and circumstance), the one situation in which most can ejaculate, no matter how recently they last did so or how frequently they have been doing so, is when they have the chance of inseminating a novel woman. Although men will not *always* accept an opportunity to inseminate someone other than their partner – their body's fear of disease, discovery or commitment sometimes causes disinclination – more often than not they will go ahead.

There is an alternative explanation for a woman's occasional interest in sex in mid- and late pregnancy, and it is the converse of the one just mentioned. Whereas most men would be interested in inseminating a mistress within an hour of inseminating a pregnant partner, they would be far less interested in inseminating a pregnant partner within an hour of inseminating a mistress. If a pregnant woman instigates sex and her partner fails to respond, it can alert her to an ongoing affair that she might otherwise not have noticed. Of course, any failure to respond could also be due simply to a recent masturbation. But it is still worth her being alerted to the possibility of an affair, even if it proves to be a false alarm. So a pregnant woman's occasional, unexpected interest in sex with her partner is much more likely to be her way of checking whether he has ejaculated recently than her trying to prevent him from ejaculating in the near future.

It is unsurprising, of course, that men eventually lose interest in inseminating a pregnant partner. Since, reproductively, they have nothing tangible to gain from intercourse with her, natural selection has so fashioned their aesthetics that they respond with less sexual interest to the shape of a pregnant women than to a non-pregnant one. As we shall discuss in a later chapter, men have been programmed to show greatest sexual interest in the female body with a waist measuring about 70 per cent of the circumference of her hips. Women with such a shape are more likely to ovulate, and are less likely already to be pregnant.

Once pregnancy begins to destroy a woman's most fertile shape, the man takes much less sexual interest in her. Nevertheless, it is often strategic for the woman to ask whether she is still a sexual object for him, even when heavily pregnant, and for the man to affirm that she is. It is all part of her ongoing assessment and reassessment of whether her partner will stay around and support her and her child. It is impossible to know, however, either how often the man really means his affirmation, or how often the woman believes him.

The heightened libido and sexual activity of early pregnancy and the gentle, careful sex of later pregnancy both emerge, therefore, as part of a jousting exercise between a man and a woman as they seek to enhance their long-term reproductive output. As we have already noted, on 90 per cent of occasions such jousting is actually unnecessary and both will benefit reproductively from doing their best for the child about to be born. On occasion, however, it *is* necessary, and one of them will benefit from victory at the expense of the other. The reason such competition always occurs is because neither can ever be one hundred per cent certain that their interests coincide.

The more sinister side to sex during pregnancy, alluded to earlier, raises the question that most concerned the couple in the scene above. How dangerous is sex during pregnancy? There are no useful or compelling data that might answer this question – medical opinions differ and vacillate. But essentially they all reach the same conclusion. As long as it is the woman who feels like intercourse, who chooses the moment and the position and who orchestrates the act, there are unlikely to be any untoward effects. Her body will be pursuing an act determined by natural selection, which at the same time will also have determined her defences against what are, essentially, three main potential dangers.

The first is that of infection from the man's penis, the seminal fluid and the sperm themselves (which can carry viruses and bacteria on their surface). Within a week of conception, the woman guards herself as far as possible against infection, giving absolute priority to protecting her womb and the developing embryo. To achieve this, her cervical mucus changes, even more than it does during her menstrual cycle. Most importantly, it thickens, becoming much more jelly-like, even fibrous. Any channels through the mucus become very narrow and fill with cell debris, so that sperm find it impossible to penetrate. In addition, the production and flow rate of the mucus increase. The net result is that during pregnancy the woman often feels wet between her legs, but with a stickier material. It is this thickening and increased flow of the cervical mucus that allow her to rid herself of just about everything introduced into her vagina during intercourse; almost all semen, sperm and any bacteria and viruses in the inseminate are ejected in her flowback.

The second potential danger is the presence of a thrusting penis in her vagina whatever the position adopted. But her body will have been shaped by evolution to seek sex only when a penis is not a threat. As far as possible, evolution will also have predisposed her body to cope with a penis on occasions when it *is* a threat – when it is a man, not she herself, who seeks intercourse. There is a limit, of course, to the protection that natural selection can offer her under such circumstances.

Which brings us to the third danger – a man insisting on violent and aggressive sex, especially in the missionary position. In terms of the damage it can cause to a pregnant woman, having a man's full weight thump up and down on her swollen abdomen while thrusting aggressively is little different from her falling down stairs or, even, being the victim of violent assault. Whenever the man initiates and orchestrates intercourse, there has to be an element of danger to the woman and the baby. But, unfortunately, there may be occasions when violent intercourse is in a man's reproductive interests. We are back to the issue of confidence in paternity: we are about to encounter the first of several situations in this book in which gentle strategic manoeuvring deteriorates into outright war.

As long as a man has a firm confidence in his paternity, it is in his reproductive interests that nothing untoward should happen to the baby. If he hasn't, his chances of reproducing with his partner may be being delayed while she is pregnant with another man's child. Then, it may actually benefit his reproductive interests if she miscarries because it will shorten the time to her next being fertile. There are no data to show whether a pregnant woman is more likely to fall victim to violent sexual acts when her partner has a low confidence in his paternity. But that is the prediction of evolutionary biology. Of course, there are other kinds of physical violence whereby a man can induce his partner to miscarry.

In the scene above, the man never contemplated anything violent. On the contrary, with a high confidence in his paternity, he was as worried as she was about the possible repercussions of intercourse. She also worried about the consequences of orgasm, concerned as she was about her baby's apparent reaction the last time they had intercourse. Again, there are no good data on how orgasm influences the baby in the womb, but the prediction of evolutionary biology is that there should be no deleterious effects. Natural selection has dictated that women should continue to have orgasms during pregnancy, and so will naturally have shaped their bodies to cope.

So why should pregnant women continue to experience orgasms, whether during intercourse, during sleep or following an urge to masturbate? Such things are major contributors to 'cervical housekeeping', as we have already seen, and a pregnant woman's cervical mucus still needs occasional attention, for which orgasm continues to be an important mechanism.

There is one last, surprising, twist to the explanation of sex during pregnancy, which concerns the first few hours and days after conception. Although sperm are generally useless to a woman once she has conceived, they are not useless *immediately* to *every* woman. Recent studies have suggested that fraternal twins are sometimes the product of two eggs produced one or two days apart. On occasion, therefore, the two eggs will have been fertilised by sperm from two different inseminations. These inseminations are usually, of course, successive inseminations, a day or so apart, by the same man – the woman's long-term partner. But one in every two hundred or so conceptions of fraternal twins is achieved via successive inseminations by *different men*. In the most conspicuous and often the most newsworthy cases, the fathers, and hence the twins, belong to different races.

So for a very few women, those who are going to produce

fraternal twins, sex in the first week after conception is designed not just to give their partner's confidence in his paternity an extra boost, but to fertilise a second egg. And even then, a woman's behaviour can sometimes conceal the fact that one of her two eggs has been fertilised by someone else. There is still the potential for conflict – this time it is not only between the woman and her partner, but also between the two men, and between the two men's sperm.

It seems that whatever aspect of pregnancy we investigate, we invariably find conflict of some sort, even where we would least expect it. This is no less true when we consider the trials of pregnancy sickness and labour in the next two scenes.

SCENE 6
Pregnancy Sickness

The woman sank back heavily against the bathroom wall. It was two thirty a.m., and for the fifth time that night the sound of the flushing toilet was ringing out loudly in the silence. Once back in the bedroom she stood for a moment, watching her partner sleeping soundly. Irritation flashed briefly in her mind. Why should he sleep so well when she was so wretched? If he couldn't share her discomfort he could at least wake up and witness it.

She toyed with the idea of flushing the toilet again, this time with the door open. Or maybe she should go back to the bathroom and clatter about a bit? She ran through the inevitable scene in her head. He would appear benign and bleary-eyed at the bathroom door. Shading his eyes from the fluorescent shimmer, he would ask her if she was OK. She would say yes of course she was OK, apart from backache, headache, heartburn and an almost constant need to urinate – in fact, most of the things she had been warned to expect during the last few weeks of pregnancy. Yes, she was fine and why didn't he just go back to bed? Desperately trying to look awake and concerned, he would ask if there was anything he could do. She would mellow slightly, regretting her sarcasm and beginning to feel bad about getting him up. No, honestly there was nothing he could do. He would hesitate for a second or two, waiting for her to look at him, smile sheepishly, then disappear back into the bedroom. After listening to him flop heavily back into bed, she would flick the light switch, then follow him.

As she closed the bedroom door the headlamps of a car flashed through the crack in the curtain and travelled smoothly around the room, interrupting her thoughts. Her irritation began to subside and suddenly she felt overwhelmingly tired. As she lowered herself gently on to the bed, she felt glad she hadn't woken him.

Getting in and out of bed was no longer easy, but the manoeuvre had become second nature. Keeping her back straight and supporting herself on her arms, she swung her legs, bent together at the knees, on to the bed and lowered herself back on to the pillows. A familiar pulling sensation across her middle reminded her that she could no longer sleep on her back. She couldn't sleep on her front, either. In fact, the only position that offered any degree of comfort was on her side with her legs drawn up so that the fronts of her thighs touched the underside of her bulge. As she was manoeuvring herself, her partner grunted, half turned over and caught hold of her knee. She slowly adjusted herself, then studied his profile in the half-light. As her body warmed up and relaxed again, her thoughts began to splinter. After a few moments he stirred briefly and moved his hand away from her knee, allowing her to draw her legs further up. She finally drifted off to sleep.

The woman had not planned her pregnancy. She had intended to have children one day, but not quite yet. True, the distant ticking of her biological clock had recently started to impinge, but she had managed to convince herself that there was still time enough. Motherhood had seemed to her like a giant leap in the dark. Once pregnant, though, she had resigned herself to it. Indeed, in some ways she found herself welcoming it, if only as proof of her fertility.

The first few weeks were uneventful. Apart from a strange tingling and soreness in her breasts she hadn't really felt any different. She had found herself marking the delivery date on every calendar in the house as a reminder of her change in status. Almost as if to force things to feel different, she had shared her news with a few people at work, announcing in the process her intention to carry on working right up to the last few weeks. Feeling relaxed but excited, she had waited for the glow and the air of serenity that soft-focus photographs in magazines had led her to expect. She began snatching sideways glances at heavily pregnant women. Suddenly it seemed as though there were babies everywhere. She noticed their satin hair and creamy skins and marvelled at the way they could scream themselves into a frenzy. She watched an old woman on a train pull out all the stops in order to elicit a single smile.

Then the nausea set in. It didn't start suddenly, as she'd been led to expect. About the sixth week of her pregnancy she had woken one night feeling ravenous. Intent on satisfying her hunger, she had crept downstairs and made herself a snack. However, this night-time urge gradually changed into an overwhelming feeling of nausea which was with her most of the time, day and night. If only it had been just *morning* sickness.

She completely lost her appetite. Indeed, eating became something of an ordeal, even though she usually felt better afterwards, if only for a while. As well as reacting badly to the sight and thought of food, her sense of smell intensified. At work she could smell the canteen even though her office was four floors above it. She began crossing the road solely to avoid the smells wafting out of restaurants. Supermarkets, and the smell of red wine, made her heave. Her weight began to drop, and eventually all she could think about was how awful she felt.

Seeking reassurance, she turned to the mothers amongst her friends. She wouldn't feel ill for more than the first three or four months, they told her. But even so, everyone had known someone who had felt nauseous throughout her pregnancy. The prospect appalled her. She became convinced that, for her, it was bound to last the whole nine months. All her partner could do was hold her hair out of the way while she vomited repeatedly into the toilet and keep her supplied with fruit juice and mineral water, even if it meant going out in the middle of the night. He also had to patiently endure the same conversation over and over again. She would say how fed up she was; he would say that it was bound to go soon.

Over the next few weeks she began to feel permanently weak and exhausted. In the mornings, she hardly had the energy to get out of bed. In the evenings she felt almost drunk with tiredness, and went to bed at the first opportunity. She spent most of the weekend curled up on the sofa in her dressing-gown. A mental sluggishness had set in. For the first time in her life she found herself having to make lists and write little reminders to herself. Dates and times became impossible to remember. At work she was no longer her usual articulate, confident self. She began to feel depressed. It seemed as if the tiny individual inside her was sapping her strength, threatening her well-being, as if its growth was at her own physical expense. She recorded every detail of her misery in a diary. When the time came, she would also record her return to relative comfort.

Her recovery had begun about the fourteenth week. Gradually her appetite returned and her energy levels climbed back to normal. In fact, apart from a niggling lower back pain first thing in the morning she began to feel quite good. She bought new clothes. Her partner took photographs of her gently swelling stomach. The baby started to kick.

This good phase, though, was to be relatively short-lived. Within a few weeks her back pain had developed into an intense and persistent ache. She also began to have sharp pains in her womb. Then one morning she bled heavily into the toilet. Mesmerised by the sight of the blood, several seconds passed before she reacted. She grabbed the towel draped over the side of the bath and stuffed it between her legs, then shouted to her partner through the open bathroom door. They waited for a while, but the pains in her womb worsened and they decided that hospital was the place to be. On the way she found herself thinking not of the baby but of herself. If she miscarried at this stage it would mean having to go through all this again. Twenty weeks of pregnancy ending in nothing. All that misery for nothing.

In industrialised cultures pregnancy is traditionally and romantically viewed as a time of serenity, a time when a woman's body is fulfilling its destiny, quietly nurturing a new individual in the safety and warmth of the womb before easing it out into the world. For a few women, of course, the reality may not be very different from this. For most, however, there is very little similarity at all. As discovered by the woman in the scene, pregnancy can be months of extreme discomfort; the whole experience can involve more pain than pleasure and induce an attitude of stoicism rather than serenity.

Why should a woman's body be programmed to commit itself to nine months of discomfort – and not just once, but as many times as are needed to produce her family? At first sight, it seems strange indeed that natural selection should have shaped something as basic as pregnancy to sometimes be so traumatic. But there is an explanation: the surprising answer is that during each pregnancy a war is being waged. The battleground is the woman's body – and here natural selection is on everybody's side.

So if the battleground is within her body, who are the combatants? Superficially, it would appear that the confrontation must be between the mother and her baby. But the fact is that the real battle is genetic, and the two armies are the matching sets of maternal and paternal genes. The conflict begins almost immediately the father's sperm, carrying its twenty-three chromosomes, fertilises the mother's egg, also carrying twenty-three chromosomes.

Each human chromosome is a helical string of DNA, a sequence of millions of molecules of amino acids. This is our genetic code, our genes, the instructions that tell the fertilised egg how to develop and what organs to form. Also encoded are the details of anatomy, physiology and behaviour that make each of us unique. In an amazing feat of manoeuvring and alignment, each one of our father's chromosomes aligns itself alongside the partner chromosome from the mother. Even more remarkably, each gene from our father pairs up with the same gene from our mother: eye-colour gene with eye-colour gene, hair-colour gene with hair-colour gene, cancer gene with cancer gene, sexuality gene with sexuality gene, and so on.

Often, of course, genes from both mother and father will be the same. Both sperm and egg will have carried the gene for brown eyes on their appropriate chromosome. Maybe both carried the gene for resistance to breast cancer, rather than for a predisposition to it. And maybe both carried the gene for heterosexuality, not bisexuality. In which case, there is no conflict between maternal and paternal genes over these features of the child. It will grow up with brown eyes, a resistance to breast cancer, and a predisposition to heterosexuality.

Often, however, the genes will not be the same. Maybe the sperm carried the gene for blue eyes whereas the egg carried the gene for brown. There is some conflict here, but not much. It probably doesn't matter that much to the reproductive success of the mother and father whether the child has blue eyes or brown; what may matter to them both is that it should be one or the other, not a mosaic of the two. During the course of evolution, therefore, these two genes have come to a tacit agreement that whenever they meet, the gene for blue eyes gives few, if any, instructions to the developing child who, as a result, ends up with brown eyes. (In fact, inheritance of eye colour in humans is not as straightforward as this familiar example suggests. There are various genes involved, and eye colour can be anything from pale blue to dark brown. More often than not, though, blue-eye genes do give way to brown, and our example illustrates well enough the principle of gene cooperation.)

Some genes, on the other hand, have not reached so amicable a settlement. On occasion, it *does* matter to the mother and to the father that it is *her* or *his* instructions, not the partner's, that prevail. In effect this means that it is the child's body that becomes the battlefield for the two sets of genes. The root cause of this genetic conflict lies in the difference between the ways in which men and women each seek to achieve their reproductive success. Both try to maximise their reproductive output, but they set about it in different ways. We shall discuss this in more detail later, but a summary here may be useful.

A woman can maximise her reproductive output only by having the optimal number of children during her lifetime. The challenge which faces every woman, therefore, is first to identify the optimal family size for her circumstances, and then to ensure that she actually *has* that number of children. That done, there is one other thing that she must do in order to increase her contribution to future generations: she must shop around for the best father(s) for her children, that is, men with the best genes and for the best partner(s), that is, with the best resources. Conceiving to a man who, from the point of view of evolutionary biology, has superior genes will give her superior children, and partnering a man with more resources will give her a better chance of raising those children into a healthy, fertile and competitive adulthood.

In contrast, a man can, in theory, have an unlimited number of children. His only constraint is in finding enough women who are prepared not only to let him fertilise them but also to raise those children without his help. Thus, since it is only men with resources to spare, or superior genes, who can attract the sexual interest of many women, it is only they who manage to have more children than the average woman. The most famous case was Ishmail the Bloodthirsty, an ex-emperor of Morocco. Maybe not all of the 888 children he claimed to have sired were actually his, but even allowing for the occasional infidelity on the part of his harem, it's a fairly safe assumption that his reproductive success was above average. The *average* man, of course, ends up with the same number of children as the average woman. Nevertheless, the principle is clear: however restricted a man is in finding women prepared to have a baby by him, he is never as dependent on any *one woman's* body to achieve his reproductive output as a woman is on *her own* body. Once a woman is unable to have any more children, that is the end of her reproductive life. However, if a man's partner becomes sterile he can simply try to find another woman to bear his children.

What this difference in the constraints on men and women means is that a woman's genes need to be much more cautious about any potential pregnancy and birth than do a man's. The mother's genes have to balance the contribution that the child in her womb is going to make to her total production of grandchildren against the contribution that any future children might make. Her genes are always trying to maximise the number of grandchildren and later descendants. If her current pregnancy in any way threatens her ability to have more children in the future, her body may decide not to go through with it.

The father's genes are, of course, also trying to maximise the number of grandchildren he will have. But because his reproductive success is less dependent on the mother's continuing fertility, his genes can be much more cavalier and aggressive with regard to making the child already in the mother's womb as successful as possible. His genes can take far more risks with the woman's body than can her own genes.

Before we discuss the nature of these risks, we need to know what options are open to the baby and its two sets of genes. We have already discussed the events leading up to the egg being fertilised by a sperm in the woman's oviduct. Let's pick up the story at the moment the fertilised egg starts to divide as it heads on down the oviduct. By the time what once was a single-cell egg reaches the womb, the new life consists of a *blastocyst* of about a hundred cells.

The mother's body prepares for the arrival of this tiny bundle of cells by thickening the lining of her womb (from $\frac{1}{25}$ to $\frac{1}{6}$ of an inch) and by increasing its blood supply. If the egg has been fertilised, the blastocyst implants in the lining two to four days after entering the womb. While waiting to implant, it receives nourishment from the mother via secretions from the womb lining. These secretions form the *uterine milk*. The blastocyst also develops special *trophoblast* cells on its surface, which secrete enzymes that digest and liquefy nearby cells in the womb wall. The trophoblasts then multiply rapidly, and invade, imbibe and digest further cells from the womb lining as they begin to form the foetal half of the placenta. This 'invasion' of the mother's womb lining is known as implantation. Once implantation is complete, the scene is set for the battle between maternal and paternal genes.

Pregnancy in humans lasts on average about 270 days. Throughout this time, the mother and baby are chemically communicating with each other across the placenta. Where the baby's half of the placenta touches and intertwines with the mother's half, which is formed from the womb lining at the point where the trophoblast cells invade, huge surface areas of blood vessels and membranes from the two individuals come into contact. The resulting network of vessels and membranes forms the whole placenta, to which the baby is joined via the umbilical cord (about 50 cm long). It is through the cord and placenta that nourishment passes from mother to child and metabolic waste products pass from child to mother. But as well as being vital channels of chemical transfer, the placental membranes are also vital barriers. Their job, honed by millions of years of mammalian evolution, is to allow beneficial chemicals across while at the same time preventing the passage of chemicals that would harm either mother or child. For example, it is the placenta that prevents the immune systems of both from rejecting each other, from misinterpreting each other as invading parasites or foreign transplants.

From our description so far, it looks as though pregnancy is a time of cooperation between mother and baby, neither trying to do anything that would damage the other. And up to a point, of course, this is how it is. It is in everybody's interests – baby's, mother's and father's – that the baby forms, grows, survives and does well. The conflict arises because maternal and paternal genes cannot agree over how many risks the mother's body should take in ensuring that the baby does all these things. The father's genes want the mother's body to worry less about *her* future, and do the best for the baby, while the mother's genes want a safer compromise.

The first detectable sign that a war is taking place in the

mother's body is pregnancy sickness. About 70 per cent of women experience some degree of pregnancy sickness which, although most common in the morning, is by no means confined to that time of day, as the woman in the scene above discovered. Usually, it declines from about the twelfth week. However, 50 per cent of women still have some symptoms by the fifteenth week, and an unlucky 15 per cent experience nausea, and 5 per cent continue to vomit, throughout their pregnancy.

Pregnancy sickness protects the child, if at some cost to the mother's comfort – it is part of the armoury of the father's genes. To illustrate this, we can consider some figures from North America. There, 10 per cent of children have some sort of birth defect. These defects may be relatively minor, such as deafness, or more serious, such as abnormally formed limbs. In a third of cases, the cause is obvious: usually either an inherited syndrome or the result of drugs taken by the mother during pregnancy. This leaves two-thirds of cases having no known cause, and one possibility is that all of them are due to toxins in the mother's food, of which there are many. Coffee, for example, contains about a hundred – and a sudden aversion to coffee is one of the earliest signs of pregnancy that the modern woman in an industrial society experiences.

A baby's organs develop mainly during the first three months of pregnancy. After that, gestation is just a matter of growth. So any developmental abnormality usually results from an event in the first three months. The mother's body is quite good at detecting abnormalities in the developing child, and when it does, its reaction is often to spontaneously abort the foetus, preparing the ground to try again as soon as possible. A large proportion of foetuses miscarried during the first three months have some sort of developmental deformity.

Women who experience pregnancy sickness are significantly less likely to miscarry, the implication being that the sickness is in some way protecting the foetus from chemicals that might otherwise interfere with its development, promote abnormalities, and so trigger a miscarriage. The placenta acts as a more or less efficient filter for unwanted chemicals, but works best at keeping out big molecules. Because it has to let nutrients and waste products pass between mother and child, and vice versa, there are many small molecules that it just cannot keep out, and many of these are dangerous to the baby. Moreover, the mother's body's own dietary requirements must be met if it is to stay in good health and keep up its reserves: most importantly, it has to keep her brain well nourished if she is to be able to function properly both during and after pregnancy. The father's genes would indeed be doing themselves a disservice if they made the baby so demanding of nutrients that the mother's brain suffered damage.

Nutritionally, the first three months of pregnancy are a dietary tightrope. The best combination of nutrients for the baby is not necessarily the best for the mother. In fact, so great is the risk that toxins in the mother's food might damage the baby's development that the safest option for the baby would probably be for the mother not to eat at all. She could then slowly erode her toxin-free fat and other bodily reserves, while circulating the chemicals in her blood, and let the baby take what it needed across the placenta. Studies in famine areas show that this can in fact happen. The baby leaves the mother just enough nourishment to protect her brain, but takes the rest for itself. While the mother becomes emaciated during pregnancy, the baby's weight at birth is relatively little compromised, at least as long as the famine is only moderate. Clearly, however, unless – as is unlikely – the mother has superabundant reserves before pregnancy begins, this option is not good for her.

The scene is set for a major battle between paternal and maternal genes. The father's genes (in the baby) try to manipulate the woman into eating and digesting very little food, and within a range that is best for the baby. The mother's genes (in her self and in the baby) try to compromise between what is best for the baby and what is best for her future reproduction. The avenue by which the father's genes try to manipulate the mother is via chemicals which are released by the baby into the mother's blood stream. This triggers changes in the mother's levels of oestrogen, progesterone and other hormones which influence her hunger, taste and sense of smell. The result is that the baby induces a sporadic stream of changes in its mother's appetite and food preferences, and, as a final back-up if she does eat or drink something to the baby's disadvantage, nausea and vomiting.

If, despite all of this defensive activity, some toxins do get through, the mother's body as often as not detects the problem and aborts. Better for her to miscarry while the baby is small and start again with a new foetus, than to risk giving birth to a damaged full-size baby. For the father, however, who through death, desertion or her infidelity, may never get another chance of having a child with this woman, it is better to protect this foetus by preventing toxins getting through in the first place – hence the usefulness of pregnancy sickness. So when the father's genes gain the ascendancy, the mother suffers sickness but the foetus receives the best possible nourishment and is less likely to be miscarried. When the mother's genes prevail, sickness is minimal, mother and foetus compromise over nutrition, and miscarriage is more likely.

It would appear that, as we left the scene above, the woman's genes were losing their battle against the paternal genes inside her baby, with the result that she had suffered great discomfort during the first three months of her pregnancy. If we didn't in fact know that she isn't going to miscarry, we might suspect that all of the protective discomfort of pregnancy sickness has been in vain. We might think that her body has detected an abnormality in the unborn child and decided to miscarry. All will soon be clear, however, for we are about to pick up the story where we left it – with the events that followed her visit to the hospital after a heavy bleed.

SCENE 7
Labour

Thirty-six hours after going into hospital, the woman was back at home, her pregnancy still intact. A scan had failed to explain the bleeding but had at least reassured her that the baby was of a reasonable size and appeared to be healthy and active.

The next few weeks were uneventful, but her near-miscarriage had unsettled her. The pregnancy suddenly seemed very fragile, and thereafter the possibility of miscarriage preyed heavily on her mind. Every night she crossed one more day off the calendar, willing the delivery date nearer and nearer. Then she would go to bed, dream in kaleidoscopic colour about the birth process, and wake at the slightest twinge in her womb.

As the baby grew, she became more and more uncomfortable. Recently, in the evenings, despite their having bought extra cushions and a beanbag for her to sit on, she had become distressed by a peculiar jumping sensation in her legs which compelled her to pace around the room and to stamp and jiggle her feet. Her breasts had become sore and heavy and she had heartburn a lot of the time. Although she didn't look very large, she was carrying a good-sized baby whose movements were more painful to her than pleasurable. Now in the thirty-eighth week, its nightly squirming kept her awake and its kicks were so strong that the inside of her womb felt quite sore. The skin across the top of her bulge was so taut it felt tender to the touch. Worst of all, the backache which had been with her for most of the pregnancy had gradually worsened until lately there had been times, particularly first thing in the morning, when she could hardly move. Her partner had to ease her gently out of bed. He had also taken to helping her on with her knickers.

This morning she had arranged to meet a friend, also in the last few weeks of pregnancy. They had planned a short walk around the park, followed by tea at a nearby café. Her friend was in high spirits and did most of the talking. For her, pregnancy had flown by. She had felt healthy and confident right from the start, with no hint of nausea or tiredness or backache. In fact, she insisted, she had felt better than ever – full of energy, relaxed, and counting the days to the onset of motherhood in happy anticipation.

The woman couldn't help but feel mildly envious. 'Pregnancy obviously suits you,' she remarked dryly when they were about a quarter-way round the park. For her, the walk was proving to be a strain. The pulling sensation across her middle was intensifying, forcing her to breathe in short, shallow pants. Her legs were aching and, glancing down at her feet, she was convinced her ankles were beginning to swell. Having persuaded her friend to head for the nearest bench, she flopped gratefully down. Later, in the café, she admitted that she couldn't wait for the delivery date, not because she was particularly looking forward to motherhood but because it would mean the end of her pregnancy.

Two weeks later, the phone rang. Even before she lifted the receiver the woman knew what the call was going to be about. A second later, the sound of her friend's voice confirmed it. Weary but elated, she recounted the story of the labour and birth of her son. Although he was a bit on the small side he had arrived right on time, after a short, straightforward labour. She hadn't even needed stitches. Hopefully, she would be allowed home the following day.

The woman replaced the receiver and sighed heavily, letting her taut features relax. She knew she hadn't sounded as pleased for her friend as she should have done, but at this moment all she could think about was herself. She was already ten days over her date, and was getting increasingly anxious. The last few days she had been feeling unwell, and her blood pressure was slightly raised. At first she had just been told to take it easy. Then, when she had developed a persistent headache and her ankles had begun to swell, she had been ordered to bed. If there was any further deterioration, she was told, she must go into hospital.

She picked up a magazine and began to flick agitatedly through it, hoping to find something to occupy her mind. But it was no use. Focusing on anything other than her condition was proving impossible. Pushing the magazines aside, she eased herself slowly out of bed and went over to the window. A cat was threading its way through the flower border. Still restless, she moved away from the window, and for the third time that day made her way into the newly decorated nursery. This bright, white, virginal room had an expectant air about it. Winding up the mobile over the cot, she tried to imagine a baby looking up at the brightly coloured clowns circling overhead. The picture didn't come easily.

The woman was in fact destined not to give birth for another week. Labour finally started with the breaking of her waters in the early hours of the morning. Shivering violently, she sat on the toilet with a blanket around her while her partner backed the car out. Later, she could remember nothing about the journey to the hospital except that every traffic light was against them. Once she was safely ensconced in the delivery ward, her labour progressed quite quickly until mid-morning, by which time she was beginning to feel exhausted and shaky.

The contractions were far more painful than she had imagined they would be, despite a pethidine injection and the use of gas and air. Sweating profusely, she asked if the nurse would help her take her night-dress off. The rim of the gas mask was beginning to leave a red mark on her cheeks and on the bridge of her nose where she held it clamped down. Her mouth and her lips were dry. As time went by she became less and less aware of what was going on around her. Gradually she lost track of time as she sank deeper into the fog induced by the anaesthetic. She was aware of people coming and going in the room, but their voices seemed far away. At one point she surfaced to dimly register some medical students peering between her open legs. During the second stage of labour the ferocity of the contractions jerked her back briefly to consciousness. The urge to bear down and push the baby out was all-consuming. The birth finally happened at six p.m., after more than seventeen hours of labour. The baby's weight was recorded as 4.5 kilograms – nine pounds and twelve ounces, the midwife told her.

Afterwards, the woman learned the full details of her labour and delivery. Her daughter was so big for a first baby that the birth had been difficult and eventually dangerous. There had been several points at which the monitor had registered foetal distress, and at one stage a caesarean section had been contemplated. As it was, her womb had suffered some damage. Fortunately, her baby was so strong that she survived her ordeal, and once she had begun to take milk in sufficient quantities she had grown stronger by the day.

But her daughter's health and strength contrasted noticeably with her own. The doctors had warned that the damage her womb had suffered might make it difficult for her to have any more children – and they were right. Although she conceived three more times over the next ten years, she miscarried on each occasion, and when she was in her early forties a year of frequent bleeding led to a hysterectomy.

Whatever the woman's problems over the years, her daughter was her main source of strength and pleasure, particularly after her partner left her to have a second family with a younger woman. Mother and daughter remained close, even during the latter's adolescence. When she left home for college, the pair met frequently, almost always taking pleasure in each other's company – they were more like sisters, one of them once remarked. Later, the daughter successfully combined a demanding career with having a family of her own, and the woman eventually became a doting grandmother to her daughter's four handsome children.

In Scene 6, we discussed the way our main character's genes lost their battle for serenity in the conflict over pregnancy sickness. But ahead of her lay a much bigger, and in many ways more important, battle with the father's genes. And as we shall now see, she again lost out to the baby's father in their separate pursuits of reproductive success.

Throughout pregnancy, a baby floats within the amniotic fluid, held in the tough amniotic sac. The chances of the womb being invaded by disease organisms are greatly reduced by the presence of a cervical plug, which, as we have already mentioned, consists of cervical mucus so thick and so cluttered with cell debris that little can pass through it from the vagina to the womb. The strong fibrous walls of the cervix also help to hold the baby in the womb. Come the moment of birth, however, the cervical walls have to soften, stretch and weaken, the pubic bones have to give a little, the amniotic sac has to burst, and the baby has to be pushed down through the cervix, along the vagina and out of the woman's body.

Natural selection has done its best for the mother in designing her to perform this natural process. Even so, the wholesale stretching and widening, pushing and pummelling, of her body during birth can be a dangerous experience. Then, after the birth she has to shed the placenta and rejuvenate the womb lining as well as return all her organs to their non-pregnancy state. If she does this successfully, she will be able to go through the process all over again with her next pregnancy. But, if she doesn't, like the woman in the scene, she may not be able to have more children. At worst, she may even die. So why has natural selection apparently failed women over this, the most critical of their requirements? The answer is that, although it has done the best it can for women, it has also done its best for men, and their long-term interests conflict.

Of course, it is in nobody's long-term interests, including the father's and the child's, that the mother dies during childbirth. In countries such as Bangladesh, for instance, in 75 per cent of cases, if the mother dies then so too does the baby. Nor is it in anybody's interests for the mother to be so weakened by giving birth that she is unable to look after the newborn. However, there is a less extreme situation, in which the *current* child has the best of all possible starts, but in which the mother's *future* reproductive ability is destroyed. For example, it is possible for a woman to be so stretched – physically, emotionally and practically – by doing the best for one child, that she becomes ill or infertile and thus unable to have the future children that would add up to her ideal family. It is estimated that, for every woman who dies in childbirth, probably about thirty incur injuries and infections, many of which are painful, disabling, embarrassing and lifelong. Clearly, these injuries disadvantage the mother reproductively, but they don't necessarily disadvantage the father. Like the character in our scene, having produced as successful a child as possible with one woman, a man can move on and try to repeat the process with another. We are back to the battle between maternal and paternal genes.

The most important indicator of a child's likelihood of survival is its birth weight, larger babies having better prospects. Even now, in the most industrialised and medically developed countries, birth weight has a major influence on a child's prospects for survival and resistance to disease. In England and Wales in 1994, for example, one in five babies weighing less than 1.5 kilograms at birth died in the first year of life, compared with one in four hundred weighing 3.0–3.5 kilograms. Nor has the disadvantage of being light at birth disappeared by the child's first birthday – it persists throughout its life. In the United States, children who weigh less than 2.5 kilograms at birth are later twice as likely as their average-weight (3.3 kilogram) contemporaries to be hospitalised between the ages of three and five. They also perform less well at school, and the girls, when adults themselves, are also in their turn more likely to have babies with a low birth weight. In Third World countries and in our historical and evolutionary past, the influence of birth weight on survival, prospects and fertility is and was even greater.

Inevitably, the size of the baby is also precisely the factor that most influences a woman's ability to have more children: a larger baby is more dangerous to her as it is being born. Consequently, because of the importance of birth weight for the well-being of the child, this becomes the prime area of conflict in the war of the genes. On the one hand, the maternal genes try to limit the size of the baby so that it is as big as, but no bigger than, her body can manage without prejudicing her future reproduction. The paternal genes, on the other hand, try to up the size so that it is as big as the mother can produce even if this risks damage that prevents her from reproducing further, but not so big that she cannot raise it.

All else being equal, there are two factors that can make a baby bigger at birth: it can either grow faster while in the mother's womb, or stay there for longer. Some, of course, do both. To grow faster, the baby's half of the placenta needs to be more aggressive – more invasive – and to take more risks with its mother's health and safety as regards what and how much it extracts from her body. To stay longer, the baby needs to manipulate the mother's hormones so that labour and birth are delayed.

The war between maternal and paternal genes has relatively simple aims while the baby is still in the womb, which can be summed up as follows. The father's genes try to manipulate the baby into extracting more, better and safer nourishment from the mother's body – and faster – and secondly into staying inside her womb for as long as possible. The mother's genes try to get the baby to be less demanding and less tenacious, thereby giving more control to her body. If the father's genes gain the ascendancy, the mother is likely to suffer more during pregnancy, go over term and have a more difficult birth, but she will produce a bigger baby with better lifetime prospects. If *her* genes gain the ascendancy, she will have an easier, even serene, pregnancy and labour, but the baby will be smaller with not quite such good prospects for its survival and fertility. The mother, however, will be better able to have another child when it best suits *her own* pursuit of reproductive success, not the father's.

The final phase in this genetic battle comes at the end of pregnancy, and concerns the question of when the baby should be born. The longer it stays in the mother's womb, the bigger it becomes, but the more difficult and dangerous the birth. The father's genes want to prolong the pregnancy, and try to judge how far the mother's body can be made to nourish the child until the moment *just before* it becomes so big that she will be unable to give birth to it. Her genes, on the other hand, try to judge the moment when the baby is big enough for its prospects to be good, but not so big that her future reproduction is prejudiced by the difficulty of giving birth.

This battle is taking place inside, and under the control of, the baby, and when it is resolved it will signal to the mother that the time has come. Studies of sheep and horses, and a few observations concerning people in which the baby had part of its brain missing, show that labour is initiated by the baby. In effect, the baby, or maybe the baby's half of the placenta, is continually weighing itself during the last few weeks before birth. And when the appropriate weight has been reached, a part of the baby's brain produces hormones which pass across the placenta into the mother, triggering her hormones to start the birth process. If the critical part of the foetus's brain is damaged or missing, labour is not initiated and the pregnancy goes on, and on. In sheep, pregnancy has continued up to the equivalent of fifteen months in humans, and the same would probably happen to a woman in a similar situation if it weren't for medical intervention.

Who wins this battle over when the baby is to be born will vary from couple to couple and from pregnancy to pregnancy. In the scene above, the main character clearly lost out in her particular battle for serenity. Her body was pushed to its limit and, although the baby was born with excellent prospects for survival and fertility, her ability to have further children was harmed. Her friend, on the other hand, sailed through her pregnancy on the tide of her genes' ascendancy over her partner's, and would be able to have more children. Her son, though, may have been less successful, reproductively, than the heavier daughter born to the main character.

The battle between paternal and maternal genes over the size of offspring is found in all mammals, not just in humans, as is the experience of suffering during pregnancy and birth. Both actually began with the earliest evolution of placental mammals – those that grow their offspring inside their bodies – about sixty million years ago. As soon as evolution pushed females into protecting and nourishing embryos inside their bodies by forming the placenta, paternal genes were given a novel and powerful way of influencing the growth and survival of their offspring. The continuous battle between the genes that was then set in motion has snowballed throughout the course of evolution and continues today in the body of every human mother.

Pregnancy and labour represent periods of high risk to all female mammals, but perhaps we should feel most sorry for female spotted hyenas. To us, they would seem to be the victims of one of evolution's cruellest tricks. In the interests of holding their own in another battle between the sexes – that of access to food and space in a highly aggressive society – evolution has boosted the level of male hormones to which the females are exposed in their mother's womb. The resulting increase in aggression and competitiveness in the battle for space, food and rank is a vital factor in their pursuit of reproductive success, leading to the highest-ranking females achieving two and a half times the success of the lowest-ranking females. However, there is a price to pay.

Because of the exposure to male hormones, evolution has so fashioned the clitoris and surrounding tissue of female hyenas that they have developed into an almost perfect replica of the penis and testes. These organs can become erect and are used for scent-marking and display just like the male equivalents. The consequence of this perfect mimicry is that a female hyena has to give birth *through her clitoris*. And with the clitoral channel only 2 centimetres or so in diameter and a foetal head 6–7 centimetres in diameter, only one thing can happen when a female gives birth for the first time: the clitoris tears. Often, birth is so difficult that the foetus may remain in the clitoris for thirty minutes before emerging. Nearly half of hyenas have difficulty giving birth to their first offspring, and 9 per cent are estimated to die as a direct result of labour problems.

By comparison, in industrialised societies, and thanks mainly to medical assistance, relatively few women (about one in two thousand) now die as a result of childbirth. But at the beginning of the twentieth century childbirth was still a dangerous event in a woman's life, as it continues to be in Third World countries. In Africa, for example, about 4 per cent of women die from the complications of giving birth. In South Asia the figure is 3 per cent, and in Latin America 1 per cent. Moreover, for every woman who dies in childbirth, probably about thirty incur injuries and infections. According to UNICEF, the toll of injury and disability from pregnancy-related causes is arguably the most neglected health problem in the world. It is likely that more than fifteen million women a year fall victim to 'maternal morbidity', and that there are several hundred million in the world today who have suffered or are suffering from the untreated consequences of injuries arising during pregnancy and childbirth.

As these figures suggest, pregnancy and labour are everywhere uncomfortable, if not dangerous. The popular expectation, among women as well as men, that all women really ought to be able to give birth in a field or wherever else they happen to be at the time, then resume their normal activities, has arisen because the fundamental nature of pregnancy has been misunderstood. If it really was just a relationship between mother and foetus, perhaps the popular expectation could be realised. But it isn't. Given that it is a battle between paternal and maternal genes, it can only ever be a risky business.

CHAPTER FOUR

Baby Wars

SCENE 8
Breast-feeding

The woman could hear the animal-like wail long before she actually woke. The sound had slowly penetrated her dreams before she eventually surfaced. Almost instinctively, she knew it was *her* baby crying. Already she could distinguish his sound from those of the eight other babies in the ward, even though he was still less than two days old. Carefully avoiding her glass of water, she reached out, switched on the bedside lamp, then cautiously swung her legs out of bed. The floor felt warm to her feet. As she looked around for her slippers, she noticed that her ankles were still quite swollen. How long would it be before she could fit into her shoes again? she wondered.

The baby was in a small transparent cot at the end of her bed, his tiny face screwed up in anguish, his fists tightly clenched. He didn't stop crying until she picked him up. As she held him close to her, hot and quivering from his exertions, he turned his head towards her and began to root for a nipple.

She glanced across the ward at the woman opposite, who had her baby on a pillow on her lap, lying curled round her body. They looked so comfortable, she would give it a try. So far she had failed to find a comfortable position in which to breast-feed. But to her surprise, this one seemed to work quite well. The baby latched firmly on to her nipple and fed hungrily. With his tiny hand resting on her breast, he held his eyes wide open as if concentrating very hard.

Slowly, she began to relax. For the first time she was actually enjoying the experience. The baby began to pause between each suck, until after a moment or two his eyes closed and his lips loosened their grip. Eventually, his head fell away from her breast. Her deep-red elongated nipple glistened with little pinpricks of milk. She wiped the milk away from her baby's mouth and put him back down to sleep. Then, slipping back into bed, she too was fast asleep within minutes.

She had been looking forward to breast-feeding. She had wanted to experience the feelings of closeness and tenderness and, having heard that breast-feeding would reduce her chances of breast cancer, she also wanted to do it for the sake of her long-term health. And this time, so far, it had gone reasonably well – in contrast to her experience with her first baby, who had steadfastly refused to have anything whatever to do with her breasts. From his first moments in the delivery room, he had shown an aversion to sucking her nipple that had both upset and frustrated her. Every time she tried to put him to her breast he would scream and arch his back, throwing his head back as far away from her nipple as he could manage, his whole body stiffening. Unable to believe how something so natural could be so difficult, she remembered crying in frustration as she watched him being bottle-fed by one of the nurses. Feeling rejected and confused, at times she had felt positively hostile towards him.

She had ended up expressing her milk into a bottle, using a large, archaic electric machine that she would wheel to and from her bedside every couple of hours. She hated the whole process of expressing, but had felt compelled to do it as the only means of ensuring that her baby actually got the benefits of breast-milk. Once her proper milk had begun to flow, she produced loads of it, but her son never once latched on to her breast, let alone suckled. She managed to force herself to express her milk for six weeks, until the supply was finally curtailed by a severe bout of mastitis in both breasts.

In a way it had been a relief when her milk dried up. At least, the decision to stop expressing was made for her. She had disliked the machine almost as much as she had missed the closeness of breast-feeding. Looking back on the experience she wondered if it had all been worth the effort, not least because her early relationship with her son had undoubtedly suffered. When at last she was forced to give him formula milk, he had seemed to thrive on it. But this time, with the new baby, things seemed to be going well.

The next day her partner arrived with their elder son to take them home. As they walked through the ward towards her, she was breast-feeding, having already packed. She was looking forward to going home; it would be nice to have her own things around her once again.

More than anything, she was anxious to finally find a comfortable position in which to feed. Her success of the previous night had been a one-off: it was fine as long as the feed was short, but after a while it gave her backache.

She had experimented with every position she could think of. Sitting propped up on cushions in bed was comfortable initially, but she couldn't stop herself from slipping further and further down. Sitting straight-backed on the edge of the bed, or in the chair next to it, worked well enough, but only until it started to give her pain in her shoulders and neck. She knew she was holding herself too tensely, not wanting to move an inch in case she dislodged the baby from her breast. If only she could make herself relax. And positioning wasn't her only problem. She also kept forgetting to make sure that everything she needed was within easy reach before she started. Without a doubt, she was ready to go home – there, at least, there would be extra pillows and someone to reach things for her.

It was during the first feed at home that she felt a sharp pain in her left nipple. Examining it afterwards, she found that it was looking rather sore. She also thought she could see a tiny crack appearing at its base. Scrabbling around in her toiletries bag, she found the cream she had bought before going into hospital. She applied generous amounts to both nipples and hoped for the best – she had heard all about the agony of cracked nipples. As she smoothed the cream on, she wondered if its pungent smell would put her baby off. Maybe she should try to wipe it off before starting the next feed?

Over the next few days, despite the cream, the young mother's nipples grew increasingly sore and cracked. Soon, aching breasts – which had become tight and heavy as her milk supply increased – added to her discomfort. She knew this would be only a temporary problem, but it didn't make it any easier to cope with. Before long, her breasts became so swollen and hard as each feeding time approached that latching on became a problem for the baby. Even when he did eventually manage it, her let-down reflex was so spectacularly fast that it made him cough and splutter as he tried to swallow the spurting milk. For a while, she dreaded feeding time.

Over the next few weeks, however, one by one the difficulties gradually sorted themselves out. Her breasts slowly stopped overproducing and her flow adjusted to the baby's demands. As the cracks healed, her nipples lost their soreness and became more pliable. She began to enjoy breast-feeding again, and to appreciate just how easy and convenient it could be. She happily continued for eight months before she began to wonder, prompted by questions from others, when she should give up. It wasn't an easy decision.

On the one hand, both she and her baby were now enjoying it, and she had no wish to deny him pleasure. She worried about how he would react to being bottle-fed. Would he miss the breast as much as she thought he would? Would it make him irritable? On the other hand, more and more reasons to give up were emerging. She was losing a lot of weight – so much that her friends had begun to tell her she was looking quite ill and run down. She had to admit she did feel permanently tired. Then there was the problem of breast-feeding when she was away from the house. For the first few months she hadn't really gone out that much. Even when she had, it hadn't been difficult to time her trips between feeds. Apart from two occasions – once when she fed him in a car park and once in a toilet in a department store – she had never failed to get home before he demanded food. But now she was going out more and for longer periods, and she didn't like the prospect of having to breast-feed in front of people. It didn't matter who they were, she just felt embarrassed. Her son was no longer tiny and it was difficult to feed him inconspicuously.

The main pressure to stop, however, was coming from her partner. At first, he had loved to watch her breast-feeding. She knew that he had been as pleased as she was when, after the traumas with their first son, this one had latched on to the breast immediately. Now, though, she knew that secretly he wanted her to stop. He wanted her back, and he wanted their sex life to return to normal. So far, he had been very patient and considerate, but she knew he was becoming increasingly frustrated. Her libido had been virtually non-existent ever since the birth, and feeling tired all the time didn't help. He had begun to drop hints. He told her how distressing he found it to see her so tired and thin, pointing out that if they changed to bottle-feeding he could help. She began to worry that he was becoming jealous of his son's apparent monopoly over her body.

In the end, albeit with great reluctance and not a little sadness, she gradually weaned her son on to a bottle.

B abies mean wars, and at no stage is the conflict more intense than during the first few months of a baby's life. This chapter is concerned with the very first baby wars that parents experience, those that happen almost immediately after the birth.

There are three scenes. In Scene 10, we consider the conflicts that can surface in some women as post-natal depression. In Scene 9, we discuss the war of attrition waged between a baby and its parents over sleeping and crying, the trouble that leads to the misery of sleepless nights. But we start with the much more subtle conflict that surrounds what should be one of the most satisfying of all stages of parenthood – breast-feeding.

In principle, nothing should be simpler, safer, more beneficial or more rewarding to a couple than having the mother breast-feed their child. Breast-milk is both food and drink, ideally balanced by natural selection to meet all of a baby's early dietary requirements. In addition, because it is carried around by the mother wherever she goes, it is convenient, always readily available, and always at the right temperature. It is alive with beneficial bacteria that aid an infant's digestion and help prevent diarrhoea, a frequent cause of infant death in developing countries. It is also rich in immunoglobulins that protect infants from disease, the mother passing on to her baby some of the hard-earned protection that she has built up during her lifetime. Breast-feeding also promotes correct teeth, jaw and speech development and reduces the risk of obesity and diabetes – as long as a baby is breast-fed for more than three months, its chances of getting type 1 diabetes, for example, decrease by 40 per cent.

So why, given all of these advantages, did the woman in the scene above encounter so many problems? She, indeed all women, could be excused for expecting that, after millennia of natural selection, the process of breast-feeding should have been shaped to perfection. So why hasn't it?

There are two main reasons. One is that some of the problems are very recent, and have not yet been addressed by natural selection; they pose difficulties for the modern woman, but not for womankind, and so we can't blame natural selection for them. Most of these recent problems are involved in some way with the decision as to *whether to start* breast-feeding, or simply to bottle-feed, and are dealt with in the second half of this discussion. The second reason, and much more within the domain of evolutionary biology, is that there is a conflict of interest over breast-feeding. This conflict surrounds a woman's decision over *when to stop* breast-feeding, once started, and it is the problems inherent in this decision that we shall discuss first.

Studies that have divided breast-fed babies into categories based on length of breast-feeding have found that those breast-fed the longest did best in terms of avoiding diseases such as gastrointestinal illness, upper respiratory illness, multiple sclerosis, diabetes and heart disease. Also, the babies nursed the longest scored the highest in IQ tests. In all, babies breast-fed for eighteen to twenty-four months were healthier than those allowed less than six months at the breast, but even these still did much better than those who were never breast-fed. None of these studies looked at children who had nursed longer than two years, so we do not yet know whether the benefits of breast-feeding continue or stop at two years of age. We do know that the law of diminishing returns is at work here – the first six months of breast-feeding are clearly much more important in terms of the baby's nutrition and immunological development than, say, the six months between the ages of three and a half and four. This doesn't mean that breast-feeding ceases to be beneficial. A child's immune system doesn't completely mature until about the age of six, and it is well established that breast-milk helps develop the immune system and augment it with maternal antibodies for as long as it is taken. On the face of it, therefore, we might expect natural selection to have programmed women to breast-feed their children until the ages of about five or six, which would be comparable to the average length of time for other primates. Clearly, however, this hasn't happened.

A survey of sixty-four anthropological studies done before the 1940s showed a median duration of breast-feeding of about 2.8 years, with some societies breast-feeding on average for much shorter times, and some for much longer. There are still many societies in the world where children are routinely breast-fed until the ages of four or five, and even in countries such as the United States some are nursed for even longer. When they are allowed to nurse as long as they want to they usually self-wean, with no arguments or emotional trauma, between three and four years of age. In modern industrial countries, however, most are weaned well before this, at a time that suits the mother or her partner rather than the child. When to stop breast-feeding is a problem that confronted our female ancestors no less than it has confronted all other female mammals throughout their evolution. The problem has not been solved, because it has no solution. And this is because – not for the first time in this book – the problem arises from a conflict of interests. When the soft-focus haze of the breast-feeding image is dispersed, we find an underlying battle in progress. And it is this battle that causes most of the problems women experience once they have settled into breast-feeding.

To the evolutionary biologist, breast-feeding and its termination represent a contest – a three-way contest between mother, father and child. Sometimes it is even a four-way contest, between mother, child, mother's partner and the child's genetic father. It arises, like all contests, because the interests of the people involved are different. But before we can understand these differing interests we need to consider some of the less obvious repercussions of breast-feeding, for it does more than provide a baby with a meal. It also regulates the mother's body chemistry in a way designed to promote her long-term reproductive output.

Natural selection has designed humans, and many other primates, to be less likely to conceive while lactating. Lactating women may take six or more months to start menstruating after giving birth. Furthermore, this first menstruation while lactating is almost always infertile. Even the next three cycles have a less than fifty-fifty chance of being fertile. A woman *can* conceive during the months when she is breast-feeding, and as time goes by the chances increase, but those chances are always lower than they would be if she were not breast-feeding, or had breast-fed for a while and then given up.

Why has natural selection decreed that human females should delay conception while nursing their young? It didn't *have* too. Many mammals regularly conceive while lactating, some even being stimulated to ovulate by the very same hormonal regime that inhibits ovulation in humans. The answer is that women inherited a basic problem from their primate progenitors: that it is normally very difficult to carry more than one child at a time when walking long distances.

91

Of course, the problem was, and still is, most extreme in those cultures in which women are responsible for collecting and carrying large quantities of food, water, firewood, or other materials. Carrying even one child at the same time is difficult and tiring – carrying two would be almost impossible. Under such circumstances, the greatest reproductive success is achieved by those women who avoid having another child until the previous one can not only walk but can also keep up.

A detailed 1980s study of the !Kung San bushmen, living in the Kalahari Desert of south-west Africa, revealed an average birth interval of about four years. !Kung San women are responsible for day-to-day foraging and often have to carry food as well as their youngest child for long distances. In this culture, women who conceived less than four years after their previous child was born were more likely to damage themselves and their long-term reproductive prospects. In shaping their body chemistry to produce a four-year gap between children, therefore, natural selection had done the best it could for them, given their way of life.

The challenge faced here by natural selection was to develop a body chemistry in women that, on the one hand, delayed conception for as long as the woman was carrying her youngest child but, on the other, speeded up conception if that child died. This might seem no challenge at all. Surely, natural selection could simply have allowed the woman's brain to tell her body whether her child was still alive and, if so, how often she was having to carry it? But it didn't. Strange though it may seem, evolution seems not to have trusted a woman's brain to tell her body about her baby's survival and requirements. It has preferred to trust the evidence of her nipples, so that having a baby suckle is the main way in which a woman's body reassures itself that her baby is still alive.

As we said at the beginning of this discussion, the act of suckling has evolved to do much more than simply provide the baby with milk. First, it stimulates centres in the mother's brain to trigger a whole series of chemical commands that tell her body to make more milk. Not only that, but the length and intensity of breast-feeding, and the amount of milk the baby takes at each meal, tell her body how much to manufacture for the next meal. Second, the act of suckling triggers chemical commands that reduce the chances of the woman ovulating and hence conceiving. This is why, if a woman doesn't breast-feed, even though her brain knows full well that her baby is still alive her body nevertheless begins to make preparations to conceive months or even years earlier than might be the optimum. A study in Chile found that none of the exclusively breast-feeding women had conceived within six months of birth, compared to 72 per cent of non-breast-feeding women. It is also why, if a baby dies but the mother immediately allows another woman's baby to feed from her – as wet-nurses did in the past – her body still delays its preparations to conceive, even though her brain knows that her own baby is dead.

With this information as background, it is now easier to see why the interests of the woman, her baby and her partner are different and thus why the termination of breast-feeding becomes a three- or four-way battle.

As far as the baby is concerned, it will be bigger, healthier, more likely to survive infancy and childhood, and itself have greater reproductive potential if it can obtain breast-milk as much and as often as possible. In addition, it is by extending breast-feeding for as long after birth as it can that a baby delays its mother's next conception. This is our first encounter with the phenomenon known as sibling rivalry, which we shall discuss in detail in Chapter 6. Here, the important point is that in preventing its mother from conceiving for as long as possible, a baby avoids having to share its parents' attention with a younger sibling, and thus gets more of their attention during those critical first few months and years when its very survival, as well as its future prospects, depend on the quality of care it receives. A baby, therefore, gains from *prolonging* the breast-feeding period.

As far as the mother is concerned, she gains most from finding the *best compromise* for maximising her *long-term* reproductive output. If she feeds her current baby too little, *its* health and future prospects may be compromised. If she feeds it too much and for too long, *her* health and future prospects may be compromised because she risks reducing her body reserves to too low a level, as well as delaying her next conception for too long, thereby losing those benefits of an optimal delay that we have just discussed.

The conflict of interest between mother and baby, however, rarely translates into a real conflict. It can't – the contest is too uneven in the mother's favour. Recent studies of rats show that chemicals in the milk as well as the behaviour of both mother and baby all communicate signals of need and intent. As soon as the baby's body detects that it is about to be weaned, its gut begins to produce the enzymes necessary to shift to a different diet, irrespective of its age. In the conflict of interests between mother and baby, the mother's decision is final, whereas the conflict of interest between mother, baby and the mother's partner is much more finely balanced. As far as the partner is concerned, his best interests as regards breast-feeding depend on his situation. Two things are important – the probability of his being the father of the woman's current baby and his chances of being the father of her next.

The principles are straightforward. First, the more certain he is of his paternity, the more his reproductive interests coincide with the child's. The interests of both are then best served by the mother breast-feeding as intensively and for as long as possible, even if in doing so she compromises *her* long-term reproduction. As we discussed in relation to pregnancy sickness and labour, if necessary the father can always switch to reproducing with another woman. On the other hand, the less certain he is of his paternity, the more his interests are served by curtailing or even preventing breast-feeding so that he has a chance, sooner rather than later, of fathering her next child. The second principle is this: the greater the man's chances of fathering her next child, the more it is in his reproductive interests for her to breast-feed less intensively and to finish earlier, thereby shortening the interval before he fathers that child.

These differences of interest between the mother and her partner are the main cause of the problems experienced *by couples* over breast-feeding, as illustrated at the end of the scene above. The feelings of exclusion and jealousy that men sometimes experience as they watch their partner breast-feeding, and the pressure they exert in order to reduce the process and terminate it early, all stem evolutionarily from this conflict. Sometimes the conflict can reach extremes. In the USA, for example, some mothers have had allegations of extended breast-feeding used against them in custody fights with the fathers of their children. The evolutionary biologist's expectation is that the greater a man's doubts that the child is his, the greater should be the jealousy and the pressure he exerts. And the more certain the man, or the less dependent he is on this woman for his next child, the less intense should be the jealousy and the pressure.

Men, women and babies have experienced this conflict over breast-feeding for as long as there have been people, and it can never be resolved because the differences of interest will always exist. Furthermore, the modern woman faces other difficulties in addition to those generated by her evolutionary past. Most of these more recent problems, which are social and technological in origin, are to do with the fact that, at least in industrialised societies, mothers have a choice when it comes to how they will feed their babies. In the past, neither women nor men had any choice. If the child was to have any chance of surviving at all the woman had to breast-feed. A wet-nurse was the only alternative. The advent of bottle-feeding with formula milk, however, has changed all this. Pressures that in the past would have affected only the question of when to stop, now apply with equal force to the question of whether or not to start breast-feeding in the first place.

It would seem that no woman should choose, or be asked, to bottle-feed if she can possibly avoid it. The poorer the circumstances of the family, the more vital the protection that breast-feeding affords. There is nothing inherently dangerous in formula milk, but it can't possibly offer all the benefits of human milk. Similarly, where as cow's milk is perfect for calves, it is ill-suited to children, as are artificial milks. The effects of the mismatch are devastating. In one study, a group of infants fed artificial milk incurred $68,000 worth of health care costs in a six-month period, while for an equal number of nursing babies the figure was only $4,000. In Brazil, where medical care is not readily available, an artificially fed baby is fourteen times more likely to die than an exclusively breast-fed one, and at least four times more likely to die than an infant receiving both mother's milk and artificial milk.

Despite such evidence, the modern woman, no matter where she lives, can sometimes find herself under enormous pressure not to follow the course of her ancestors and breast-feed. Even in Brazil, where the dangers of artificial feeding are so high, only 4 per cent of babies are exclusively breast-fed during their first four months. The proportion ranges from 90 per cent in Rwanda to 1 per cent in Niger, and from 53 per cent in Bolivia to 3 per cent in Haiti.

The pressure to bottle-feed can come from all directions. One of the most interesting aspects of the problem is the fact that, as soon as this alternative is available to a society, that society passes through a phase in which there is intense social pressure on women *not* to breast-feed. The pattern is persistent, and even now breast-feeding is still not the norm in most industrialised societies. In the United Kingdom, for example, in 1990 only 63 per cent of new mothers even tried to breast-feed. After two weeks, only 50 per cent of them were still nursing, and after six weeks only 39 per cent. Only one in ten mothers breast-fed their babies for more than nine months. This low proportion of modern children being raised on the breast persists despite recent medical attempts to persuade women of the benefits of breast-feeding. In the past, social pressures strongly favoured bottle-feeding: a few decades ago in Europe and the USA breast-feeding was portrayed as unhygienic. Other pressures range from warnings about the difficulties of breast-feeding, through antagonism towards women who dare to breast-feed in public, to the commercial promotion and exploitation of bottle-feeding and formula milk.

Sometimes, it is obvious that to bottle-feed is *to the detriment* of both mother and child. The most poignant recent examples come from the Third World: while still in hospital after delivery, mothers have been pressurised into bottle-feeding despite the fact that, once out of hospital, they would not be able to afford formula milk, nor would they have access to the clean water needed for making up the feeds.

In many places such as some parts of the USA, nursing mothers encounter disgust, hostility and prudishness about breast-feeding. To the women concerned this kind of attitude is no trivial matter, and can place them under much greater pressure than the mild embarrassment experienced by the woman in the scene. Nursing mothers in the USA have been asked to leave, and have been threatened with arrest for indecent exposure, at malls, restaurants, public parks, courtrooms and so on where bottle-feeding is regularly accepted. Indeed, public opposition to breast-feeding is so pervasive that several state legislatures have enacted laws in order to clarify that it is not a form of indecent exposure. Moreover, the claim that there is something sexual and improper about a woman breast-feeding her child past early infancy has given rise to reports of abuse being filed against some mothers, though nobody as yet has been found guilty. A Minnesota mother, for example, was accused of abuse for breast-feeding a six-year-old in public; the child was in fact three, and when the age was established the case was closed. In Tennessee, accusations against a mother for nursing a four-and-a-half-year-old were ultimately dropped; in Florida, a woman was cleared of abuse for breast-feeding a six-year-old.

To the evolutionary biologist, such public pressure against breast-feeding is interesting in its own right. It can be cynically interpreted in terms of evolved self-interest: both men and women in the general population gain from pressurising the female population *as a whole* not to breast-feed – for the following reasons.

It is in every man's interest for the female population, except for the mother(s) of his children, *not* to breast-feed. The fewer women who are breast-feeding at any one time, the more there are who are fertile and the greater, therefore, the choice of potential reproductive outlets available to each man. Women also benefit from pressurising other women not to breast-feed. Because, on average, those who do so are likely to be reproductively more successful than those who do not, they are more of a reproductive threat to every other woman. So whether a woman breast-feeds her own children or not, she could gain reproductively by pressurising other women to bottle-feed. Social pressures against breast-feeding and in favour of bottle-feeding are, then, not surprising, and are as much the product of natural selection as everything else we have discussed.

It would be a mistake, of course, to conclude that women only ever decide to bottle-feed in response to pressure from others. Some women logically, and others more intuitively, decide that their personal interests will be best served by feeding their babies formula milk from a bottle rather than natural milk from their breasts. And in fact there are occasions when, although the decision to bottle-feed is not in the best interests of most babies, it *can* be in the long-term interests of certain women. It is not an easy decision. There are costs and benefits to breast-feeding for the modern woman, just as there are costs and benefits to bottle-feeding. The relevant factors are a subtle mixture of ancient legacy and modern innovation.

One of the *benefits* of breast-feeding that we have not yet considered is one that the woman in the scene above regarded as particularly important. She had heard that successfully breast-feeding a child could be beneficial for her long-term health. This is hardly surprising. Since a woman's body is genetically programmed to lactate after giving birth, failure to allow it to work through this part of its program can have detrimental long-term effects. One benefit of breast-feeding, for instance, is its influence on a woman's ability to regain her pre-pregnancy weight, shape and attractiveness. In fact, if they don't breast-feed, some women never return to their pre-pregnancy state. And if their waist circumference does not return to 70 per cent of the hip measurement, their attractiveness can be reduced. Even more seriously, breast-feeding influences a woman's chances of developing breast cancer. In a study published in the *New England Journal of Medicine*, women who had lactated had a lower risk of *pre*-menopausal breast cancer than those who had not. Further, in this study the earlier and the longer the woman had lactated – whether because she had breast-fed a number of children or because she had nursed each one for many months – the more protection she had against breast cancer. Lactation did not appear to influence the chances of *post*-menopausal breast cancer.

It is no coincidence that these consequences of breast-feeding are beneficial, for they are ancient legacies shaped by natural selection. Nor is it a coincidence that the following consequences are detrimental, for they are linked to relatively recent social and technological change that natural selection has not yet had time to influence.

The sore, cracked nipples experienced by many modern mothers often lead them to abandon their attempts at breast-feeding. Mastitis, too, can be a problem. At best, it is painful, and at worst it makes the woman very ill and terminates her milk production.

We might be inclined to think that problems with nipples and breasts look like a failure of natural selection. If evolution has dictated that women should breast-feed, why hasn't it endowed them with nipples and breasts adequate for the job? The answer, of course, is that it has, but that it has been unable to anticipate the modern woman's environment. The inadequacy of her breasts is not the fault of evolution, but of social conventions concerning dress. This, in turn, is not a fault in the evolutionary process, but a product of man's success at invading colder and colder climates, which he could only do because he discovered fire – and clothes. Sore nipples are the price many modern women have to pay for humankind's success at colonising the globe. Breasts evolved to be exposed to the elements. Nipples and the skin around them should be tough, hardened by years of exposure to sun, rain and wind. Then they work. They are a bit like feet. Enclose them in socks and shoes, protect them from the elements, and make them sweat for years on end and they never harden. Expect them then to do the job for which they evolved – to run over hard rock for hours on end – and they fail. They crack, they bleed, and they become infected. Similarly, wrap breasts in clothes, protect them from the weather and make them sweat for years on end and *they* never harden. So when they are required to do the job for which they were designed – to be sucked, nibbled and pulled about by the wet mouth of a baby – they aren't up to it. They crack, they bleed, and they become infected.

The second consequence of breast-feeding that can be to the detriment of the modern woman is that it interferes with her ability to return to work, or to resume the search for a new or better partner. Both of these, as already noted, can be important factors in the woman's long-term reproductive output, because they help to improve her child's environment and care.

Just because something has not been shaped by natural selection does not mean that it has to be disadvantageous. Nor is it inevitably true that because something is recent it will not fit in with evolved strategies. In at least one sense, bottle-feeding is just such a phenomenon. Women have been saddled with a body chemistry that links their opting for bottle-feeding with an increased chance of rapid conception, and the accompanying risk, in centuries past, of having to carry around more than one child. Although the transporting problem may not be totally unfamiliar even now, cars, prams and push-chairs have almost liberated the modern woman from this ancestral legacy. The result is that the woman in an industrial society can afford to be much more opportunistic about conceiving successive children. If she encounters a suitable opportunity to conceive again only a few months after giving birth, she has relatively little to lose compared with her nomadic ancestors. Whereas breast-feeding may prevent such rapid conception, by bottle-feeding she frees herself from such ancestral constraints and may conceive two children in rapid succession if circumstances favour such a strategy.

These costs and benefits of breast-feeding and of bottle-feeding in the contemporary environment present the modern mother with a delicate decision to make, one that will have repercussions for her long-term reproductive success. To the ancient question of when to stop breast-feeding is now added the question of whether even to start. Without doubt, some mothers *may* enhance their reproductive interests by bottle-feeding rather than breast-feeding, and every woman has the onerous task of deciding whether *she* is such a mother.

Unfortunately for her, in making her decision she is on her own. Given that the bottle-feeding option is far too recent for natural selection to have shaped her decision-making, mistakes will inevitably often be made. Over the next few millennia, though, we can expect even this element of parenthood to receive the honing it needs as natural selection weeds out any genes that predispose their possessors to make the wrong decision. Thus the genes of women who make an accurate assessment of the relative merits of breast- and bottle-feeding *for their situation* will gradually spread over subsequent generations.

Another set of genes that have been given a new lease of life by the advent of bottle-feeding are those that were possessed, presumably, by the first son born to the woman in the scene above – the genes that predispose their possessor, as a newborn baby, not to latch on to its mother's breast. Whether, in the evolutionary past, hunger would have driven such babies *eventually* to feed, or whether they would simply have died, is unknown. One thing is clear, however. In the modern world, once such babies discover the ease of feeding from a bottle, they refuse and even fight the breast. Nowadays, such babies are treated much less harshly by natural selection, and are at little or no disadvantage compared to babies who readily breast-feed. Indeed, with the technological advent of expressers, they can even be fed their mother's breast-milk, albeit via a bottle, thus gaining the same nutritional and immunological advantages as their breast-fed contemporaries. But because it is so much easier for them to suck from a bottle than from a breast, they can gain these advantages for much less effort.

The other problem experienced by the woman in the scene is that of position. In part, like sore nipples, this difficulty is also a consequence of our modern way of life. A sedentary lifestyle has given many people such weak backs and muscles that they find holding any fixed position painful and tiring. More interestingly, climate, clothes and convention dictate that breast-feeding be turned into an event. The woman has to stop what she is doing, partly undress, and find somewhere socially and spatially suitable.

Primates, and women in particular, were not designed to breast-feed in this way. Neither female anatomy nor a baby's appetite was shaped for such ceremony by natural selection. Breast-feeding evolved to interfere as little as possible with the female's activities. Whether monkey, ape or human, whether walking, sitting or even sleeping, she was designed to carry the baby with its head near her nipple so that food was just a root away at any time of day. As she continued with her daily routine the mother scarcely needed to notice whether the baby was feeding or not. However, even if modern women *could* walk around naked (at least from the waist up) while breast-feeding, many would have neither the strength nor the stamina to travel far while doing so.

It is because natural selection made breast-feeding an ongoing and spontaneous procedure – 'milk to go' – that it simultaneously gave women their characteristic waist, hips and breasts. Whereas the babies of other primates can cling to their mother's body hair as they travel, human babies and infants tend to perch on their mother's hip, supported by a restraining arm. Hips *are* perches. This is why the ideal female shape, as already mentioned, gives a waist considerably smaller than the hips and why males have been programmed to find such a shape attractive. There is a similar reason why women have breasts.

Breasts are cushions, not glands. The padding that gives them their characteristic shape has nothing to do with milk production, so that the size of a woman's breasts before pregnancy gives no indication of her ability to produce milk. It is the accumulation of fat and other tissue, rather than of what will ultimately be milk-producing tissue, that, starting at puberty, gives breasts their shape and *size*. Human females are unique among the primates in developing pendulous breasts at puberty, then retaining them throughout life. All others, including the great apes, develop pendulous breasts only at the onset of lactation, and they stay that way only until lactation ceases. The main reason that the primate breast is pendulous during lactation is for ease of suckling in a range of positions. It needs length and manoeuvrability to reach the baby's mouth as the mother walks, sits and sleeps. A nipple flat against the chest, as in males, would be of little use.

Once evolution stood our ancestors on their back legs and made them walk vertically, women encountered a problem not often experienced by their pre-human ancestors: how to stop their baby's head, which was particularly wobbly while the baby was asleep, from forever banging against their ribs. Part of evolution's scheme for bipedal walking, therefore, will have been selection for a cushion for the baby's head. And what better cushion than a swollen breast? Moreover, because women from time to time carry infants long after they have been weaned, and because post-pubertal girls carry their younger brothers and sisters before they themselves have reproduced, human females have breasts from puberty onwards.

Inevitably, women lose their characteristic waist–hip ratio during pregnancy, their 'waist' eventually becoming much larger than their hips. It is in their long-term reproductive interests to regain that ratio as soon as possible after giving birth, and at least by the time they would next benefit from conceiving. So how do they do it?

This is one situation in which a woman's conscious wishes match her subconscious. Both encourage her to lose enough weight to return to her pre-pregnancy weight and shape. There is much that can be said about weight loss during lactation, not least that it reveals an interesting and unexpected twist, an instance of the way modern life has inadvertently outwitted natural selection – though to nobody's benefit.

The main targets of a woman's concern once she has given

birth are the fat deposits on her buttocks, thighs and abdomen that accumulated during the later stages of pregnancy. Even if she doesn't breast-feed at all, her body is programmed to reduce these deposits. Not surprisingly, the more she breast-feeds and the less she eats, the faster they disappear. The fat deposits are actually reserves of energy, important buffers against hard times after giving birth, as we noted in our discussion of Scene 7. They are there to protect both the woman and her baby if food becomes scarce during lactation, enabling her to carry on producing milk at the necessary rate even during times of famine. Taking most of the burden of famine on herself in order to protect the baby, she uses up more and more of her fat reserves. So efficiently has natural selection designed her lactation system that under moderate famine conditions a baby's growth rate is reduced by only about 10 per cent.

There is a limit, however, to how much food deprivation a lactating mother can cope with – and that limit is reached when the last of her fat deposits has been used to produce milk. Evolution has predisposed her body to keep a close eye on how much and how quickly she erodes those deposits. Poor nutrition during lactation may have relatively little effect on the amount of milk she produces, but it may make her so thin that she is in no state to embark on another pregnancy, even once she stops breast-feeding. So natural selection has programmed women not to ovulate if their fat reserves have been eroded too far. Until they have been built up again, her body will rarely allow her to ovulate and conceive.

And here is the interesting twist, one that poses a new problem for natural selection. In the past, a woman's body was programmed to monitor her fat reserves via the simple device of monitoring her blood sugar levels, which would usually have been higher when her fat reserves were high. This is an adequate mechanism and, as long as the woman was on a healthy, *ancestral* diet, it allowed natural selection to prevent her from ovulating while her fat reserves were low. Studies of hamsters, though, have shown that whereas acute starvation does indeed block ovulation, the simple addition of glucose to the drinking-water fools the body into thinking that it still has adequate reserves of fat and induces it to remove the block to ovulation. So if a woman with low fat reserves eats too many of the sugary foods available in a modern diet, her body, too, might be fooled into thinking that her reserves are higher than they are. Inadvertently, she might trigger an ovulation and even a pregnancy that normally her body would not have allowed.

There is one final question to do with breasts, nipples and breast-feeding that has nothing to do with parenthood but which is interesting nonetheless. Why do men have nipples? Some even produce tiny quantities of milk. Is it because at one time males as well as females used to breast-feed?

The males of all higher mammals, except rats and mice, have nipples, which is a sure indication that males of the very first such mammals had them too. Yet the earliest of these creatures, like most of their modern counterparts, led such a free-ranging life that they would rarely even meet their offspring, let alone show them parental care or feed them. We can rest assured, then, that male mammals never breast-fed their young. So why *do* males have nipples? The disappointing answer is: males have nipples because females have nipples.

Natural selection finds it difficult to evolve something in only one sex. Usually, if something evolves because it is of benefit to one sex, the other inherits the same thing by default. Then evolution sets about fashioning the item differently in the two sexes, according to their separate needs. This is why, for example, males and females have essentially the same range of hormones, but in different proportions. It is also why male and female genitals are shaped from the same tissues, the clitoris and the labia minora being shaped from the same foetal tissue as the penis, and the labia majora from the same foetal tissue as the scrotum. And it is why males have milk-producing tissue – and nipples. They are just less developed in males and relatively, but not entirely, functionless. Roughly half of men have nipples sensitive enough to be involved in sexual stimulation. It is possible, also, that the milk-producing tissue in men produces substances that help to regulate their body chemistry and behaviour, as it does in women. This, by itself, would be enough for evolution not to try to rid men of their nipples completely. As far as parenthood is concerned, however, male nipples are not part of the story.

Sleepless Nights

On the verge of waking, the naked woman shifted her position, instinctively avoiding the baby sleeping next to her. Her right breast, turgid with milk, seemed to brush against his head. Comfortable on her bed of leaves and warmed by the nearby fire, she was subconsciously reassured by the familiar nightly backdrop of snoring men and jungle noises.

Suddenly, her dreams were pierced by a howl, and then another. There were dogs around. She reached out to pull her baby closer, but he wasn't there. Waking in a panic, she thrashed around in the shadows cast by the fire, seeking the reassuring feel of his warm body. But where was he? Had he rolled away? Or had a dog plucked him from under her breast as she and the others had slept? Leaping to her feet and peering through the darkness, she tried to wake the men, but none of them stirred. Imagining her baby being carried off in a dog's mouth, teeth crushing his fragile body, she ran frantically in circles, then dashed towards the edge of the clearing, adding her own shouts to the howls of the dogs. Were they fighting over her baby, pulling him limb from limb? They had gone quiet – but now she could hear her baby screaming. She must get to him. His agonised cries weren't far away, so why couldn't she see him?

Wet with the sweat of panic, the woman was suddenly awake. Her dream had been so real – but it was only a dream. Her brain, muddled from lack of sleep, slowly focused. Their baby was in the next room, screaming as if he really was being attacked by dogs. By her side, her partner was snoring loudly. As exhausted as she was, he was oblivious to their baby's cries.

She groaned. It was only an hour since their son had at last fallen asleep. They had fed him, changed him and laid him in his cot. Then they had closed the nursery door, and for a few blissful minutes afterwards he had lain quiet, distracted by the chimes of the clockwork night-light that projected nursery characters on the ceiling as it played. As soon as the light had stopped turning, however, he had begun to cry. Then to scream. She had picked him up, put him down, tried to feed him again, rocked him, checked his nappy again – but nothing had worked. He continued to scream.

In the end, they had just shut the door, gone to bed and waited for him to cry himself to sleep. He had done, but it had taken a while. She had lain awake, agonising over whether or not to go to him. Was she being cruel? Was she doing him untold damage? Would he hurt himself, crying so much? He sounded distraught, but she was so tired that her worries over his well-being alternated with feelings of hostility towards him at the way he was ruining her sleep.

For the first few nights after they had brought him home from hospital, he had slept well. They had, of course, had to get up twice a night to feed him, but in between times he had slept. They had been tired, but they had coped. Increasingly, though, he had settled less and less well in his cot until, now, the nights were really stressful – just a few random hours of sleep, if they were lucky. A week ago, her partner had been so desperate for sleep that he had got up, dressed and taken him for a drive. The baby had slept perfectly well in the car, as he always did, but as soon as he was transferred back to his cot he had begun all over again.

There was no shortage of sympathy and advice from friends who had been through it all themselves, but none of it seemed worth following. They briefly considered letting him sleep in their bed, between them, but didn't really like the idea. They were worried that they might roll on to him, or that they would be storing up trouble for the future. Once he knew he could sleep in their bed, he might refuse ever to go back into his own. As the months passed, they became inured to the lack of sleep. Some nights were better than others, but still they *never* had a full night's sleep. Then, when their son was about eight months old, things deteriorated further. He seemed to have developed the ability to yell non-stop for hours at a time. As an experiment, they moved his cot out of the nursery and put it by the side of their bed. This helped considerably for a week or so, but then began a new phase. They would wake to find him standing in his cot, staring into the darkness and screaming as if they were a million miles away. Every time they laid him down, he stood up again and continued where he had left off.

Finally, one desperate night, they had pulled him out of his cot, put him in bed between them, and ignored him. Voicing his displeasure for a little longer, he hadn't settled immediately, but it wasn't long before he went quiet. Moreover, he had slept for the rest of the night. The next night, they laid him between them as soon as they went to bed –

and had their first full night's sleep for months. Soon, they were allowing him to fall asleep on the sofa next to them, then taking him up to bed with them when they went.

From that moment on, sleepless nights were a thing of the past. Admittedly, they had to endure other discomforts as he thrashed around between them. Occasionally, in his innocent sleep, he would punch one of them in the eye, head-butt, kick them in the groin or scratch whatever his sharp fingernails made contact with. Admittedly, also, he was two before he accepted a bed by the side of theirs, and three before he would sleep in his own room.

By the time their son had moved out, they already had their second baby, a daughter. She slept peacefully in bed between them from the day she was born, breast-feeding as and when she felt like it. This time it was they who offered advice, usually unheeded, to distraught and haggard friends.

Humans have been spending nights with their babies for as long as they have been around. With such a long period of evolution behind them, modern humans might reasonably have expected any major problems to have been solved. Yet still the average parents in modern Western societies suffer some of their worst experiences of parenthood during the first few weeks, months or even years of life at home with a new baby. Most will be able to identify with some, if not all, of the trials of our couple in the scene above. The utter exhaustion of having to continue with a daily routine after nights of broken sleep will be excruciatingly familiar.

Why should babies be programmed to make the nights, and hence the days, so much of a nightmare for their parents? Intuitively, we might have expected it to be as important to the baby as it is to its parents that the latter stay healthy, alert and sympathetic. The answer is, of course, that a baby *is not* programmed to make life difficult for its parents. What it *is* programmed to do is to alert them to the fact that it has a problem, and the way it does this is to cry. Why it *cries*, instead of pulling a face or waving its hands in the air, we shall discuss later. First, though, we need to consider the range of problems that might make a baby feel it is worth the effort of crying to alert its parents.

A baby has such limited needs – food, comfort and safety – that it should have been easy for natural selection to shape mother and baby in a way that minimised all dangers and stresses. And, by and large, it has actually succeeded. The misfortune is that the evolved solutions are not easily accommodated within modern parents' environment and way of life.

First, until the advent of clothes, then bottle-feeding, natural selection had solved both mother's and baby's potential problems over food. Throughout most of human and primate evolution food for youngsters was just a nuzzle and a nipple away, as we have already seen. Young babies, like all young primates, were continually carried by their mothers, usually in a position within reach of a nipple. Morning, noon *and night* all they had to do was root, nuzzle and suck. Rarely will they have needed to cry to let their mothers know they were hungry, and at night, the mothers scarcely even needed to be awake.

Second, again until the advent of clothes, natural selection had little difficulty dealing with urination and defecation. During much of human evolution both mothers and their babies went naked and slept on the ground. Urination and defecation while on the move during the day posed no problem, and during the night were no more than a minor irritation. Babies would never have been soaked in their own urine or smeared with faeces, any more than are the babies of any other primate. In cultures which are still naked, a mother becomes exceptionally good at anticipating when her baby is about to pass urine or faeces, and can usually adjust its position for minimum inconvenience and discomfort to either of them. The colonisation of the colder regions of the world, however, and the necessary adoption of clothes changed the situation and raised a problem that can be minimised technologically with nappies, but never solved evolutionarily.

Finally, natural selection has done all it can to solve the problem of safety. If the woman in the scene really had been sleeping naked on the jungle floor, she wouldn't even have questioned what to do with her baby. In such an environment, in any unsafe environment, there is only one place for a baby to be: in contact with an adult's body, either held or carried. At night, ancestral nomadic mothers would automatically have put their babies right next to them, preferably in bodily contact so that they would know immediately if they rolled away. Even better, the baby would have been placed between themselves and an older child or other adult. For this reason, natural selection predisposed babies to look for reassurance from three main sources – body heat, body smell and/or motion. If a baby has satisfactory evidence from these three sources that it is safe, then it can relax and sleep in peace, until it gets hungry or otherwise uncomfortable. This is one reason why babies sleep so readily in a car, as found by the man in our scene. The feeling of motion fools their bodies into thinking they are being carried and are therefore safe.

Of course, *we* know that babies are safe in our homes at night, at least in so far as there is no danger from marauding wolves, coyotes, cats and the like. Not surprisingly, though, this is not so obvious to a baby. Natural selection in our evolutionary past favoured those babies who responded by crying to *any* feeling of separation from their parents, particularly the mother and particularly when in the dark. Those were the babies who survived, reproduced and passed on their genes so that babies down the generations would respond in that way. Those who quietly accepted their isolation were more likely to have been attacked or carried off by predators and were less likely to have descendants alive today. As far as a baby and its genetic program are concerned, therefore, they are still in the ancestral environment, with all its dangers, and no amount of 'discipline' or explanation will convince either of them otherwise.

So automatic will it have been during evolution for babies to sleep by their mother's side that natural selection could afford to use her presence to help the baby perform certain vital tasks. Babies pace their breathing with their mothers, to the extent that babies separated from their mothers sometimes develop abnormal and dangerously long gaps between taking breaths. This might seem a silly trick for evolution to play – but it wouldn't be silly if evolution could assume the mother would always be by her baby's side.

We can see, therefore, that because modern babies soil their nappies, sleep on their own and have to ask to be fed, they have *more reason* to alert their parents to problems than their ancestral counterparts had. But why do they do so by cry-ing instead of by some more peaceful means? Why *do* babies

cry, and why are we programmed to find the sound so stressful?

There is no mystery, of course, over why a baby uses sounds
rather than gestures to alert its parents. Gestures would be fine if
the baby could guarantee that its parents were within sight and
vigilant. But because it has no such guarantee, particularly at
night it needs to make a noise. There is, of course, an inherent
danger in noise. In an unsafe environment, crying does more
than draw the parents' attention to the baby's location – it also
attracts the attention of predators and other dangers. Cunningly,
however, natural selection has found a way for babies to exploit
this danger – because more often than not parents will do anything
to protect their child. In effect, a baby cries to galvanise its possibly
recalcitrant parents and thereby safeguard its own survival. It aims
to force its parents into acting, and into acting sooner rather than
later, relying on their wanting to quieten it before it attracts danger.
If parents leave a baby to cry, they initiate a war of attrition that
lasts either until the baby eventually stops or until they give in
and respond.

Modern parents, safe in their comfortable homes, delay their
response far longer than babies are programmed to expect. In
our evolutionary past, it will have been important that parents
tended to a crying baby quickly, so their hormonal response to
the sound needed to be of the fight-or-flee type. Such responses
are by their very nature stressful, and particularly when not acted
upon and satisfied. It is for this reason that a baby's cry is one
of the most stressful sounds a human can hear. Hormonally, it
is equivalent to seeing a tiger approaching while being tied to a
stake and unable to fight or flee.

Modern humans, living in their concrete environments and
forced by climate and social pressures to wear clothes, can do
little more than they already do about the problem of their
baby soiling itself. They can, however, avoid forcing it to sleep
apart from them, and breast-feeding mothers can also allow their
baby to spend its nights near the breast. By and large, those
that pursue such ancient practice discover that sleepless nights
are largely avoidable. But for those who prefer to ignore their
baby's finely tuned sensibilities, sleep deprivation is a virtually
unavoidable penalty of modern emancipation.

SCENE 10
Post-natal Depression

The young woman walked slowly along the pavement pushing her four-week-old baby in its pram. The pram, brand-new, shiny and expensive, glided smoothly along. She had looked forward to this experience while she was pregnant, and had pushed it up and down the kitchen a few times, imagining her baby looking back at her. She had smiled. It had made her feel like a five-year-old again, pushing an assortment of dolls and teddies around the garden in a lurid pink pram with a shiny black handle.

Today, the young woman had come out because she had thought it might make her feel better. But so far it hadn't. In fact nothing seemed to make her feel better at the moment. She didn't feel just a *bit* miserable. She felt a heart-wrenching hopelessness that made her want to cry out to complete strangers as they passed by – but she didn't, of course. Instead, she stared fixedly ahead, gripped the pram handle and carried on walking.

Unsure of where she was going, she turned hesitantly into the greengrocer's and stood gazing at the colourful array of fruit and vegetables. Before the birth she would have walked briskly in, list in hand, grabbed a few bags and quickly filled her basket with all the weekly vegetables and fruit they needed. But now she couldn't even decide which type of apple to buy. Was it the green crispy ones they liked, or the softer red ones? Making decisions, even the simplest ones, had become almost impossible for her. It was as though her mind had slowed down to such an extent that it was in danger of stopping completely. She stood for a moment or two longer, as if paralysed, then slowly became aware of something pushing into her back and a voice saying, 'Excuse me please dear.' Moving aside, she dragged the pram round and walked out of the shop.

That morning had seemed especially difficult. She had woken early with a churning stomach and an intense feeling of foreboding. Her first instinct had been to curl up into a ball and spend the whole day in bed. She was convinced that a good long sleep would help her feel better. But soon her stomach and a full bladder had forced her to get up. On her way to the toilet she had stopped by the carry-cot and looked down at her sleeping baby. A thought briefly crossed her mind. Maybe he wouldn't wake up. Maybe it would be the best thing that could happen – best for everyone. But at that moment the baby had stirred. He kicked, then stretched. His mother stood motionless for a moment, then bent down towards the cot and picked him up.

Once downstairs, she began to breast-feed him. Reaching for the remote control, she switched on the television. As she stared, unseeing, at the screen a feeling of intense sadness overwhelmed her and she began to cry. At first her crying was quiet, apparently controlled, but within a few moments it had become loud and desperate. The baby, his eyes now wide open, detached himself from the nipple and began to cry too. Putting him down on the sofa beside her, she wiped the back of her hand across her streaming eyes. Why was she feeling this way? Why was she feeling so *terrible*? All she knew was that it had started just after the birth.

The birth had been more painful than she could ever have imagined. Her attempts to talk about the experience had fallen on kindly but essentially deaf ears. Everyone was far too interested in the baby. During the first few days she had felt a peculiar kind of numbness, a detachment, almost, from everything around her. No matter how hard she tried she could feel nothing for the tiny infant clinging to her breast. She looked at him rarely, but when she did it was as if she was gazing at some alien being that had no connection with herself at all. She couldn't believe she had actually given birth to him. Visitors had come and gone, telling her how lucky she was to have such a perfect, beautiful baby, but she hadn't *felt* lucky. She felt completely unable to cope, as if things would never be normal again.

Her partner had been sympathetic. At the birth he had helped her through the pushing stage, encouraging and talking to her. His excitement had mounted as the birth progressed. Afterwards, he had carried his newborn son proudly around the room as if bearing a trophy. All she had wanted to do was sleep.

Once home, her feelings of isolation had increased. It was as if a glass barrier had formed, imprisoning her in her own silent nightmare. When her son was six days old her partner had left on a pre-arranged business trip abroad. He hadn't wanted to go, but in the end he had had no choice. As he packed she wandered around with their sleeping infant in her arms, following him from room to room. She wanted to plead with him not to go, but she hadn't. Besides, she knew he couldn't get out of it. They both knew this trip was his first chance to prove himself worthy of his recent promotion. There was no way he could simply back out and stay at home with her. His increased salary was vital to their future plans. Even so, when he tenderly kissed her goodbye, promising to phone every night, she had been unable to look at him.

After he had left, she had sunk further and further into despair. Tiredness overwhelmed her. She began to spend all day in her dressing-gown; there seemed no point in getting dressed – or washing, cleaning her teeth or brushing her hair. The smallest of tasks defeated her. She was barely able to feed and keep her baby in clean nappies. In her few active moments, when things had penetrated her consciousness enough to bother her, she panicked at the state of the house, at the chaos around her. She had spent hours just sitting, hunched up, staring into space while the baby cried in his cot. This is how it had continued until this morning, when with an incredible effort of will she had ventured out to the shops. It had taken her almost five hours to get herself and the baby ready.

On the way home from the greengrocer's her head seemed suddenly to clear. She knew now: she was a complete failure as a mother, totally incapable of looking after her son. He would almost certainly be better off without her. The only option was to leave him where someone would be sure to find him, and care for him in the way he deserved. And then her own life could get back to normal. All she had to do was get rid of him. This, she convinced herself, would make everything better. Her step quickened – she felt strangely excited. Her mind began to cast around for ways of abandoning him. She was walking along a busy road in the centre of town. A moment later she would cross over and turn into a side street. Her eyes fixed on the point ahead where she would have to stop and turn the pram round at the edge of the kerb. As the noise of the traffic thundered through her head she thought how easy it would be to gently push it out into the road. It seemed such a perfect plan, so simple. Within a few seconds, it would all be over. It would be best, she reassured herself, best for everyone . . .

Looking back, she would never know what made her pull the pram back, at the very last moment, to the safety of the pavement. Perhaps it was instinct, perhaps fear. What was clear to her later was that it had been the turning-point in her illness. She had walked home in a state of shock that didn't begin to lift until her partner had phoned later that afternoon. Between bouts of hysterical crying she had managed to tell him what had happened and how she had been feeling since he'd left. A wonderful sense of relief had washed over her at being able to tell someone of her misery. And when her partner turned up only hours later, having cut his trip short by a week, her long road to recovery really began.

Ever since the time of Hippocrates, clinicians have noted mood disturbances in women who have recently given birth. The same disturbances have been described for many cultures, and appear to span the whole range of socioeconomic groups. In modern industrial societies about 50 per cent of new mothers experience mild mood changes known as 'baby blues'. Symptoms peak from three to five days after giving birth and last anything from a few hours to a couple of weeks. Mothers who experience baby blues are sometimes sad, weepy, moody, irritable, tired, or angry towards the baby, partner, or other family members.

The woman in the scene above, however, was suffering from a much more serious condition known as post-natal (or post-partum) depression. It occurs in about 10 per cent of new mothers, can strike weeks or even months after the birth, and can last for several weeks, months or even years. Women experiencing post-natal depression have much more severe and intense feelings, such as loneliness, powerlessness, guilt and acute embarrassment. They may also experience a range of negative feelings towards their newborn baby. In the past, post-natal depression often led the mother to neglect, abandon or even kill her baby. By the end of the nineteenth century in England there was near-panic over the number of dead babies found abandoned, presumably killed by their mothers. Nowadays, such an extreme finale to the illness is rare. So how does post-natal depression fit into the evolutionary biology of parenthood?

The simple answer is that it is part of female family planning, some aspects of which were discussed in the context of stress and conception (and others will be dealt with in the next chapter). Post-natal depression is one manifestation of the way natural selection has predisposed female emotions and psychology to judge how many children she should have, and when and with whom she should have them. As we noted earlier, a woman's subconscious aim is to produce precisely that size of family that takes maximum advantage of her status and circumstances, and to make her reproductive attempts coincide with the more buoyant phases of her life. To this end, she has the body chemistry to seek sex or not to seek it, to ovulate or not to ovulate, to implant the fertilised egg or not to, to miscarry or not to, as the situation merits. Finally, she has the urge to look after her newborn baby – or not to. The days and weeks after giving birth represent her last real chance to appraise whether or not to try to raise the child. Once she has begun to invest milk, time and energy into this child, it becomes increasingly disadvantageous to her long-term reproductive output to abandon the attempt and try again when circumstances improve.

Even if circumstances remain favourable in early pregnancy, they may still deteriorate before the baby is born. The last three months are often associated with marked changes in a woman's psychology. First, there are the well known spells of 'nest-building' – strong urges to prepare the environment into which the baby will be born. Also, she may go through spells of intense reappraisal of her situation, of which primary targets are her partner, home, and general environment. These phases often manifest themselves in worry, depression and irritability. In addition, she may be preoccupied with the future. The main strategic aim of these phases is to test the woman's situation, her partner and her other support systems for signs of fragility, indicating maybe that now is not a good time to reproduce. Any major deterioration in her circumstances at this time can lead to outright depression and the later neglect or even rejection of the baby. Post-natal depression appears to give the woman who is unsure a last opportunity to weigh up her situation and to change her mind before throwing herself wholeheartedly into caring for her baby. By withdrawing into herself and becoming aggressive towards her baby and partner, she tests to the maximum his willingness to help her raise the child.

The one solid research finding to emerge from the study of post-natal depression is that it is most likely to occur when the woman has poor support, from her partner, her friends or the wider society. Major environmental stress is also a factor, but it is less significant than poor social support. In pre-industrial societies, it is those cultures which traditionally give a ritualistic show of support for all new mothers that are characterised by the lowest rates of post-natal depression.

More often than not, of course, women pass through the last three months of pregnancy and the first few weeks or months of motherhood with little more than mild attacks of 'the blues'. Their bodies have had no difficulty deciding that now is a perfectly good time to raise a child, and see no need to test their support to its limit by embarking on post-natal depression. Even a woman who is sufficiently doubtful about her situation to become depressed more often than not eventually judges it to be favourable enough, and emerges from her depression as a good and attentive mother. If her situation fails the test, however, the new mother may become overwhelmed by an irresistible urge to neglect, abandon or even kill her new baby. This urge has been so widely recognised, both historically and geographically, that many legal systems around the world accept that a woman may not be responsible for her actions in the phase immediately after giving birth.

Probably nearly every case of infanticide during the first year of a baby's life is preceded by the mother's post-natal depression. Throughout human history, infanticide has been, and still is, one of the major forms of population control employed by women. In hunter-gatherers – people who live by hunting and foraging, as did all our ancestors until about fifteen thousand years ago – about 7 per cent of children were killed by their mothers. Even in Western industrialised societies, infanticide was common until relatively recently. According to the World Health Organisation, it was *the* most prevalent means of family planning in late-nineteenth-century Britain.

Such behaviour is not unique to humans. Infanticide, like all other forms of natural family planning, has been inherited from our mammalian ancestors. Anyone who has kept pets such as rabbits, gerbils, hamsters or mice will know that if the mother is at all stressed soon after giving birth, she is likely to kill, even eat, some or all of her litter. This is not a maladaptive practice. It reflects the mother's subconscious decision not to raise the litter in the current circumstances. She opts instead to delay her reproductive attempts until circumstances improve.

A woman's situation does not have to be absolutely desperate for her to suffer post-natal depression. Everything is relative. The woman in the scene above, for example, did not have a hard life. Many women struggle to raise their children in much worse conditions than this woman would ever have to. The important factor for the individual woman is not how things are in an absolute sense, but how much better they might be for *her*, if she waits a while.

In the scene, the woman's partner had just been promoted, and perhaps in a few years they would achieve the comfortable position they both looked forward to. But other scenarios are possible. Maybe the woman needed reassurance that her partner's promotion and the financial improvement it could bring were not in reality simply going to lead to her spending much more time alone, with minimal help from him with the children. She may even have needed reassurance that his new-found status and increased opportunity were not, in fact, going to lead to his being unfaithful to her, perhaps on a future business trip abroad. Maybe deep down she was afraid he would eventually desert her and her child. Her situation had changed dramatically while she was pregnant, and she had not yet had a chance to judge what her new circumstances really meant for the future. Her body, therefore, decided to rigorously test just how successful her attempt to raise this child might be. It seriously questioned whether her long-term security, health and reproductive success might be better served if she did not stretch herself now, but waited for a better, more secure moment. In the end, her situation and support systems passed the test, and she opted to raise the child – as most women do. But at one point on the way home from the greengrocer's she was just a pram push away from not doing so.

Post-natal depression, as well as clinical depression and seasonally affective disorder (SAD), have been the targets of much recent research. They emerge as prime examples of how little control our consciousness has over states triggered by the body. The currently favoured explanation for depression is that it is due to chemical changes in parts of the brain – a reduction in serotonin, for example. These changes are generated chemically by the body, either internally, as after childbirth, or in response to environmental events such as winter day-lengths or long-term stress. Whatever their origin, changes in the brain generate thought patterns and behaviour totally different from the individual's normal character. In particular, it is now accepted that there is no point urging her to 'get a grip' on herself or to 'pull herself together'. The brain chemistry of depression prevents the very thought processes that might allow her to do so.

There are only two ways of changing the thought patterns. One is to change the brain's chemistry by administering antidepressants. The other is to find the environmental trigger that will cause the body to change its chemical instructions to the brain. As far as SAD is concerned, this can often be done by exposure to bright light. As for post-natal depression, it will often respond to a strong show of support from the woman's partner, friends and, nowadays, social services. Once her body receives the evidence that she will have the support she needs to raise a baby, it changes her brain chemistry, and her mood and behaviour become appropriate for motherhood.

We do not know what happened to the woman in the scene in the years after her depression. The chances are, though, that she successfully raised her child, both of them benefiting considerably from her partner's new-found prospects. In which case, her body had made the right decision as it stood by the side of the road, hand on the pram handle. It is worth noting that the change in circumstances that took place during her pregnancy was not *inevitably* going to be to her advantage. Her partner could have reacted to his new horizons by rarely seeing her or leaving her for another woman. The woman's body probably did the right thing by withdrawing into itself, thus testing her partner and his support. Her depression was an intensely unpleasant experience for her, but that didn't prevent it from being to her long-term advantage.

CHAPTER FIVE

Families
and Dynasties

SCENE 11
All's Fair . . .

The two teenage girls sat in the corner of the field and watched the cart-horse as his penis grew larger and larger. Soon, it seemed, it would touch the ground. Momentarily silent, they continued to watch as the horse swayed, making his huge appendage swing backward and forward. The dark-haired girl, prettier than her fair-haired companion, turned and with a giggle made a wickedly perceptive comment for a girl of her age, first about the horse and then about one of her elder brother's favourite pastimes.

Their laughter, and the horse's erection, were dramatically cut short by the most frightening thing that had yet happened to them. Almost without warning, an unfamiliar sound that had begun as a barely perceptible distant drone burst deafeningly over the trees at the far edge of the field and filled the skies above them. Penis rapidly shrinking, the horse bolted across the field while the girls, holding hands so as not to stumble, fled in a panic across the rough ground towards the row of cottages where they lived. Halfway home, the skies once more silent, they paused first for breath and then to confirm to each other what they both knew had happened. They had heard about aeroplanes, but this was the first time they had seen one.

'Race you!' cried the dark-haired one as they resumed their homeward dash, each wanting to be the first to tell her mother what she had seen. For a while, they were running side by side, but twenty yards or so from home the dark-haired girl, always the faster of the two, started to forge ahead. As she did so, her friend deliberately caught the back of her heel and tripped her up.

'I win!' shouted the fair-haired one, on reaching the door of her cottage.

'Only because you cheated!' the other responded. But it was too late, her friend had gone inside.

The two girls, born within days of each other, had been inseparable companions all their lives. They were thrilled when, the summer after they had seen the plane, at just fifteen they were both taken on as live-in domestic servants at the manor house. Not that such employment had ever really been in doubt. The houses in which they lived were owned by the big estate, and their fathers, as well as most other people in the village, were employed in one way or another by the squire.

Their friendship continued as close as ever over that first winter of service. It even survived the eighteen-year-old gardener who arrived the following spring. Like most men, he was attracted first to the striking dark-haired girl. Whenever he found the pair of them together, it was her he spoke to first and her he flirted with. She enjoyed his company and once, when she knew her friend was watching from an upstairs window, she allowed him to kiss her as she leaned against the trunk of the magnificent cedar that stood in the middle of the huge lawn. But most of the time she kept him at arm's length.

From the moment of witnessing that first kiss, the fair-haired girl was determined to prove to herself, and to her companion, that she was equally if not more capable of winning the gardener's attention. Whenever they met around the house or garden she would find any excuse to touch him as they passed or talked. As summer approached and the weather warmed up, she met him daily in the garden when she went to collect the vegetables. On her way she would undo the top buttons of her blouse in the hope that he might see her breasts as she bent towards the soft earth. He was slow to notice, so intent was he on winning the attention of her prettier friend, but eventually her campaign began to work and one night in early summer she lost her virginity to him on the lawn under the stars.

Her victory, sweet as it was, was only partial. She knew her hard-won lover still lusted after her dark-haired friend. He talked about her often, even after they'd just had sex. Even more frustratingly, her friend had given no sign that she even knew she had been beaten. In an effort to force acceptance, if not acknowledgement, the fair-haired girl made a point of giving her friend explicit details about the affair, embellishing so as to make the relationship seem more exciting, and more serious, than it was in reality. Irritatingly, all her friend did was laugh, then warn her not to get pregnant and point out that, although the gardener was fun and good-looking, he could hardly support her and a baby – even if he could be trusted to stand by her. To defend herself, remembering something her mother had once told her, the fair-haired girl replied that everybody knew a girl couldn't get pregnant until she had had her first period – and she hadn't.

Nor did she have a period that summer – but she did get pregnant. And the events leading up to the conception heralded the end of the girls' friendship.

Hardly had she lost her virginity to the gardener than the squire's son arrived home from university. Once the girls had set eyes on him – twenty years old, confident, handsome and rich as he was – they could think of little else. Secretly each longed for him to take her in his arms, proclaim his undying love, then transport her into a life of luxury and leisure. He had other ideas.

The fair-haired girl had quickly begun to enjoy her physical explorations with the naïve and gentle young gardener. And although her lover was still over-attentive to her friend, she was loath to give up her only avenue to the new-found thrill of sex. But from the moment the young son of the house arrived it was him she craved, and she grew increasingly jealous when it became obvious that he too found her friend attractive, not her. Moreover, this time her friend was responding.

It was true that the dark-haired girl felt more sexual excitement in the presence of the squire's son than she had ever felt before. Three nights after their first flirtatious encounter, she had masturbated herself to sleep against a backdrop of images of herself naked beneath him. She still managed to appear cool and distant in his presence, though, and parried his flirtatiousness with conversation rather than coyness. Still a virgin, she had heard many stories from her mother about young servant girls who became pregnant and were then dismissed and left to fend for themselves. She was not going to let that happen to her.

Two weeks after the son had returned home, his parents went away for a few weeks. With the cook and butler off duty for the evening, the two girls had served him dinner on his own in the dining-room. When the meal was over, he had asked the dark-haired girl to stay a while. As the other one went back to the kitchen, frustration and anger overwhelmed her. Picking up a plate, she hurled it across the room, then sat and cried, imagining the sexual liaison that was about to take place. Her fantasy was misdirected, but the jealousy and hatred she felt for her friend at that moment were to last for the rest of her life.

There was no doubt that the son was hoping to have sex with the dark-haired girl that night. He flirted, then suggested that she should help him prepare his bedroom for the night, even mildly threatened her – but all to no avail. As a last resort, he tried the ploy that had never failed before. He told her she was the most beautiful girl he had ever seen, that he thought he was falling in love with her – and how would she like one day to be mistress of the house? The girl trod the tightrope of resistance impeccably. She did all the right things – took him seriously, laughed, and moved – at all the right moments, and parried his threats and advances with wit and insight. Not once did she make him feel embarrassed or offended, and when eventually she left the dining-room the feeling between them was one of friendship, not of thwarted lust.

For a week or so after that evening, there was a closeness between them that belied their difference in status. Occasionally, the son would misinterpret her friendliness, and would momentarily overstep their tacit understanding. But most of the time he simply enjoyed the company of this young, beautiful and interesting girl whenever her duties allowed her to spend some time with him. He still fantasised about their being naked together in his bed – as, in truth, did she. But until she felt she could really trust him not to desert her if she became pregnant, she was not prepared to risk either of their fantasies.

The fair-haired girl, however, mistook the pair's closeness as an indication not only that they had had sex, but also that he was taking his relationship with her seriously. Increasingly jealous, she grew determined to ruin whatever dreams of a life with this man her one-time friend might have: she would do the same with the son as she had with the gardener – make him notice her and, whenever possible, criticise her former friend. In the end, she would win him from her – she was quite determined. Using every excuse and every ruse that the beady eye of the butler would let her get away with, the fair-haired girl would bump into her prey as often as she could. And when in his company she employed every provocative device she knew to attract his attention.

The dark-haired girl realised what her companion was trying to do but refused to play the same game. By now happily confident in her superior looks and personality, and convinced that her friendship with the young man was genuine, she despised and yet was amused by the other girl's antics. She even allowed herself to dream that one day friendship might turn into genuine romance and that eventually she might, just might, be mistress of the house. But her dream was to be short-lived. The change began the night that her friend, the top of her dress unusually loose, bent down to pick up a glass from the floor in front of the son's chair, then apparently lost her balance and fell forward on to his lap. Her ample breasts practically falling out of her dress, with one hand on his genitals she slowly pushed herself up then apologised and ran in apparent embarrassment from the room.

The dark-haired girl's hopes were finally dashed when, one stiflingly hot and humid afternoon, the senior servants were in the village and the son was out riding. She was supposed to be cleaning an upstairs room, but the heat was slowing her down. A stifled giggle from outside took her to the wide-open window.

At the back of the house a field of corn, now tall and golden, came to within twenty feet of where she stood. She could see the young gardener chasing her friend into the field. He quickly caught her and after a mock-forced kiss, they virtually tore off their clothes with a sexual urgency that the dark-haired voyeur could not have begun to imagine. But when they were naked, instead of instantly engaging in intercourse, the girl pushed the man backwards into the thistles, then ran off deeper into the corn. He gave chase, and the pair zigzagged through the field as he tried to catch her. The dark-haired girl watched in fascination as the other girl's breasts bounced and swayed as she ran and dodged. She was curious to know if the man was erect as he ran but, frustratingly, the corn, just over waist high, always hid his groin. One brief glimpse of his buttocks was all she got.

The chase lasted for some time, but in the end the girl gave in, at first just standing there, then kneeling as he stood laughing and breathless in front of her. Then the pair sank to the ground – and disappeared from view, lost below the golden harvest. The stillness of the countryside combined with the direction of the almost imperceptible breeze caused every sound the hidden couple made to float up into the room where the dark-haired girl stood, transfixed. Torn between embarrassment, jealousy and curiosity, she stared in their direction open-mouthed, listening to every whimper, groan and cry until first her friend climaxed and then, seemingly an eternity later, the man's grunts peaked and died away.

She would have left the window then, but the snort of a horse drew her attention to the garden below. It seemed she had not been the only witness to this scene. Partly hidden by trees and shrubs, the son of the house, astride his horse, was also looking across the field. Holding her breath, she wondered how much he had seen and what he would do. She didn't have long to wait. Scarcely had the young gardener gone quiet than the son bellowed his name. When there was no response he shouted again, ordering him back to the garden.

The dark-haired girl heard panicked whispers from the couple, each asking the other where they had left their clothes. She saw the corn move as the naked gardener, stooping low, followed first one track then another, but they had chased each other for so long after removing their clothes that he might as well have been trying to find the exit to a maze. In the end, cursing and still stooping, the man made a wide detour across the field to his cottage, about two hundred yards away.

Evidently, the squire's son could also see what was happening, for he waited until the gardener had nearly disappeared from view before shouting at him to 'get a move on'. After half a minute or so he ordered the servant girl by name to come out of the field. Still hidden from sight, she didn't answer the first time, but at the second call she shouted back that she couldn't find her clothes. The squire's son dismounted, climbed over the fence, and made his way into the field along one of the tracks that the lovers had made in their scramble. When he reached the point where they had stripped, he stopped and looked nervously round. The dark-haired girl caught her breath when she realised that he, too, was undressing. Naked, he now called to the girl that he had found her clothes and that if she wanted them she had to come and get them. She rose from the sea of corn, arms crossed in front of her, hands over her breasts. After a moment's hesitation, she walked slowly towards him. With still some distance between them, she halted and asked for her clothes to be thrown to her, but he refused, saying there was a price to pay for being caught neglecting her duties.

The next few moments were to change the lives of both girls. She didn't want to have sex with him, lied the naked girl, still a few yards from the man and half hidden in the waist-high corn. 'Why not?' he asked her, pointing to the place where he had seen her and her lover sink to the ground. She could hardly object on moral grounds, he said, not after her 'performance' out there. She said that the problem wasn't morality, but disease. Everybody knew he had been having sex with her dark-haired friend, which meant that he would almost certainly be infected by now – and she wasn't going to risk infection too.

'What disease?' he asked, but when she told him he said that it didn't matter anyway because he hadn't had sex with her friend. But the other girl had been bragging to everyone that he had been chasing her, the fair-haired girl lied again – but when she had eventually given in, she had told them, he had had no idea what to do. So was he saying her friend had made it all up? Of course she'd been making it up, he blustered – he had never wanted sex with her, anyway. But if *she* thought he didn't know what to do, why didn't she come over and find out? With the smile of victory on her lips, the girl slowly dropped her hands from her breasts and moved the last few steps towards him. Putting her arms around his neck, she pressed her body to his and asked him to prove himself.

Hearing herself so maligned made the dark-haired girl feel sick in her stomach. She wanted to shout from the window that it wasn't true, but she froze, then ran from the room. In doing so, she missed her friend's second intercourse in fifteen minutes. She missed hearing the squire's son tell the girl to turn round and bend down, her saying she didn't really like it that way, and him replying that nothing would make him lie down in the thistles. For some time the dark-haired girl lay distraught on her bed, crying in anger and frustration.

After what she saw as her victory in the cornfield, the fair-haired girl had sex with the young master many more times that summer. She also continued having sex with the gardener – and it was as well she did. Her dreams of the son of the house one day proclaiming his undying love evaporated the day she told him she was pregnant. He threatened her with dismissal if she ever told anybody that the child was his and advised her to find someone to marry her as soon as possible. Fortunately for her, although he knew that the child she was carrying might not be his, the gardener agreed to marry her before her son was born. They both stayed in employment at the house, and eventually the young man became head gardener. By the time the fair-haired girl was thirty she had had five children – the son of uncertain parentage, three daughters, and then her favourite, another son who, if the truth was known, was also of uncertain parentage. This time, however, her husband did not know.

Even though they were both earning, their early days together were a struggle. Their combined income was only just adequate, and the family always seemed to be plagued by illness. Their youngest daughter died of measles as a baby, and their eldest daughter was not only partially crippled by polio when she was three, but for years afterwards also endured one urinary infection after another. Their other three, however, emerged from the ravages of childhood relatively unscathed. Later, as adults, they also survived the Second World War.

In the years following the war the eldest son and his 'father' got involved in the business of supplying produce to local grocers. Unknown to them they had been aided by some behind-the-scenes string-pulling by the new squire, he of the escapade in the cornfield. Despite the childhood diseases that had left her unable to have children, the eldest daughter married into a long and loving relationship with a young man who, after gaining and losing a succession of jobs, became the village postman. The other surviving daughter married a policeman and the youngest son, always the most able of the fair-haired woman's children, qualified as a schoolteacher and landed a good job at a school in a nearby town.

The dark-haired girl was dismissed from service, without explanation. But she had no difficulty finding re-employment – or a husband. Just by going and asking she got a job in a local shoe-shop and, within a year, had settled down and started a family with the go-ahead son of the shop's owner. Their eldest child, a girl, was nearly ten years old before they had their second, a son. In the interim, her husband became increasingly successful and by the time their son was born they owned a chain of shops and were reasonably wealthy. They had lived in a number of different towns as the chain had grown and spread, but now they had moved back to their home town to a splendid, spacious house that they had had built to their own specifications.

So far in this book we have illustrated a number of aspects of parenthood, each scene being followed by a discussion of the way the characters' behaviour has been determined by natural selection. We have talked generally about reproductive success and output, but have not really considered how such success is measured. In the next few chapters, the phenomena to be discussed will call for a clearer picture of reproductive success than we have needed up to now. While elaborating the concept in this chapter, we shall take the opportunity to discuss mate choice.

The first and second of the three scenes in this chapter follow two women from childhood to death as we try to decide which of the two will be the more favoured by natural selection. One of the most important elements in this discussion will be the apparent paradox that people may sometimes increase their reproductive success by having *fewer* children. The third, Scene

13, illustrates the dangers of taking this paradox to its logical extreme.

Parenthood is a contest between people and between the genes for which they are the champions. Natural selection awards prizes, and the rules are inflexible. Bouquets go to those with high reproductive success, brickbats to those with low. Most people are more or less unaware that they and their genes are competing with their contemporaries for parental prowess. Maybe a surge of pride when a child does something exceptional or a rush of embarrassment when he proves totally inept occasionally brings home the competitive nature of parenthood, as may the pride shown by grandparents in the number of grandchildren they have managed to produce. Most of the time, though, people pursue parenthood simply because their genes drive them to do so, with little conscious thought for the way their behaviour is going to be judged by natural selection. But judged it will be.

Reproduction *is* a contest between people, and parenthood is an important stage in that contest. Often, however, the success or failure of parenthood is determined long before people actually start to reproduce. It is influenced first by what happens to them during their own childhood, and second – and arguably more strongly – by their choice of a reproductive partner. Indeed almost all of a person's success as a parent very often depends on who they choose as their mate. And, as illustrated in the scene above, very often in *this* phase of the contest the competitive element is clear to all concerned. Not only do people have to choose a mate, they then have to win them from other rivals. And it would seem from our scene that all *is* fair in love, if not in war. Which of us have never suffered the agony of longing to be a particular person's partner, only to be thwarted by a rival? And which of us have never experienced the joy of being preferred over a rival by the object of our fantasies?

So how does mate choice influence our reproductive success? How do we choose a mate who will give our future parenthood the boost it needs? Why do we find some people more attractive than others? Why do people differ in who they find attractive? And why are some people considered to be attractive by nearly everybody, while others are fancied by hardly anyone?

In the scene, the fair-haired girl considered the gardener as a potential partner from the very beginning, and was jealous that he seemed to prefer her friend. The dark-haired girl, on the other hand, had no interest in him. There are two possible explanations for this difference between the two girls as regards who they did and who they did not find attractive. The first is that the girls differed in confidence and ambition; the second is that they really were looking for different qualities in a man. The main reason people differ over who they find attractive is to do with compatibility.

Compatibility figures at many different levels. A couple have to be compatible behaviourally, emotionally and physically, each one's weaknesses being compensated by the other's strengths. It also figures at the genetic level. As we shall explore in detail when we consider incest, nearly everybody carries dangerous genes. However, these cause neither them nor their children any problem – as long as they are not matched with a similar gene. Avoiding reproduction with someone who might carry the same dangerous gene as oneself is therefore an important element in mate choice; and people do often seem to be less attracted to mates who share their problematical genes. Natural selection seems to have developed genetic complexes which are able to recognise and avoid dangerous liaisons. The system isn't foolproof, of course, but it is better than pure chance.

So maybe the two women differed in their feelings towards the gardener because the fair-haired woman saw him as compatible whereas the dark-haired woman didn't. But the alternative explanation is also a possibility: that the dark-haired woman was so confident in her own greater attractiveness that she *knew* she could do better than settle for the gardener. But the fair-haired woman, too, *hoped* she could do better, and when the squire's son arrived on the scene, both girls found him attractive and both wanted him. Why?

In choosing a man with whom to share her life, a woman has two major criteria to satisfy. On the one hand, she needs a man who can help her to raise her children. On the other, she needs genes that in combination with her own will produce attractive, fertile and successful children. The better the environment and the better the help she gets, the more fully each child will achieve its genetic potential.

A woman's difficulty is that she has a much wider choice of men to provide her with genes than she has of long-term partners. She could probably persuade many men of her choice to give her their genes – it takes only a few minutes. The fair-haired girl, for instance, had little difficulty collecting sperm from the gardener and only a little more difficulty in collecting the squire's son's. A woman's choice of long-term partner, however, is restricted to those men who are unattached, or ready to desert their current partner, or who have so much time, energy or wealth that they can support more than one family – and most men in most societies are not in such a position. The gardener, for example, scarcely had enough to support even one woman and her family.

Surveys consistently show that in looking for a long-term partner women prefer men who have, or have the potential for, wealth, status, stability and durability. In the past, in all cultures, the children of women paired with men at the top of the scale had a far greater chance of survival, health and subsequent fecundity. The same holds true in today's modern industrialised societies.

As we have already mentioned, children are most likely to grow into healthy, fertile adults if they are born into a favourable environment, which means in particular plenty of space and an adequate supply of nutritious food. They then run the lowest risk of contracting diseases, and have the greatest resistance to those they do contract. In modern societies, space and good nutrition depend on wealth. Even now, the chances of a child from a poor family dying before reproducing are double those of a child from a rich family. In the historical and evolutionary past, these differences will have been even greater, though wealth will have been measured in terms not of money but of crops and livestock – or simply in terms of access to the best areas for food, water and shelter. In the scene above, the gardener and his wife struggled to keep their family fed and healthy in their early years, whereas the dark-haired woman, with her wealthy shop-owner partner, had no such problem.

Women's preferences are clear, but few will find in the same man all the characteristics they favour. One may be wealthy but uncaring. Another may be of high status but unstable. Yet another may be poor, but stable and caring. Inevitably, therefore, a woman has to opt for the best compromise. Of course, she does not have to stay with her first partner. Again, studies show that when a woman leaves one partner for another, she invariably moves up the scale to a better compromise. And all the time she is also searching for a partner within the limitations set by who she herself can attract.

The dark-haired girl did not find the gardener a suitable compromise – she could do better. The fair-haired one, perhaps recognising her more limited potential in attracting men, did consider him acceptable, both for sex and as a long-term mate, even though she still hoped to do better. When the wealthy son turned up the dark-haired girl wanted him only as a *long-term* partner, someone whose wealth and status would give her future children and later descendants every advantage. When she didn't get clear signals that he wouldn't abandon her, she would not risk conception. The fair-haired girl knew, consciously or subconsciously, that the only way she could land such a high-status partner would be to conceive to him. At the same time, she could not risk losing the gardener, and so gave them both a chance of paternity. As it turned out, it was just as well she took out such insurance. When she failed to win the squire's son, she accepted the gardener's offer to support her. Presumably the gardener made her his offer, even though the child might not be his, knowing that if he didn't it could be years before he found another acceptable mate.

In contrast, and even though she too failed to win the major prize, the squire's son, the dark-haired girl did eventually obtain a good alternative partner. And at least he was likely to be more faithful than one as sought-after as the rich son. Just what other benefits she gained from her eventual choice we shall discover in a moment.

First, we should consider one of the most important factors determining what happened in the scene – the difference in attractiveness between the two women. What was it about the dark-haired one that men found so attractive? What criteria do men use in choosing partners and lovers, and how do these criteria differ from those used by women?

Basically, men select women for their health, fertility and fidelity – though not consciously, of course. And although when they see a woman for the first time they don't immediately remark on her potential for bearing and raising children, the features that their bodies are programmed to find attractive are precisely those that *reflect* this potential. Unlike a woman, a man uses similar criteria whether he is selecting a partner or a lover: with both, his primary concern is with looks and behaviour. An important feature is body shape, particularly the ratio of waist to hip, as already mentioned. Irrespective of a woman's size – and in some cultures they prefer thin women, in others fat – men prefer someone whose waist measurement is about 70 per cent of her hip measurement; or, to put it another way, whose waist is significantly narrower than her buttocks. This preference is remarkably constant both throughout history (to judge from statues, paintings and 'girlie magazines') and from culture to culture (to judge from rock-paintings and figurines). The explanation is that this preferred shape reflects a good hormone balance, good resistance to disease, and high fertility.

In addition to shape, men all over the world also respond strongly to clear eyes, healthy hair and skin, and the symmetry of the face and body – again, features that are strong indicators of health and hence fertility. Men of most cultures also respond to breast size and shape, though preferences vary and, as we have already noted, there is no simple link between the appearance of a woman's breasts and her ability to lactate and sustain a child. Finally, men respond strongly to character traits that might indicate potential fidelity – these, however, are relatively easy to fake, at least for short periods.

In choosing a man to help raise her children, a woman is primarily concerned with the security he can offer and is only secondarily impressed by looks. In choosing a short-term partner for sex, however, looks are much more important. The features she finds most attractive are clear eyes, healthy skin and hair, firm buttocks, a waist that is only a little smaller than his hips, shapely legs, broad shoulders, quick wit and intelligence. She is also attracted by symmetry in his physical features. These various qualities are all reasonably reliable indicators of genetic health, fertility and competitiveness, and hence they imply a genetic constitution that would also be desirable in her children.

One of the most interesting features of the new research on mate choice and attractiveness in humans and other animals is the importance of disease, and resistance to it, during early life. Not only do diseases influence the 'glow' of people's eyes, hair and skin, they also influence their symmetry, and symmetry is now emerging from studies around the world as one of the most important elements in a person's attractiveness.

Of course, some parts of the body are genetically programmed to be bilaterally asymmetric – that is, the right side is different from the left. Only the left side of the chest cavity, for example, contains a heart. Parts of the left and right sides of the brain interact with different parts of the body and, in men, the two testes are of different sizes and hang at different heights. And, of course, the nerve-wiring networks of the left and right sides of the body and brain are different enough to make some people right-handed, others left-handed. All of these asymmetries are genetic and passed on from parents to offspring in accordance with rules of genetic inheritance that may be simple or complex. Other parts of the body are programmed to be symmetrical but become asymmetrical through differential usage, which is itself programmed. Right-handed people, for example, tend to have larger biceps on their right arm than their left and, depending on their pursuits, often larger right thighs than left.

Many other parts of the body are programmed to be symmetrical, and are uninfluenced by most environmental factors. The lengths of right and left index fingers, for instance, are under the control of the same gene and hence should be identical, so that the only reason for their being of different lengths must be that their development has been disturbed in some way. The same applies to the remaining fingers and toes, the length and width of the ears, the widths of the wrists and ankles, the lengths of the bones in the arms and legs, the sizes of the breasts, and the various features on left and right sides of the face. So what can disrupt the grand design of the genes to produce a perfectly symmetrical body in these particular respects? Two things – accident and disease.

As far as accidents are concerned, the process of repair is likely to create asymmetry. For example, if bones are broken during early life, the process of healing and regeneration often makes for greater size. In fact, often this is necessary to make a bone as strong as it would be had it never been broken. The result is usually asymmetry between the broken bone and its intact 'alter ego' on the other side of the body. Torn muscles and ligaments can also heal to a larger size; and a damaged back, by making spinal discs press on nerves, can cause leg and other muscles to be less well developed or even to shrink in size on one side of the body only.

Throughout life, the body is exposed to attack by a myriad of micro-organisms, and because these rarely attack both sides of the body equally, their presence tends to promote asymmetry. The fewer diseases people encounter and the more genetic resistance they have to the diseases they do encounter, the more symmetrical they remain. The more successful they have been in avoiding and resisting accidents and diseases, the greater will be their genetic 'fitness', compared with their less symmetrical contemporaries.

The underlying principle of attractiveness is therefore quite straightforward. People are genetically programmed to find attractive those features that indicate that the target of their attention is healthy and fertile and possesses 'good genes'. These 'good genes' will be passed on to any children the two parties may have together. Studies of other animals, ranging from birds to insects, show that they too are responding to similarly informative features, and that symmetry is one of the most potent for all.

The dark-haired girl in the scene was physically and generally more attractive to men than her friend was. She had all those qualities of looks, physique and character – a good waist–hip ratio, clear eyes, healthy hair and skin, symmetrical face and body, quick wit and honesty – that signalled to men that she was likely to be healthy, fertile and faithful. Undoubtedly, there would have been some men who, for reasons of compatibility, would have preferred her friend, but the majority did not. This meant that she usually had the first pick of any men who knew them both, and needed to take fewer risks to attract their attention as a prospective partner. Although the fair-haired girl was not unattractive to men, she had to run the risks of rape, disease and desertion in order to gain the same attention. In the event, she escaped the worst of these dangers but had to settle for the gardener as a lifetime partner. In contrast, and with relatively little effort, the other girl managed to attract a competent and eventually successful and wealthy man to help her rear her children.

Thus far, everything in the scene appears to make sense, yet the way the characters' lives unfolded seems to reveal a paradox. If the dark-haired girl not only signalled greater health and fertility via her greater attractiveness, but also, as a consequence, managed to obtain a 'better' partner, why did she seem to have lost the contest for reproductive success? After all, by the time she was thirty she had had two children, while the fair-haired woman had had five (even if a bout of measles had robbed her of a daughter). It would seem, therefore, that the latter had won the contest hands down – or at least the one being played out under the rules of natural selection. Surely the events depicted in the scene contradict every comment made in our evolutionary analysis? Or is there a subtlety to natural selection that we haven't yet considered?

Life would be so much easier for the evolutionary biologist if the reproductive success on which natural selection acts could be measured simply in terms of the *number of children* had by different individuals. But the reality is far more subtle, as the next scene will illustrate. We are about to see what happens to our two women and their dynasties.

SCENE 12
Quality or Quantity?

Rather than have more children, the dark-haired woman and her husband chose to invest heavily in their son's education and officer training. The Second World War came and went, and he emerged from the army unscathed as a distinguished and handsome twenty-five-year-old, ready to take a major role in the running and development of his father's growing shoe empire.

By this time, their daughter, who lived nearby, had already given them their first two grandchildren. The son, however, was in no hurry to settle down. He lived on the move, staying in expensive hotels, as he travelled from town to town keeping a close eye on the finances of his father's shops. He enjoyed the freedom – and he enjoyed meeting the numerous pretty girls around the country who vied for his favours.

One of his favourites was a young girl, just twenty, who worked in the shop in his home town. Each time he dropped in he got to know her better and they would talk more and more, and it was soon a regular part of his visit that he would drive her somewhere and buy her lunch. This very much displeased the shop's manager, who himself secretly lusted after her – but the usurper *was* the owner's son. The girl had a boyfriend, a local schoolteacher, but was resisting his pleas to settle down, saying she wasn't yet ready for commitment. With typical arrogance, the son half-suspected that he might be the reason for her reticence, that she was harbouring some slim hope that one day their friendship might escalate.

It was mid-winter and dawn had broken on a blizzard. By midday, when the skies cleared, a pale sun shone down on a town completely shrouded in snow. Undaunted, the son drove his shop assistant off for lunch as usual, twice skidding on the deserted roads. Afterwards, he drove past his parents' house in order to pick up some papers. On being assured his parents were out, the girl needed no second invitation to get out of the car and look inside the house that in her dreams she fantasised about inheriting. Neither of them was properly dressed for such weather, so they stepped carefully as they went up the garden path, treading in old footprints.

As they stood outside the front door while the son struggled to find his keys, a mass of snow, warmed by the sun, slid serenely off the roof, on top of them. They were shocked and uncomfortably wet but unhurt. Once inside, the young man added some wood to the dying fire in the morning room, and soon they were kneeling in front of it, trying to dry out.

Partly through discomfort and partly through a growing sexual excitement, the girl needed little encouragement to accept his suggestion that their clothes would dry more quickly if they took them off. He would go and find something for them to wear, he said. She had been expecting him to return with at least a couple of dressing-gowns, and laughed when he came back with two large towels, then poked fun at his coyness when he slipped behind the sofa to undress. His fingers still numb with cold, he struggled to undo his belt and trouser buttons. The girl stayed in front of the fire, and deftly undressed under her carefully wrapped towel without revealing more than her legs and shoulders. Even before he had removed his trousers, she was naked under her towel.

Watching his fumbling, she derived amusement from his obvious nervousness. She offered to help, and made towards the sofa. Embarrassed, he wrapped the towel around himself and told her to stay where she was. Misunderstanding his coyness, she ignored his warning and within seconds the pair were engaged in a good-humoured chase around the room. Her towel fell off seconds before she caught him. Then, laughing and breathless and offering only token resistance, he let her unbutton and remove his last garment. Minutes later, now breathless from passion, they were on the floor behind the sofa, having sex.

He had just ejaculated but was still inside her when the door opened. The dark-haired woman had seen her son's car outside the house, and had made straight for the morning room. Seeing a woman's clothes in front of the fire and the towels in disarray, she instantly recognised their significance. But instead of leaving, she allowed the voyeur in her to scan the room. Familiar with, and somewhat proud of, her son's philandering, when she spotted them still naked and coupled behind the sofa she gave an embarrassed laugh, made her excuses, and left the room.

A month later, the next time the son saw his shop assistant, she told him she thought she might be pregnant. Although she hadn't mentioned her fears to her schoolteacher-boyfriend, she confided, she had already told him that she would marry him – if he still wanted her. It wasn't too late for her to change her mind, though, she said meaningfully, staring into the son's eyes, desperately searching for signs that he might yet want to marry her himself. He paused, then looked away, asking how certain she could be that he was the father, if she really was pregnant. It had to be him, she replied. It was months since she had allowed her boyfriend to be intimate with her. They should wait and see whether she was really pregnant, the son said cagily. The girl was disappointed and angry. She couldn't wait that long, she told him. She knew that if she wasn't careful, she could find herself pregnant and alone.

Surprising himself, the young man asked his mother for her advice. Much as he liked this girl, he said, he wasn't ready to be tied down. He was having too good a time to give it all up for family life. His mother agreed with him – so adamantly, in fact, that he was quite shocked. He couldn't be certain the child was his, she told him. He was a good catch and he wouldn't be the first man in his position to be tricked into marriage by a scheming woman. Even if he did like the girl, he could do a lot better. So he took his mother's advice, even though secretly he believed that the child, if the girl *was* pregnant, was his. On his next visit to the shop a month later, the girl told him what he least wanted to hear, insisting again that he was the father. As gently as he could, he told her that he couldn't marry her and that she should go ahead with her plans to marry the schoolteacher.

The girl was upset by his decision, but not surprised. She had known that if he had wanted her he wouldn't have stayed away for a whole month. As the days had passed and her pregnancy became certain, she had increasingly resigned herself to life as a schoolteacher's wife. Then, fearing she might lose even that option, she had had sex with her fiancé, in the hope that he would think the baby was his. Her son was born two weeks late, but her husband believed the child was three weeks or so early and never once questioned his paternity. Nor did it ever strike him as strange that his wife's boss – she worked part-time in the shoe-shop on and off for years – took such a close interest in his son's schooling and, when he was old enough, gave him an apprenticeship.

From a discreet distance, the dark-haired woman took as much pride in the boy's progress as she did in her legitimate grandchildren. Her son, who had managed to convince her as thoroughly as he had convinced himself that he really was the boy's father, eventually married into a well connected and wealthy family. He and his beautiful young wife had two children, both girls, but the woman could tell from her son's attitude that his illegitimate son was his pride and joy – especially when he followed in his footsteps as a womaniser. By his mid-thirties the young man had had six children with three different women.

Now in her late eighties, and thirty-five years after the day she had walked in on her son and the girl in the morning room, the woman sat at breakfast reading the local paper. An obituary caught her eye. Despite herself, it triggered a wave of nostalgia: the childhood friend with whom she had once watched a horse's erection and seen her first aeroplane was now dead. Hate her as much as she had throughout her long life, she could not help but feel sad at reading that she had died. The obituary listed the fairhaired woman's family: two sons and two daughters, five granddaughters and one grandson, and twelve great-grandchildren – six of them belonging to the grandson – and said how proud she had been of them all.

The woman smiled. She had never forgiven her former friend for the lies she had told the squire's son that sultry afternoon so long ago, and enough comments had reached her over the years to leave her in no doubt that the hatred was mutual. The other woman had always been jealous of her, first on account of her looks, then later her wealth. One remark in particular had annoyed the dark-haired woman: despite her wealth, the other had said, she hadn't managed to produce the dynasty of grandchildren and great-grandchildren that the fair-haired woman claimed was *her* real achievement in life.

The woman smiled again. It was true that she had had only two children. It was also true that as far as the world was concerned she had only four grandchildren and eight great-grandchildren. But she knew better. The grandson who the fair-haired woman proudly thought had given her six great-grandchildren wasn't hers at all. He had been conceived behind a sofa on a snowy winter's day, and his real father was the dark-haired woman's son. The poor cuckolded schoolteacher was the fair-haired woman's. In fact, *she* had only six great-grandchildren, the dark-haired woman fourteen.

She chuckled, and laid the paper on the table as emphatically as her frail old hand would allow. 'I think *I* win,' she muttered to herself.

Natural selection does not rush to award its prizes. Reproductive contests are neither won nor lost when a person has finished having children. As this scene illustrates, reproductive outcomes may not unravel themselves until children have produced children, or even until those children have produced children.

The two women whose fortunes we have just followed were born within days of each other, in the same village, to parents of similar (modest) means and status. They even began their adult lives doing the same job, in the same house. The only major difference between them was their genetic makeup and thus the attributes with which they were each endowed. And it was those attributes that led them to perform differently in the eyes of natural selection. The dark-haired woman eventually won their contest 14–6 in terms of great-grandchildren, even though she had been losing 5–2 in terms of children, and drawing 5–5 in terms of grandchildren. Even without the fecund illegitimate grandson, she would still have won 8–6, despite her apparently weak start. With him, she won hands down. So why did it turn out like this? Was this reversal in the two women's reproductive fortunes in just three generations simply luck, or was there some important principle at work?

First, the scene above is not intended to be a moral tale. Conceiving before having a long-term partner, having sex with two different men in fifteen minutes, and having a large family can all, with the right protagonists and in the right circumstances, be perfectly good and successful reproductive strategies. The fair-haired woman did not lose simply because of her early rush of sexual activity, nor because of the underhand methods she employed to lure men from her more attractive rival. Natural selection makes no moral judgements, and in different circumstances with different people such an underhand strategy could well have given the fair-haired woman victory. But in this case, it didn't. So what were the factors that led to evolution eventually favouring the dark-haired woman?

There were, in fact, several, the first two of which we have already discussed. First, the majority of men found her more attractive than her friend. Second, she managed to recruit a successful man to help her rear children. Third, she produced the size of family – two children – that allowed her to invest a great deal in their upbringing and education, and particularly in her son's. Fourth, her children were healthy, fertile and attractive. All these factors are linked, as we shall now discover.

Given the first two factors, the dark-haired woman was able to rear her children in a spacious and healthy environment. And given that this meant that they were less likely to contract diseases or to suffer so badly from any they did get, they were more likely not only to survive but also, on account of their greater symmetry, to be fertile and attractive. Of the fair-haired woman's five children, one died in childhood and another was rendered infertile by the succession of urinogenital diseases she suffered during childhood. In part, these misfortunes will have been due to their standard of living. As we noted earlier, even in this final decade of the twentieth century children in the lowest socio-economic groups have twice the chances of dying before they are adult than those in the highest. In the years leading up to the Second World War when the two women in the scene were having and raising their children, the difference was even greater.

The third factor, having only two children, allowed the dark-haired woman to invest so much time, effort and money into each of them that they had every chance of realising their full potential. She achieved this by delaying the conception of her second child until the family fortunes were on the increase, and then having no more.

The dark-haired woman's behaviour illustrates the strategy that is the main point of this chapter: having *fewer* children can actually be a positive step towards more successful reproduction, as long as there is a consequent increase in their quality as potential reproducers. In other words, a woman does not necessarily achieve greatest reproductive success simply by having as many children as possible as quickly as possible. Avoiding conception can also, therefore, be an essential element in successful reproduction, especially for a woman.

Most people think of family planning and contraception as modern inventions. In fact, families were being planned long before the existence of contraception technology. The female body was avoiding conception for tens of millions of years before humans had even evolved, and women inherited these natural traits from their mammalian ancestors. Sexual abstinence, not ovulating, not implanting the fertilised egg into the womb, spontaneously losing the foetus during the first three months of pregnancy, miscarrying later, or even abandoning or killing the child after birth, have always been, and still are, powerful aids to family planning. All of these responses, some of which are considered in more detail in other chapters, are 'natural' means by which a female can avoid having or raising a child when to do so would be inopportune.

There is a general principle which all women's bodies strive to follow, one that we have mentioned before and will now explore more fully. The challenge that faces every woman is first to identify the optimal family size for her circumstances, then to ensure that she actually *has* that number of children. If she has fewer, she will naturally have fewer descendants. Equally, if she tries to have a larger family, she may create an overcrowded household and risks spreading herself and her resources too thinly. The resulting disease and infertility again mean that she ends up with fewer descendants.

For most of human history, from about one million years ago until as recently as fifteen thousand years ago, all people lived as hunter-gatherers. Societies were made up of small, scattered bands of people. They had a good protein-rich diet, and most deaths were due to accident, predation and inter-group warfare rather than disease. The children of hunter-gatherers had an excellent chance of survival. Using nothing but the natural methods just listed, women gave birth to only three or four children in their lifetime. Of these, two or three survived. So small families are not a new invention.

Large families did not appear until about fifteen thousand years ago, when agriculture brought a change of lifestyle. In the most fertile agricultural areas, large and concentrated communities developed which lived on a carbohydrate-rich diet. Disease and infant mortality were rife. The average family size was about seven or eight children, but double figures were commonplace. One advantage of large families to agriculturists was that, when the children were grown, there were many hands to do the manual work that is a feature of such a way of life. Whole families might be wiped out in days by virulent disease, but on average two or three survived.

With the advent of 'modernisation', the infant mortality rate began to fall and so too, a few decades later, did the birth rate. In Western Europe the decline in the birth rate was again the product of *natural* family planning, for it preceded by up to a century the availability and use of modern contraception. All the stresses discussed earlier will have come into play to help the woman achieve her optimal family size. For example, the average working-class woman in Britain who married during the 1890s in her teens or early twenties will have had about ten pregnancies. On average, three of these will have ended in miscarriage and two of the seven babies born will have died during birth or infancy. Even of those who survived past infancy, only about three-quarters will have survived to adulthood. The reduction in family size to the levels found in modern industrial societies was not due, therefore, to improved contraceptive technology, but to women subconsciously planning smaller and smaller families in response to the improved survival prospects of their children.

In 1995, an international conference on world population growth in Cairo acknowledged that the best way of reducing family size in Third World countries would be to improve living standards and life expectancy. Women would then subconsciously respond to their greater expectations by producing smaller families. To achieve this, they would use all of the natural methods of family planning listed above, plus any modern methods available. However, it is possible that modern contraceptives make little real difference to the *total* number of children women elect to have in their lifetime. Some of the lowest conception rates – those of Spain, Italy and Japan, for instance – occur in countries with very limited use of modern contraception. In Japan, oral contraceptives are not yet available for contraceptive purposes – only for treating menstrual irregularities. In Africa, also, the conception rate owes more to the different standards of living in the different countries than it does to the availability of modern contraceptives.

This is not to say, of course, that contraceptives, particularly the oral kind, are not an invaluable weapon to the modern woman in the conscious organisation of her life. They give her more control over when and with whom she conceives than she could possibly achieve using only her natural methods. But for most women, the number of children they have is determined much more by their

environment and by the chances that the children they *do* have have
to survive to adulthood with their fertility intact.

The fourth factor that led to the dark-haired girl being reproductively more successful than her friend – that her children were
healthier, more fertile and more attractive – is the real key to her
success, and it is the combined result of all the factors we have
just discussed. Her daughter, born early in her relationship with
the shop-owner, probably did *not* reap the full benefits of her
mother's success. Nevertheless, she inherited many of her good
genes, attracted a successful partner, and had two children. In
contrast, having delayed until wealth was assured before having
her second child, the dark-haired woman was able to give him
many advantages. Being raised in an affluent, spacious home, he
will never have been short of good food. He will have reaped the
benefits of their wealth and status by being less exposed and more
resistant to accident and disease. His resistance derived also from
the good genes he inherited from his mother. With this background,
he should have been physically more attractive and, because of his
family's wealth and status, more attractive as a long-term partner.
Whether they were shopping around for genes or for resources,
therefore, women should have been irresistibly drawn to him –
and they were. He eventually had two children in a long-term
relationship and one in a short-term liaison in which he managed
to cuckold another man, the son of the fair-haired woman. In his
early life, with 'a girl in every town', he may have had even more
children without his mother – or even himself – being aware of their
existence. In which case, the dark-haired woman's victory over her
rival will have been even greater than she knew.

Since the child that we know he produced during his early
philandering, a boy, was raised by the fair-haired woman's schoolteacher son, he was free to concentrate on his legitimate children.
But when the boy was older and his real father could help him
without arousing suspicion, he received support from both men,
became successful and attractive in his own right, and ended up
producing six children from three different relationships. It was
these six which gave the dark-haired woman such an emphatic
victory over her lifelong rival.

We can now appreciate the dilemma that faced the fair-haired
woman over her family planning. Her standard of living was

sufficiently low that if she had had only one or two children, even if she had invested as much time, effort and money as she had available into raising them, she could still not have guaranteed that they would escape the ravages of accident and disease. She might have ended up without any offspring at all. She needed to have five in order to be reasonably certain that two or three would survive to adulthood with their fertility intact. If she had been lucky, all five might have done so, in which case she would have reaped greater reproductive rewards. As it was, three survived, with their fertility intact. Reproductively she was by no means a failure, but she didn't match up to her rival. The dark-haired woman could afford to have only two children. Her standard of living dictated that any child of hers was very likely to survive. Heavy investment in two children was therefore a good move, and the boost such help would give, particularly to the son's status and attractiveness, was always likely to bring great reproductive rewards – as indeed it did.

Thus, the dark-haired woman reaped the benefits of her good genes, good courtship strategy and good family planning, as well as profiting from the production of fewer, but healthier, wealthier, more fertile and more attractive children.

SCENE 13
A Single Mistake

The old man reached for his stick and slowly pulled his failing body upright. Swaying slightly, he reached out for his second stick, then began to shuffle across the room, his shoes making a scuffling sound on the old brown linoleum. It was a late summer's afternoon. The smell of freshly mown grass was drifting in through the open window. In between each mechanical pulse of the mower a radio could be heard babbling unintelligibly in the distance.

He was tired. He had been dozing fitfully in his chair, dreaming of his childhood days, when a shaft of brilliant sunlight had fallen across his eyes and roused him. The same beam was now picking out a collection of brownish photographs arrayed on an old dresser in the darkest corner of the room. Three of the photographs were larger than the rest. Their ornate frames were thick with the accumulated dust of years. After his wife had died he had continued for a while her weekly practice of dusting them, until it had begun to seem pointless.

The largest photograph was of an adolescent boy leaning against an old wooden gate, obviously posing. Tall grass grew at his feet, and the wind had tousled his thick hair into a mass and given him a fresh, rosy-cheeked complexion that made him look younger than his seventeen years. As he gazed at it, the old man could recall in the minutest detail the events surrounding the photo. A keen amateur photographer, his son had persuaded him to take this picture of him one day while they were out walking in the hills. It remained the old man's favourite reminder of his son's childhood, and because today was the day it was, he had been drawn to it often.

The middle photograph of the three was of a sheep dog that the man had once owned. He loved dogs and wished he was fit enough to have one now. The other showed two small boys side by side – the man and a friend as ten-year-olds. In their younger days the two had been inseparable. Their friendship had lasted well into their teenage years and hadn't really started to fade until they met their wives. Unfortunately, the women didn't get on at all. So the two young men had met less and less often, until gradually their contact was reduced to little more than a polite nod to each other across the street. Each got on with their separate lives, earning a living and raising their families. The old man had had only the one son, born when he and his wife were in their early thirties. His friend, always the devoted parent, had had two sons and three daughters.

Then, about two years ago the old man's wife had died quite suddenly. Among the mourners at the funeral was his old friend. They spoke only briefly that day, but before long they began to spend time with each other again. The other man, concerned for his old friend, invited him to visit him at his home during this lonely period. The old man knew his friend was trying to be helpful, but in truth he found the visits a strain. The other man had such a large family that he and his wife were rarely on their own in their house. With their five children all living locally and each having at least one child, the house was often full of noise. The contrast with his own situation was so striking that he began to make excuses and turn down invitations. He actually found it quite irritating that he was expected to listen for hours on end to detailed descriptions of the latest antics and achievements of this or that grandchild. Eventually, he made a point of avoiding his old friend altogether. Indeed, nowadays he led a very lonely life. Today, however, was Wednesday, and on Wednesdays he had *his* visitor.

In the kitchen, the old man made himself a cup of tea, then sat down heavily in the old leather chair next to the hearth. As he drank he closed his eyes, and would have nodded off had not his reverie been interrupted by two sharp taps on the window. His eyes flicked open as he instantly recognised the sound. He stood up to greet his visitor as he came through the door, then the boy set about making himself a cup of coffee. No stranger in the old man's kitchen, he knew exactly where everything was kept. Before sitting himself down in the only other chair in the room, he shifted a pile of old newspapers from the seat. The man enjoyed the boy's company because he reminded him of his own son at a similar age. Their talk was more like that between old friends than between two people separated by sixty years. After a few moments' chat, the boy produced a pack of cards, and they began to play.

After a while the boy noticed that the old man seemed unusually distracted. Was anything wrong? he asked. The old man, apparently surprised at his question, merely continued with the game. The boy refused to be put off, however, and pressed him to tell him what the matter was. Eventually the old man got to his feet and shuffled back into the living-room, then returned a moment later with the photograph of his son. Today was his son's birthday – or would have been, he said simply.

Unsure how to respond, the boy asked what had happened to him. The old man sighed, then told his story. He had so often relived the details given to him by one of his son's friends that it was almost as if he had been there himself.

It had been New Year's Eve, and his son had gone out celebrating with some friends. One of them had managed to borrow his father's car for the evening. The young men were in high spirits, as the car had snaked its way along the high-sided country lanes towards the nearby town. The evening had fulfilled its early promise. They had spent it dancing, singing and weighing up their chances with the local girls. The New Year had been almost three hours old when they had left for home.

The air had seemed strangely thick and damp and the atmosphere menacingly still. Before long they had found themselves in a fog so dense that the driver, no longer able to see where he was going, had to stop the car. A thick white blanket enveloped the vehicle and in the silence the men began to feel uneasy. After a few moments' deliberation, the man's son had insisted on taking the wheel. Craning as far out of the window as possible, he could see just enough to drive slowly along. This had worked for a mile or so but, unknown to any of them, the car had gradually drifted over to the wrong side of the road. Then it happened. Concentrating hard on the short stretch of visible road, the driver had failed to notice a large overhanging branch directly ahead. In an instant it had jerked the young man's head back, breaking his neck. His son's life was over in a flash.

After unburdening himself of his story, the old man fumbled silently for his handkerchief. He and his wife had never really reconciled themselves to the death of their only son. The young man suddenly felt at a loss for words, as though he was intruding. It was all a long time ago now, the old man muttered, sensing his unease. He began to deal the cards again.

For whatever reason, the sad, lonely man in this scene was a reproductive failure, whereas his boyhood friend was a success. The latter produced five children and many grandchildren, while he produced one child, but no grandchildren. The genes that orchestrated this man's looks, his chemistry and his behaviour were not destined to be passed on by him to subsequent generations. In contrast, his friend's genes for looks, chemistry and behaviour would grace many a descendant. Yet, on the face of it, our main character and his wife had pursued the policy that had proved so successful for the dark-haired woman in the previous two scenes. The difference is that this couple had taken the strategy of producing fewer children to its extreme: they had produced only one.

It could, of course, have been successful. The one child obviously has many material advantages. He or she gets all of the parents' attention, the maximum share of the family resources, and is given the ideal springboard from which to fully realise his or her genetic potential. Against this, he or she misses out on all the things that can be gained from having siblings. On the whole, though, the advantages should outweigh the disadvantages. If a couple are going to follow the single-child strategy, there is some advantage in that child being a son. As we shall see in relation to parental favouritism in the next chapter, there is some reproductive benefit in many societies from lavishing care, attention and wealth on a son rather than a daughter. So our couple had got that part of their strategy correct.

How often the potentially greater quality, from the point of view of evolutionary biology, of a single child more than makes up for the lack of numbers – in the way that *two* 'high-quality' children did for the dark-haired woman in the previous scenes – is difficult to judge without good data on reproductive success. One thing is certain, however. Whatever advantages there might be to having just one child, there are also dangers, as the old man in this scene had discovered.

Parenting is difficult. Full of pitfalls, it requires vigilance and efficiency from day one – and never more than when the parents have only one child. One mistake, or just one stroke of bad luck, and a lifetime's reproductive effort can be lost. In the case of the man in the scene, of course, reproductive failure contained a strong element of bad luck. He was pursuing a valid strategy – one high-quality son – and he was by no means a bad parent in any conventional sense. He didn't neglect, abuse or murder his son. In fact, he obviously cared for him deeply. Nevertheless, natural selection will have marked him down as a failure. Whatever the circumstances that led him and his wife to delay their family and to have just one child, their course of action would always be risky, and as it transpired it was disastrous.

In modern industrial societies, people are increasingly having only one child. Most do so voluntarily, though in China it is actually government policy. There, 'one family, one child' legislation has successfully reduced the mean number of children, though only to an average of 1.6 per woman, not 1.0. Even so, the commonest family size in China is one child (just), whereas in the remainder of the industrialised nations it is two. For example, 43 per cent of women born in Britain in 1950 ended up with two children, three to four times as many as had only one. Interestingly, as more and more Chinese have only one child, the sex ratio of children there is changing dramatically: now there are sixteen boys for every ten girls, instead of the eleven for every ten that prevailed when family size was larger.

The very fact that more *Chinese* are having only one child means that universally more people are having only one, because a quarter of the world's population *is* Chinese. But it does not look as if the trend is likely to catch on everywhere. In Britain, for example, whereas one in five women born in 1920 had only one child, only one in eight born in 1950 stopped after the first – a decrease of over a third. Bearing in mind the difficulty the Chinese government have encountered in enforcing their one-child policy, such figures suggest that, as long as they are fully fertile, people are reluctant to have only one. The implication is that most people are programmed to be less impressed by the possible advantages of having a single child than they are by the dangers.

CHAPTER SIX

Family Strife

SCENE 14
Sibling Rivalry

The young girl burst into her elder sister's room wearing only a towel, which she held tightly around herself. 'Can I have it now please? Come on, you promised,' she said, holding the door half open. Her sister carried on writing for a few seconds as if she hadn't heard, then replied without looking up.

'I'm not sure about it now, I think I've changed my mind – and by the way, why don't you knock next time? You know you're not supposed to burst in like that.' She returned to her writing, an air of finality in her voice.

The younger girl, her eyes glinting, came towards her, then grabbed her roughly by the arm and swung her round.

'Hey! Stop it, you're hurting,' exclaimed her sister, wrenching her arm free. 'I can change my mind if I want to, can't I?'

'Not when you've promised, you can't,' warned her sister. 'Anyway, I haven't got anything else to wear and I've bought things to go with it. It's not fair – you're just jealous because I look better in it than you do!'

'Me, jealous of *you*?' laughed the elder girl, trying to look incredulous. 'You must be joking.'

There was a second's pause, then the irate teenager said, 'Right, that's it, I'm going to get it myself', and strode purposefully towards her sister's wardrobe.

'Don't you dare touch my clothes!' shouted the other, leaping up from her desk. She made towards the wardrobe, then turned and rushed out of the bedroom and ran along to the top of the stairs. Leaning over the banister, she shouted down to her mother. 'Mum, Mum, she's going through my clothes! Mum!'

Downstairs their mother sighed, put away the last of the crockery and walked slowly to the bottom of the stairs. She had been listening to her daughters arguing for a good five minutes. It could only be a matter of time before one of them would be begging her to intervene. Suddenly the commotion grew louder as the two girls came galloping downstairs, each trying to push her way in front of the other. In the tussle the younger girl's towel slipped, exposing her pubescent breasts and making her stop suddenly to recover herself. She walked sedately down the last few steps, her face slightly pink. Their mother got in first.

'For goodness' sake you two, whatever is it now?' she asked.

'Mum, it's her fault,' complained the towel-clad one. 'She's only changed her mind because she knows *he's* going to be there. It's not fair.'

'What! Don't be ridiculous, and who's *he* anyway?' retorted her sister, pulling a face.

'You know, the one you're crazy about,'

'You mean the one *you're* crazy about, not me,' came the indignant reply.

The younger girl appealed once more to her mother. 'She's just worried that he'll see me in it and fancy me more than her. It's not my fault she hasn't been invited – and she did say last week I could borrow it.'

'Rubbish!' screamed the elder girl as she stamped back up the stairs. A moment later she flung the dress over the banister. 'There, you can have it if you like. See if I care, you stupid cow!'

'Hey, you mind your language young lady,' shouted her mother as the teenager disappeared back into her room. Meanwhile, the younger girl gathered up the dress and bounded triumphantly back up the stairs, two at a time.

Half an hour later the door slammed, marking her departure. The elder girl, after finishing her assignment, spent the rest of the evening soaking in a hot bath, studying her body and wondering how her sister was getting on. Her mother, meanwhile, slightly annoyed that her younger daughter had left without so much as a goodbye, spent much of the rest of the evening thinking about her children. Indeed, without their father here to distract her – he was working late yet again – she found it difficult to take her mind off them.

It had always been the same. Sometimes they got on, but more often than not they didn't. There was always *something* they could find to argue about. Just lately the main area of contention had been the relative size of their bedrooms. The elder daughter's was slightly larger – which was perfectly reasonable, she claimed, because she was the elder. The younger, however, complained bitterly about the unfairness of it. It wasn't *her* fault that she was younger, she would say, and at every opportunity she would use the smallness of her bedroom as an excuse to moan about the injustices of being the younger child. She needed the extra space, she would argue. Her furniture was larger and she definitely had more visitors than her sister. It just wasn't right.

Their mother had heard about the problems of jealousy that could arise when there was too small a gap between children, but this hadn't stopped her from getting pregnant again when her firstborn was barely eighteen months old. She remembered how thrilled she had been at giving birth to a second daughter. She had always wanted a sister herself and imagined her two daughters being lifelong best friends. She could envisage them helping each other, sharing secrets. But it wasn't to be. No matter how fairly she and their father had tried to treat them, the younger girl had remained convinced that in some way she had lost out to her elder sister. In her turn, the latter's resentment towards the newcomer had never really subsided.

From the very beginning, the elder girl had seemed to regard the other as a threat. It was as though she realised that having a little sister around could only mean less attention for herself. Her mother remembered with sadness how her firstborn had reacted to her breast-feeding the new baby. In the very early days she had seemed content to just ignore the whole process, but after a while she had begun to show her jealousy. As soon as her baby sister was feeding happily she would want things, little things. She would ask for a drink, a toy she couldn't reach, or to have her sock put back on – anything she could think of to stop the breast-feeding, if only for a minute or so. When this ploy stopped working, she used to try to force herself between the two, determined to climb on to her mother's knee.

By far the worst incident had taken place when her elder daughter was two and a half. It had been a hot summer and they were spending the afternoon in the garden. She had taken the radio, a blanket and some toys outside, planning to have a picnic later. The little one had been fast asleep in her pram when she had nipped back inside to wash a teat. While she was standing at the sink, through the window she saw her elder daughter pick up the radio and toddle over to the pram. With horror, she realised instantly what was going to happen. Rushing out of the kitchen, she reached the corner of the house just in time to see her daughter flinging the heavy object into the pram. Luckily, after catching on the side of it the radio had flopped on to the sleeping baby's stomach and did nothing more serious than wake her up. For years after this, she never left the two girls on their own together.

Soon after this incident, the older child had begun a phase of what the mother called 'baby behaviour'. Whenever she was dealing with the younger one, the elder would lie on the floor, kicking, screaming and flailing around until she managed to gain her mother's attention. Reluctantly, they had even had to put her back into nappies for a while after she discovered that soiling her clothes or the floor worked particularly well. Then, as a four-year-old, she had become more strategic in her attempts to win her parents' attention away from her sister. One of her main tactics had been to encourage the toddler to do something naughty, then run off and complain about it to their mother. When she arrived to find out what was going on, the big one would insist that it was nothing to do with her.

The two sisters never became good playmates. They would argue incessantly over toys. The elder often used her superior bulk and strength to wrest things from her sister's grip. She also seemed to take delight in ruining any little games that the other one had devised for herself. As the younger one grew up she began to retaliate by interfering with her sister's games and being a nuisance when she had friends round to play. On the odd occasions when they started a board game together, the younger one would infuriate her sister by not following the rules properly and threatening to tip the board up when she grew tired of playing.

Even now that they were both into their teens things were much the same, even if the objects of their disagreements were different. They seemed incapable of ever seeing each other's point of view and their squabbles still dominated the mood of the household. Maybe this was how it was always going to be, thought the mother sadly as she prepared to go upstairs to bed.

T his chapter is a collection of five scenes, each dealing with a different aspect of family life as children develop from infancy, through childhood, and into adolescence.

Few would disagree that family life is a mixture of good and bad times. The good moments, when everybody's interests coincide, bring considerable pleasure and require little interpretation from an evolutionary biologist. It is through such accord that all members of the family potentially enhance their reproductive output *through being part of a family*. They learn from each other, support each other and by offering a cooperative, united front to the outside world they can compete for resources for the family as a whole far more effectively than if they all acted independently. There is much more, however, that evolutionary biology can say to help us understand the less harmonious aspects of family life, and it is on these aspects that we shall concentrate now.

We shall illustrate some of the interactions between parents and children, dealing in Scene 15 with parental favouritism and violence and in Scene 16 with the often taboo subject of incest. We end the chapter with two scenes illustrating situations that bring their own unique problems – 'blended families', in which there are step-parents, and lone-parent families – and in the process we also consider the question of child abuse (Scene 17). But we begin by looking at sibling rivalry.

Sibling rivalry is one of the more obvious manifestations of 'baby wars'. There are few people who have not seen or experienced for themselves the wide variety of ways in which brothers and sisters can compete with each other. They bicker, fight and take each other's possessions, just as we saw in the scene above. Occasionally, they even kill each other. Whatever their ages, they can usually find something to fight over, and the rivalry can begin early. Most children are fairly safe from their siblings while still in their mother's womb – but not twins, who may each invade their mother's body in such a way as to try to gain the lion's share of the nutrition on offer, or even jostle for the best position in the womb.

As babies and toddlers, siblings compete for their parents' attention and affection; then they add food and toys, or even just the best place to sit or stand, to their list of things to squabble over. As juniors and early teenagers they contend with each other over space and parental gifts, and as late teenagers they may compete for friends of the same and the opposite sex, as well as for more material things such as access to the family car. Finally, as adults they may compete for their inheritance. Sibling rivalry is a powerful force from birth until death.

There is nothing uniquely human about it. Nor is it a new phenomenon. Every offspring of every animal that lives in families, whether mammal, bird or insect, exhibits sibling rivalry. Moreover, it shows itself in every aspect of family life. Soon after birth, it can be seen in baby mammals as they fight over access to their mother's nipples. Nestling birds, as they strive with open bill to cajole their parents into giving *them* the lion's share of food, are displaying it too. In older animals it can be seen, for instance, in young lion cubs' rough-and-tumble play and in the fights of sibling birds that live in extended families as they compete for the parental territory.

To the romantic, sibling rivalry should have no place: the family is a unit, and if everyone pulls together that unit as a whole should make its way in the world far more successfully than if it fights internally. And, up to a point, families do behave cooperatively in this way – it is one of the benefits of forming a family group. But, as the evolutionary biologist sees it, sibling rivalry is inevitable. So why has natural selection programmed humans, and all other species who live in families, to compete with each other in this way? The basic explanation is very simple. Each sibling is trying to maximise its own reproductive output and is prepared to do everything it can to succeed, even if it means compromising the success of its brothers and sisters.

The restraining force on these sibling contests derives from the parents, just as it did in our scene. The reason that parents provide such restraint is that their interests are different from their children's. Evolution has programmed parents to referee the contests between their children according to rules that promote the parents' total reproductive output rather than any individual child's. Natural selection will favour those parents who observe, overview, intervene and orchestrate where necessary so as to maximise the total number of grandchildren they obtain. To a large extent, this simply means that parents gain most from making sure that none of their children suffers too badly from sibling rivalry. Inevitably, though, the situation is not that simple, as we shall discover in the next scene when we deal with parental favouritism. But for the moment, let us assume that the best strategy for both parents is to referee so fairly that each of their children gets an equal share of the family resources on offer.

Each child, on the other hand, is doing its best to get the *lion's share*. In part, this means that it must try not to alienate its parents *too* much by grossly disrupting *their* overall strategy. To do so will be counterproductive, if they then disfavour that child. Up to a point, also, a child has to be careful not to alienate its siblings too much. Siblings can be useful – if only to borrow clothes from! More generally, a pair of siblings can often each do better in contests within their peer group if they cooperate rather than act alone. They can also exert greater pressure on their parents if they act together. Sibling relationships, therefore, are a tightrope between cooperation and conflict, and the most successful children are those who tread this tightrope with the greatest care.

Rivalry is costly. It takes time and energy and risks alienating the rest of the family. Unless there is something worthwhile to gain from it, it may not be worth the price to be paid. For example, how much food, space, money, support and attention there is to go round will be a central issue. We might expect sibling rivalry to be greatest in families from low socioeconomic groups. With a relatively little cake, there is much greater pressure on all to get as big a slice as they can. Rivalry should be at its lowest level in families from high socioeconomic groups, but even here it will still be a feature of family life. However large a share of the resources a child manages to win, it will always benefit from having more – fierce sibling rivalry over the inheritance of large family fortunes is the stuff of life as well as of drama.

Three other factors will influence the extent of rivalry between any two siblings: the difference in their ages, whether they are of the same or different sexes, and how they are related genetically. The first two are straightforward. The closer siblings are in age, the more their needs overlap, the greater the pressure to compete, and the more even their chances. Similarly, siblings of the same sex also have more to gain from competing – again, their needs overlap more than they would if they were brother and sister. The third factor, however, is not so simple and is much further-reaching: the level of conflict between siblings depends on their relatedness. Rivalry is greatest between step-siblings, next greatest between half-siblings, then full siblings, and least intense between identical twins. The explanation for this comes later in the chapter.

No family will totally avoid sibling rivalry, unless there is only one child. Children will always find situations in which they can gain by promoting their own interests at their brothers' and sisters' expense. Within any given family, the extent of sibling rivalry will depend on a complex interaction between the costs and benefits of conflict and cooperation. This in turn will be influenced by the family's status and the number, ages, genders and genetic relatedness of the children. Even if there is nothing else to compete over, there must always be a limit to the total parental attention on offer. From time to time, all siblings will find it necessary to compete for a greater share of this important resource.

In addition, the nature and extent of rivalry will also depend on precisely how the parents orchestrate their children's interactions. In this discussion, we have assumed that both parents will referee equally and fairly. More often than not, however, it is in the parents' interests to be less even-handed. Moreover, mother's and father's interests over which child to favour and which to disfavour may not always coincide.

SCENE 15
Parental Favouritism

The young girl sorted carefully through the photographs. She knew what she was looking for. It was there somewhere.

This Saturday afternoon she had found herself alone in the house and at a loose end. The rest of the family, her elder brother, little brother, mother and father, had gone out for the day. They had been going out a lot recently, since her elder brother had come home on vacation from college. It was as if every day had to be special, just because he was home again. Normal life was suspended – no more arguments, no more boring Sundays, no more thrown-together meals. Everything had to be special.

In the days before his return, her parents had talked about nothing else. Her mother had carefully prepared his bedroom and filled the freezer with masses of home-made bread and cakes and pastries – 'just in case he felt like something sweet'. She had phoned relatives to say that he was coming home and that they might 'just be popping in to see them' some time in the next week or so.

The girl stopped looking for the photograph and stood up. Leaving the tiny box room, she crossed the landing and opened the door of her elder brother's room. The bed had been neatly made, the floor hoovered. She immediately thought of her own room, bed unmade, stuff everywhere. His was the largest bedroom in the house. She still shared hers with her little brother. Unlike him, who was too young to care, she really resented it. After her elder brother had gone away she had pleaded with her parents to be allowed to have his room. After all, it would be unoccupied most of the time. But no, it was his room and that was how it would stay. Besides, there were always the vacations and, who knows – what if he was to come home for good? It was all very unfair, she thought. She was fifteen and she needed her privacy. None of her friends had to share rooms with their little brothers or sisters.

Her eyes fell on the computer in the corner. Now this was a real source of argument. Originally it had been bought for the whole family, but within a few weeks it had ended up in her brother's room. From then on he had had almost sole access to it – all she could do was snatch the odd moment when he was out. In justification her father had argued that her brother would make better use of it, because he needed it for his assignments for 'A' level course work. Anybody would think she didn't have school assignments to do. But hers weren't as important, of course, because *she* wasn't expected to go to university.

At the moment, she was saving every penny she earned from her part-time job on a market stall in order to buy her own computer. Obviously it wouldn't be as good a machine as her brother's but it was all she was likely to get. It had never occurred to any of them that her brother should get a job. In any case, most of his spare time was taken up with his sporting activities. Her father was particularly proud of the boy's athletic achievements. Most Saturdays, when his son had still been at school, had been spent ferrying him back and forth from this or that training circuit or athletics meeting. The evening meal would be taken up with talk about her brother's performance that day. Rarely would the events of *her* day be the subject of conversation. She was sure her parents weren't being deliberately dismissive when they behaved like this – and anyway, she asked herself, if it bothered her so much why didn't she tackle them about it? Somehow, though, she knew that doing so probably wouldn't make any difference to the way they treated her.

Suddenly her thoughts were disturbed by the sound of a key turning in the front door. They were back. She went to the open window and craned out. The sound of voices drifted up, her father's in particular. 'So who's the lucky girl, then?' she could hear him asking her brother.

She didn't catch the reply because her brother was already on his way into the house. Leaving the window she sighed, then began to make her way downstairs, to put in a token appearance. So her brother had plans for that evening. She wondered idly who 'the lucky girl' was. He had a number of girlfriends that he would call up during his vacations. Who would it be tonight? How long would she spend getting ready? And how long would she wait tomorrow for the promised telephone call that would never happen? Yes, her brother had lots of girls. She felt sorry for them all.

Dinner was delayed that night in order to give her brother time to shower and get ready before he went to collect his date. A late dinner suited neither her own plans nor her stomach. She leaned against the kitchen unit, nibbling a biscuit, while her mother bustled around fretting lest any detail of the meal wasn't quite right. Usually they ate in the kitchen, but since her brother had been home they had eaten in the dining-room every evening.

By the time they started dinner, she was running late for her evening out and had to leave halfway through. As she got up from the table her mother interrupted the conversation to ask her where she was going, obviously forgetting that they had talked about it earlier in the day. Just before closing the front door she heard her brother say something, then her parents laughing. Had she remembered her key? her mother called out, still laughing. She paused and almost replied, but the question wasn't repeated so she just closed the door and left.

Ten days later she found herself alone in the house again. The rest of the family had set off some hours earlier to take her brother back to college, a day's journey. The night before, she had hinted that she might like to go with them. It was a Sunday and she was well on top of her school work. But at the last moment there hadn't been enough room in the car. She wasn't that disappointed, though. After they had left, she went up to the box room. The photographs she had been sorting through a fortnight or so before were still scattered over the floor. She knelt down and picked them up – it had to be there somewhere. Then she spotted it, the picture that her father had taken of her elder brother on his first day at school. Really, it summed up everything – she knew there was no comparable photo of either herself or her little brother. For some reason, they had never been quite as important.

T he parents' behaviour makes the outcome of this second scene involving sibling rivalry very different from the first, in which the mother refereed as fairly as possible between her two bickering daughters. In this scene, the parents do everything they can to advance their elder son, while ignoring the needs and complaints of their daughter.

So what should parents do in order to maximise their reproductive output? Should they referee as fairly as possible? Should they show favouritism? Or should they simply allow their children free rein to establish their own hierarchies? Unfortunately, at least from an evolutionary perspective, there is no simple answer. Everything depends on the family's circumstances, the relative potentials of the different children, and their number, ages, genders and relatedness.

In our previous discussion of sibling rivalry, we identified two central principles. First, each child should strive to maximise its personal reproductive output, even at the expense of its siblings; to do this, it needs to tread the tightrope between selfishness and cooperation as successfully as possible. Second, the parents should referee their children's rivalry with a view to maximising their own reproductive output.

Some of the time, parents will do this by being even-handed, by striving to give all of their children as equal a footing as possible. At other times they will take the more positive action of supporting the weak and restraining the strong. The advantage of equalising the children's potentials is that, up to a point, each is an equal ticket in life's lottery for the award of grandchildren. There are random elements, such as accident and disease, that can strike any child at any time: in this respect, life and death, which children survive to adulthood, really is a matter of chance. When a child dies, those parents who have refereed their children's rivalry to ensure that the survivors have had as good a start in life as the dead child will still be reproductively the most successful. Those who have favoured a particular child, who then dies, will be left with ill-prepared survivors, the unsupported victims of their sibling's rivalry, and will be less successful in their total production of grandchildren.

Suppose there are two children in a family who, were they to receive equal support from both parents, would in their turn also each have two children – a total of four grandchildren for each parent. Now suppose that the parents show a little favouritism with the result that the favoured child eventually produces four children and the relatively neglected child none. All else being equal, the parents would have neither gained nor lost anything from their favouritism, since they still end up with four grandchildren. However, their favouritism makes them vulnerable to the random threat of accident and disease. If they lose the favoured child, they end up with no grandchildren, and their lineage is extinct. If they hadn't shown favouritism, on the other hand, they would have had two, no matter which child they lost.

The rule is, therefore, that if favouritism cannot increase the total number of grandchildren, it is safer not to show any. But everything changes if favouritism *can* increase the number of grandchildren: then it can become worth running the gauntlet of accident and disease. If, in the example above, the favoured child had produced four or more children as against the disfavoured child's one, the parents would have ended up with five or more grandchildren instead of the four that fairness would have produced.

So natural selection has favoured parents who are alert to the possibility that one or other of their children may have much greater potential than its siblings. Under such circumstances, many find themselves irresistibly drawn towards encouraging and helping that child at the expense of the others. Of course, rarely do parents consciously think in terms of their support generating more descendants, but this is what their bodies are pursuing. The parents' brains will register that if they just do this or that, one of their children could be exceptional in some way. And exceptional people, whatever their expertise, are on average reproductively more successful than less exceptional people, particularly if their abilities create status and wealth.

We see the principle of favouritism in action in many other animals, some of the most extreme cases being various species of birds of prey. In some birds, the mother actually puts more hormones into the yolk of the first egg she lays so that this chick will beg for food more aggressively than its siblings. Many hawks and eagles lay two eggs and have two chicks, but from the very beginning one is favoured over the other. The parents preferentially feed the more promising chick, and soon the disfavoured one dies from neglect. In most years, the parents cannot find enough food to feed both chicks, and thus enhance their reproductive success more by favouring the stronger chick than by trying to treat them equally. Only in years of plenty, when food is easy to obtain, do they attempt to rear both. And only if accident, disease or predation robs the parents of their favoured chick before the runt has died will they give the smaller chick their full attention. In these birds it is usually the first chick to hatch who is favoured – and natural selection has brought about a similar policy in humans.

A difference in genetic potential between their children is not the only reason parents may show favouritism. Birth order can also be a factor. Throughout history, in a wide variety of cultures, the lion's share of parental lands and resources has been inherited by the eldest child. In Western societies, the favoured child was usually the eldest son. In some agricultural societies it was often the eldest daughter. In yet others it was simply the eldest. Similar tendencies are still evident today. At one extreme we have the inheritance of monarchies; at the other, situations such as that illustrated in the scene above.

Favouritism based on birth order is unsurprising to an evolutionary biologist. An individual's reproductive success is properly measured not by the *number* of children or grandchildren but by *reproductive rate*. A person can, for example, have twice the reproductive rate of another either by producing twice as many grandchildren in the same length of time or by producing the same number of grandchildren but in half the time. Although so far in our discussion it has been appropriate to talk simply in terms of reproductive *success*, it is crucial here to bear in mind that when we talk of reproductive success, we really mean reproductive *rate*. And one way in which parents can attempt to increase their reproductive rate is to give every advantage to their oldest child in the hope that he or she will be reproductively successful: because if their oldest child is reproductively the *most* successful, they have more grandchildren sooner and the parental reproductive *rate* is likely to be greater than if any other of their children is the most successful.

While natural selection was predisposing parents to favour their oldest child, all else being equal, it was simultaneously predisposing children for sibling rivalry in a way that has had fascinating consequences. Painstaking biographical and questionnaire work extending over twenty years has enabled scientific historians to discover that birth order has a major influence on a person's character. In soliciting parental support, firstborns typically imitate parental behaviours and attitudes. Laterborns then need to differentiate themselves from their elder siblings. This drives them naturally into a position of opposition, to adopt stances that are in some sense revolutionary. Put simply, firstborns are conservative, laterborns are rebellious.

There is now considerable documented evidence that revolutionary ideas, such as drove events ranging from political revolutions such as the French Revolution to ideological revolutions such as Protestantism, appealed to people differently according to their birth order position in the family. On the whole, the people who supported such revolutions were laterborns and those who opposed them were firstborns, irrespective of their age. For example, before Darwin's publication of *The Origin of Species* in 1859 gave evolutionary ideas some status, they were ten times more likely to be advanced by laterborns than by firstborns of similar age and background. Decades or so later, when these different revolutions had established themselves, roles were reversed. Then, the tenets of the new establishment were more readily embraced by firstborns and opposed by laterborns.

When a synthesis of this research was first published in 1996, it received some media attention. Many commentators were tempted, in discussing the findings, to assert that the study provided an example of environmental rather than genetic determination – a triumph of 'nurture' over 'nature'. But it is not so. What natural selection has done is to shape a *conditional response*. In essence, everybody is genetically programmed in the same way, first to determine his or her position in the family hierarchy, then to respond accordingly. And the appropriate response is: if a firstborn, adopt parental values; if a lastborn, question parental values; and if somewhere in between, compromise. The response of laterborns can do nothing to reduce parental favouritism towards firstborns, because such favouritism is often in the parents' interests, as we have discussed. What the laterborns' response does do, however, is define a stance around which they can develop and hone a consistent array of behaviour patterns. Essentially, they seek the opportunities and resources overlooked by their parents and older siblings, seeking to excel in novel and unexpected ways.

Genetic potential and birth order are not the only factors that influence parents' favouritism. Gender is another. More often than not, parents benefit from preferentially bestowing wealth and status on their sons rather than on their daughters. As noted earlier, men of higher wealth and status obtain partners earlier, start to reproduce earlier, are less likely to be cuckolded, and are more likely to cuckold others. In all ways, therefore, such men have the potential to be reproductively more successful than their lower-status contemporaries. This is as true of modern industrial societies as of pre-industrial ones.

There is a fascinating consequence of the female preference for, and greater fidelity to, men of wealth and status: namely, that women may actually bias the sex ratio within their family to take advantage of the preference. From the fact that high-status men achieve greater reproductive success than others, not only through their long-term relationships but also because they have the same above-average opportunities as did their fathers to cuckold other men, it follows that a woman paired to a high-status man will achieve greater reproductive success if she produces sons rather than daughters. A really successful son can enhance a woman's reproductive success far more than even the most successful of daughters. The greatest number of children ever claimed by a man is 888, as mentioned earlier; that by a woman, 69 (over 27 pregnancies).

We might, therefore, expect higher-status couples to produce more sons than lower-status couples, and this is precisely what worldwide studies have shown. Take, for instance, the data given for the men and women listed in such publications as *Who's Who*. Usually the bias is statistical rather than obvious – about 115 boys for every 100 girls – but sometimes it can be impressive. The presidents of the United States, for example, have between them produced 90 sons and 61 daughters, the equivalent of 148 sons for every 100 daughters.

So why don't all women produce an excess of sons? Actually, to some extent they do. On average, about 106 boys are born for every 100 girls. But because boys are more likely to die during childhood, by the time they start to reproduce the proportion is about equal. Even so, the average woman is less likely to have a boy than is a woman paired to a high-status male, and women without a partner at all, as well as women paired to low-status males, are more likely to produce a daughter.

Showing favouritism towards the eldest son, therefore, will often enhance the parents' reproductive rate more than would favouring a daughter. This does not mean, though, that there are never genetic, social or ecological situations in which parents benefit most by showing greater favouritism to daughters.

One of the most recent studies of such a situation concerns gypsies in Hungary, for whom poverty and the concomitant disease and infertility lead to their reproductive success being lower than that of the wealthier, settled Hungarians. Gypsy sons find it difficult to obtain mates among the Hungarian population, but daughters find it less difficult. On average, a gypsy is likely to have more grandchildren via daughters than via sons, and gypsy women are more likely to give birth to daughters than to sons. A gypsy daughter is particularly likely to produce more grandchildren for her parents if she is healthy, attractive and educated, for it is these who are most likely to marry the wealthier settled Hungarians. And among the gypsy population, more favouritism is shown towards daughters than sons. In particular, daughters are breast-fed for longer, and more of the family resources are invested in their education.

So far, we have discussed parental favouritism as if mother and father will always be in agreement over which of their children is most promising, as they were in our scene. But this is by no means always the case and, as usual, the critical factor is paternal certainty. Whereas the mother can have equal confidence that all of her children are vehicles for her genes, her partner cannot, and this difference in part explains one of the features of parental favouritism: fathers are *more likely* to show favouritism than are mothers. A father's treatment of his children can be very strongly biased according to how confident he is that this or that child is actually *his* genetic offspring. Even if his conscious appraisal is that all of his partner's children are equally likely to be his, his body may evaluate each child's characteristics differently. The apparently illogical empathy that he may feel for one child rather than another may well be the outcome of his body's appraisal of paternal certainty.

Friction can be caused between the mother and the father if they differ in their favouritism. This can also fuel conflicts between the parents and their children, and amongst the children themselves. For much of the time, the smooth surface of family life betrays little of this intricate network of underlying conflicts. Occasionally, as we have seen, sibling rivalry compounded by parental favouritism and paternal uncertainty may make waves, but more often than not the waters settle and family life returns to normal, to the mutual benefit of all its members. From time to time, however, any one of the conflicts can erupt into a confrontation so violent that the family is never the same again.

Neglect, aggression and violence are in effect the flip side of favouritism. Parents can implement their preferences in two ways – by acting positively towards a favoured child or negatively towards a disfavoured one. Aggression and murder are the obvious extremes of negativity. On the whole, parents are most likely to show the positive face of favouritism when the family's circumstances are buoyant, the negative one when circumstances are poor. Sometimes, when the behaviour of the disfavoured child so threatens the reproductive success of the favoured child, to the parent violence or murder may seem the only solution. And such extreme behaviour is most likely when there are few resources in the family to go round. In other words, parental mistreatment of children is most common in low socioeconomic groups.

In one sense, such violence is an unfortunate extension of the family planning that we have discussed earlier and that is so important to the reproductive success of both parents. The prize of maximum success goes to those couples who get the number and timing of their reproductive attempts just right. Sometimes, however, long after the children have been born, conditions deteriorate and a family size that at one time seemed right may at some later date seem too large. In effect, parents occasionally react to their deteriorating circumstances by reducing their family to a size that their bodies assess they can manage. Although such a violent reaction, shown by many other mammals as well, has more to do with family planning, the selection of which offspring to kill is clearly an extreme manifestation of parental favouritism.

Furthermore, whatever criteria a mother uses in so violently discriminating against one of her children, those used by the father may be different. Given that he has the additional pressure of paternal confidence to contend with, he may well react violently towards a child in whom that confidence is low, particularly if it is mistreating one in whom he has higher paternal confidence, and therefore favours.

SCENE 16
Incest

Unaware of the approaching thunderstorm, the man was reliving in his dream the argument he had had with his partner. The accusations of infidelity were coming thick and fast.

The storm grew nearer, lightning now illuminating the ceiling. In his dream, the ever-louder thunderclaps became the crash of the plates she had thrown at him and that still lay in pieces on the kitchen floor. In the instant before he woke, the explosion directly overhead was translated into the slam of the door as she had left, car keys in hand. Heart pounding, he awoke to see his bedroom door slowly open.

'We're frightened, Mummy,' said the eight-year-old. 'We want to get into bed with you until it stops.' Thunder terrified her. Behind her, the five-year-old boy and two-year-old girl, clutching her teddy-bear, stood and waited for the reply.

'Mummy's not here, darling,' said the man. 'She had to go and see a friend, but she'll be back soon. You can get into bed with me until she comes home.'

The morning after the thunderstorm, he found a message on his answering-machine saying that she was going to join her lover in his new life abroad. A month later, he received a postcard saying she was sorry, she couldn't help herself, but her new partner meant more to her than anything – and would he please give the children her love – and a good life.

Until that moment, the man had been unable to believe that she could just walk out on him and their children. And for a while afterwards, he still thought her maternal instinct would win through and that one day she would just turn up, desperate at least to see the children again. But the postcard forced him to examine his life and to try and work out how he was going to raise his family single-handed. Perhaps it wasn't impossible. As a writer he could work from home, and he was successful enough to manage financially.

There was no immediate family. He was an only child and his parents had died about ten years earlier, leaving him a sizeable inheritance. His partner had been adopted. On discovering her history when she was a teenager, she had gradually become disenchanted with her adoptive parents and left home at the first opportunity, never to return. Nor were there any close neighbours. He and his partner had been thrilled when they had found the tumble-down cottage, nestling in woodland. Access to the nearest road was down a dirt track just wide enough for their Land Rover. The cottage had cost them nearly half of his inheritance to buy and renovate, but when it was finished they couldn't believe how lucky they had been. At times, usually in winter as he drove the two older children back and forth to school, a thirty-minute journey, he wondered if he was doing the right thing by them, continuing to live in such an isolated spot. But in summer he had no such doubts. He would take time off from his writing, to sit or potter naked in the huge, wild garden while his children, also naked, would play for hours on end.

His only major problem was over sleeping arrangements. In the days after their mother's departure, the children had been so distraught at bedtime that he hadn't the heart to stop them from sleeping in his bed. He suspected it made them feel nearer to her, though, rather than to him. But the night he disentangled himself from their spreadeagled limbs to go and sleep in the elder girl's bed in the next room, they came and fetched him, saying they couldn't sleep if he didn't come back.

Two months after his partner had gone, he had at last managed to persuade the children to try sleeping again in their own room. But when he was woken by the eldest one's sobbing he let her get back into bed with him, and within the hour his bed was again full of children. Soon, he gave up even trying to make them sleep in their own room. Anyway, he was rather enjoying sharing his bed with them all. He felt like a mother hen, collecting his brood around him for the night. In a strange way, he even felt it was necessary. Living where they did, they sometimes thought they could hear prowlers. From time to time, though, he yearned to be able to stretch out in bed unimpeded. He had never worn pyjamas, and the night that the youngest, now three, innocently scratched his genitals with her ragged fingernails, he vowed to regain the freedom of his bed. In the end, they compromised. The two oldest accepted his bribe of a bunk bed, as long as it could be put next to his. So he crammed everybody's beds into his room, and told all three that they had at least to start off each night in their own.

But not many nights passed without one of them climbing into his bed at some point. The most frequent visitor was the oldest, now nine, who had started to have nightmares. And sometimes he found himself back to square one, with all three snuggling up with him. But at least there were still times when he could stretch his body across the bed and spread out as much as he liked. And, if he was honest, most important of all he gained the freedom, when he felt like it, to play with his genitals and think erotic thoughts – about sharing his bed not with children but with one, or even several, women.

Over the next three years, the children's memory of their mother and their belief that one day she would return gradually faded, and they became a close and self-sufficient family. The elder girl became more and more of a mother to her brother and sister, sharing the cooking and shopping with her father and taking the lead in buying their clothes. It amused him how, becoming more and more like her mother, she began to boss him around and show irritation at his untidiness and occasional lethargy.

That summer was the hottest for years. Their bodies turned a wonderful shade of brown and for a few weeks the man had his bed to himself as everybody opted for the relative coolness of solitude. One by one, also, the children followed his example and stopped wearing their pyjamas.

It was that summer that he noticed the first signs of breasts and pubic hair on his twelve-year-old, and that they woke one morning to find blood on the sheets. He was impressed, not only by the fact that she knew immediately what was happening to her, but also by the confident way she handled the process of buying and using tampons. He was even more impressed by the matter-of-fact way she responded one morning on discovering that he had ejaculated on the sheet. 'Is that semen, Dad?' was her sleepy response. He had been trying to clean it up before she noticed. But the incident clinched it. It really was time she stopped getting into his bed, especially now that she seemed to have given up wearing night-clothes completely. She complained that he still let her brother and sister get in with him when they wanted. He didn't want her in his bed any more in case she bled on his sheets, she said sullenly.

For once, however, he insisted and she obeyed. But within a week a succession of bad dreams had her creeping back again in the small hours.

She then pleaded to start the night in his bed to stop them from happening. In the end he gave in. Why shouldn't they all sleep together anyway, if that's what they wanted? But first, he bought a king-sized bed. And then he told all three that they must never tell anybody that they sometimes slept in his bed – especially with no clothes on. If they did, he said, people would come and stop them. They might even stop them from living with him. By now he was quite successful, and occasionally his work was in the media spotlight. The prospect of having to explain publicly something that had evolved quite naturally from their family situation appalled him.

From then on, the elder girl slept with him, and the others usually spent the night in their own beds, only occasionally joining their sister and father.

Over the next four years, his two younger children grew increasingly self-sufficient. His son had become interested in wildlife and would go on long walks through the woods making detailed notes of everything he saw, and his younger daughter spent long hours reading in her room. As his elder daughter turned into a shapely young woman, he lived a thousand torments. Many of his anxieties he knew he would have experienced even in normal circumstances. He worried that their isolation was affecting his children's social development, and urged them to make more friends at school and visit them more often – though not to invite them home. He half-heartedly pressed the elder girl to find a boyfriend, but then felt jealous whenever she mentioned this or that boy. It both worried and relieved him that, as far as he knew, she never had anything to do with any of them, seeming content with her life at home.

Most of his agonising, though, was sexual. It alarmed him the way his elder daughter, now the image of her mother, would so trustingly get into his bed naked. She never felt safer than when she was cuddled up next to him, she said. Increasingly, part of him wanted to tell her that they really should stop sleeping together, but the other part would have been devastated if they had. Her childlike innocence belied her adult body, and no matter how hard he tried to discipline his thoughts, she had become the main object of his sexual fantasies. The thought of her not sleeping with him – of one day sleeping with somebody else – was unbearable. But how could he tell her that while she was lying there, feeling safe and secure in his arms, he was fantasising about doing with her everything he had done with her mother in that house a decade earlier?

Many years later, he marvelled that he had managed to restrain himself for so long. His daughter was fifteen when he finally began to crack. She had remarked that he seemed to be having wet dreams increasingly often. He couldn't disillusion her with the truth. He wasn't going to tell her that he had been waiting until she was asleep, then climaxing by rubbing his erection gently against the nearest part of her body.

Once he had started using her in this way, his activity escalated. With increasing daring, he would allow his hand to rest on her breast or pubic hair. Or he would wedge his erection between her buttocks or, given the chance, her thighs. At first, he did these things only briefly and while she slept, but soon he gained greater excitement from pretending *he* was asleep and 'accidentally' doing things while *she* was awake. Not once did his daughter show any sexual response, but neither did she complain, except once with a 'Be careful, Dad' when, with his penis wedged between her thighs from behind her, he ejaculated over her pubic hair.

His main torment, though, was psychological. One thought was preoccupying him so much that he became unable to write. He kept reliving the night his daughter had been conceived, probing his memory for every nuance of conversation.

He had been at a party and, on a visit to the toilet had heard a woman sobbing in one of the bedrooms. Once he had calmed her, she told him she had just been raped – that she hadn't wanted to go all the way, but that the man had been just too strong for her. He had stayed with her, fetching her a drink, trying to soothe her, to help her decide what to do. There was no point in going to the police, she said – she couldn't face them, and in any case, she thought she had managed to pull away just before he ejaculated, so there were probably no sperm inside her. As they continued to drink in the dark solitude of the bedroom, his soothing had become stroking, her gratitude had become response, and before they knew what was happening they were having sex. She went home with him that night, moved in with him a month later, and eight months after that gave birth to their daughter. If she had not been conceived on the night they met, it could not have been long after. But it might have been before.

The thought that it was not him but the rapist, or even some previous lover, who was his 'daughter's' father had always been at the back of his mind. But now that he had become so sexually infatuated with her, the thought had become an obsession. Every night as he lay by her side, his whole body yearning to inseminate her, the possibility that she wasn't his child consumed him. He wanted to tell her, but worried that if she knew he might not be her father, she might leave his bed rather than be tempted to occupy it as his lover.

It happened when she was sixteen. He had always been liberal-minded over alcohol and although his younger daughter, now ten, hated the stuff, his son was beginning to develop a taste for it. His elder daughter enjoyed wine, though rarely got drunk. By now, the son was sleeping in a room of his own. The youngest still insisted on having her bed in her father's room, but now rarely got in with him, not least because her elder sister wouldn't let her.

One night when he had opened an extra bottle of wine at dinner, he had to physically put his elder daughter to bed, trying hard not to wake her sister as he undressed himself and then struggled to remove her clothes, one by one. How he restrained himself from making love to her as she sprawled naked on the bed, he would never know. But while she was in her drunken sleep, he did something he had not done before. While ejaculating against her back, he placed his fingers in her vagina. Minutes later, he too fell asleep.

They woke at three to the sound of an approaching thunderstorm. As the lightning grew more frequent and the thunder intensified, he could feel his daughter becoming ever more tense in his arms — she had never lost her fear of thunder. A loud clap had her turn and face him, asking him to hold her. Another clap and she was clutching him tight. Through the open window, they could hear and smell the torrential rain as it hit the trees. With nature following its course outside, it seemed to him almost as if she didn't notice his penis gently and slowly move itself further and further inside her. All the time the storm raged, they lay still, arms, legs and genitals locked together. He didn't thrust and she didn't move, save to flinch at each clap of thunder. He didn't want to ejaculate, but only because he wanted to savour for as long as possible the physical and emotional union for which he had waited so long. All through the thirty minutes that they were joined, he stroked her hair and gently kissed her face, more like the comforting father he used to be than the lover he now was. Twice she whispered words he couldn't hear above the noise of the rain, once a few minutes after he had entered her and once when eventually, unable to hold back any longer, he shuddered and ejaculated inside her. But her sounds were not those of a woman on the crest of sexual excitement; rather, they were murmurs of affection and contentment.

That night triggered a sexual relationship as intense and active as any between a young woman and a man twenty-five years her senior could be. In the heat of the moment he convinced himself the girl wasn't his daughter, that she was just a young and attractive female, no different from any other. But still he didn't tell her. She seemed so content with their situation and was so obviously relishing having him teach her about sex that he was afraid his paternity doubts could drive her away from him.

On all occasions except the first they took contraceptive precautions, though pointlessly, as it turned out. He noticed the signs first, and within six weeks of her losing her virginity a home test confirmed that she was pregnant. From the moment he saw that thin blue line, everything changed. He knew there was a genetic risk of some sort to incestuously conceived babies. She seemed not to realise this – or if she did, she didn't mention it. Only once did he suggest she might have an abortion, but she reacted so badly that he never raised the subject again. She wanted his baby, she said, and she was going to be the mother to his child that her own mother had never been. They told her brother and sister, and anybody else who asked, that the father of her baby was someone from school whom she refused to name. The man read everything he could about the possible genetic problems of incest, and derived some reassurance from discovering that the dangers were only more likely, not inevitable.

As the months passed and his daughter swelled, his distress mounted, not only from fears for the health of the forthcoming baby but also over whether he should let her in on his anxieties. On the one hand he was worried she might hear about the dangers to the baby; on the other, he feared the impact of telling her that he might not be her father – the last thing he wanted was that she should have an emotional crisis while pregnant. Most of all, he was worried that, somehow, somebody would find out about their relationship and he would end up in jail. He wondered if it would be a legal defence if he could say he was not his daughter's genetic father.

She was in her seventh month when, not for the first time scouring the library for information on paternity-testing, he found what he was looking for. He had thought that because he could not get tissue from the children's mother it would be out of the question, but evidently, with tissue from the three children and himself there was a good chance of being able to determine paternity. Somehow or other he managed to pull a hair from the head of each of his children, and sent them off with one of his own to a distant laboratory. Six weeks later, still not having received a reply, he phoned the lab only to hear them deny ever receiving the samples. He collected another set and waited as anxiously for the result as he was now waiting for his daughter to give birth. In the end, she got there first, giving birth to a perfectly healthy son two weeks before her time.

Suddenly, the results of the test seemed unimportant as, absorbed in the minutiae of fatherhood, he made preparations for his daughter's return from hospital. He found the test results waiting on the doormat when they arrived home with the newborn. He put the envelope to one side, failing to find the privacy or the motivation to open it for several hours.

Eventually, locked in the bathroom, he opened it. Scanning the mass of disclaimers explaining that in the absence of tissue from the mother all probabilities were lower than normal, at first he had difficulty finding what he was looking for. His sadness when he did made him wish he had remained ignorant. His son, it seemed, was almost certainly his, but his younger daughter, the engaging eleven-year-old whom he adored, was not. Evidently the infidelity of which he had accused her mother on the night she left home had been justified.

He tore up the piece of paper and flushed it down the toilet. As he listened to his baby son crying in a distant room, his thoughts and emotions were in a turmoil. After nearly seventeen years of doubts and suspicions, he finally knew the truth about the paternity of the girl who was now his lover.

F ew words in the language of human relationships arouse the emotions more strongly than 'incest' does. Every culture so far studied prohibits matings between certain categories of people. Yet, in fact, incest has no strict biological definition. It is delimited not by biology but by law, as sexual intercourse between persons too closely related to legally marry. And because marriage laws vary from society to society, acts that are incestuous in one may not be in another. For example, English law defines incest as sexual intercourse between a male and female whom the man knows to be his daughter, sister, half-sister, granddaughter or mother. First cousins can therefore have intercourse or marry and not be guilty of incest, just as they can in Japan. In America, the definition of incest varies from state to state, but in most states first-cousin marriage is considered to be incestuous (except in Rhode Island, where Jews can marry first cousins). Just as today England and the different states of America differ in precisely what they define as incest, so too did pre-industrial societies. The main differences usually concerned cousins: in medieval times, for example, even sixth cousins were not allowed to marry. Most societies, however, prohibited father–daughter, brother–sister and mother–son matings.

Although all cultures have some incest taboo, from time to time

173

sub-groups within societies have been exempted. In Egypt, for example, brother–sister marriages were sanctioned for thousands of years among the ruling dynasties. Cleopatra was probably the most famous of the Ptolemies to marry a sibling – she was both sister and niece to her husband. Similar incest was exercised by the ruling families of ancient Hawaii and the Incas of Peru. The Hindu-Sakta sect in India and the Mormons in Utah (until 1892) also practised brother–sister incest. However, incest has rarely become a majority strategy, except, for instance, in ancient Egypt and Persia, where it was eventually also adopted by 'commoners'. It has been estimated that in the Greek-Egyptian city of Arsinoë eighteen hundred years ago, two-thirds of the marriages were incestuous, mainly between brother and sister. But it seems to be a characteristic of the human species -- and most others, as we shall see – that intercourse between close relatives is normally avoided.

It is very difficult to present figures on how often intercourse between close relatives *does* occur in modern industrial societies. On the one hand, many cases must go unreported – estimates suggest 75 per cent of father–daughter incest and even more of brother–sister. On the other hand, many of the reported cases may be unfounded. Whether incest is actually more or less common than the figures suggest we shall probably never know. Not the least of the biologist's problems is that sociologists do not always make a clear distinction between incestuous intercourse, with the resultant chance of conception, and other forms of incestuous sexual interaction. More often than not, intercourse is included with other forms of serious sexual abuse, as the next scene will illustrate. As a very rough indication, the best estimates from the USA seem to suggest that about one female in every fifty who has an older brother will be inseminated by him, one in 150 by her father, and – the story of Oedipus notwithstanding – hardly any by her son (but then, Jocasta wasn't Oedipus' genetic mother, anyway).

Most reported cases of father–daughter intercourse are probably coercive: that is to say, fathers *forcing* sexual acts on naïve or helpless young girls. This seems to be less true of brother–sister incest. Non-forced incest, as portrayed in the scene above, will be much more rarely reported. How often incest in any form occurs in humans, therefore – and, more importantly from the evolutionary biologist's point of view, how often it leads to pregnancy and birth –

is unknown. Again, the best estimates are that about one in five cases of father–daughter incest end in pregnancy and more, perhaps half, of brother–sister.

At the end of this section, we shall address the question of why some people engage in apparently incestuous acts and some don't. Biologically, the appropriate starting-point for discussion is perhaps to ask not why incest occurs, but rather, why incest, particularly as instigated by males, is not *even more* common than it is. There are two reasons for wondering this: the first is subtle, and the second might be described as sinister.

The first reason is mathematical and concerns the number of genes we pass on to the next generation every time we produce a child. Normally, each of our children carries only 50 per cent of our genes, their other 50 per cent coming from our partner. Obviously, if we could mate with ourselves, our children would contain *nothing but* our genes, which would allow us to pass twice as many on to the next generation every time we reproduce as when we reproduce with somebody else. But mating with a close relative is nearly as good, genetically. If the couple in the scene really were father and daughter, then their son would carry 75 per cent of the father's genes and 75 per cent of the daughter's, because father and daughter share so many genes. This would seem to be a big improvement on the normal 50 per cent.

The second reason is that males are driven by their genetic programming to be forever alert for extra females with whom to reproduce. A young girl, whether a daughter or a younger sister, is an ever-present, naïve, vulnerable and potentially fertile female. She would seem to be an easy target for a male's sexual attention.

So why is it that, despite these two reasons for expecting incest to be relatively common, more often than not fathers and daughters, brothers and sisters, and particularly mothers and sons, *do not* try to reproduce with each other? The answer is that both human males and females and those of other species have a genetically programmed aversion to incest. This shows itself not only in a lack of sexual interest in close relatives, but also in an aversion to the whole idea, and it applies almost as forcefully to non-coercive incest as to coercive.

The sexual abuse of children by members of their family is illustrated in the next scene. Here, we concentrate on the aspect of incest that is more rarely discussed and about which much less is known, that between consenting and affectionate individuals. Compared with violently abusive men, the main character in the scene above is relatively benign. He used no force, no coercion, and little subterfuge. Nor could there be any doubt of the strong affection he felt for his charge, or she for him. Yet it is inevitable that even he, despite the arguably mitigating circumstances generated by his struggles as a lone parent, despite adoring all of his children, and despite the fact that his attraction to his daughter was reciprocated, will be loathed and despised for his actions by the majority of the readers of this book. This in itself is an indication of the strength of our innate aversion to such behaviour, of the negative feelings programmed into the psyche by our genes.

So, why are we programmed to have such an aversion to incest? The simple explanation is that it is a poor avenue to reproductive success. It is disadvantageous, and, as always, the brunt of the disadvantage falls on the female. The main reason incest reduces reproductive output is that it endows couples with an increased chance of producing a child with a genetically transmitted disease. Such children either die young, are infertile, or are unable to attract a partner. To appreciate why, we have to understand the existence of *hitch-hiker genes*.

For every aspect of their development, people receive two sets of genetic instructions: for example, their father's and their mother's instructions about how tall to grow, and what colour of eyes to have. Sometimes, as with height, the two sets of genes compromise. At other times, as with eye colour, one set dominates. For example, the instructions for brown eyes usually dominate those for blue (which are therefore called *recessive*), no matter whether it is the father or the mother who passes them on. So when brown-eye and blue-eye genes meet, the presence of the blue-eye gene invariably stays hidden. If successive descendants carrying a hidden blue-eye gene meet a succession of brown-eyed partners, the presence of the blue-eye instruction in the lineage can sometimes escape detection for generations. Nevertheless, it remains and is passed on. In effect, therefore, the gene *hitch-hikes*, unseen and unexpressed, until it is eventually matched with another blue-eye gene to produce a child who now has *only* the instructions for blue eyes.

This hitch-hiking of recessive genes through the generations can have sinister overtones. Every so often, genes mutate and become different from the genes of either parent. Suppose, for example, a gene for one eye colour, say blue or brown, mutates to become a gene for red eyes. If it is a dominant gene, the mutation will be obvious in the very next generation. But if it is recessive, it can hitch-hike through many generations before it meets another copy of itself, producing an unfortunate child with red eyes.

Red eyes may not be very aesthetically pleasing, but they are not dangerous. Unfortunately, however, many hitch-hiker genes *are* dangerous and may well kill or maim any child who inherits two copies of them. Most of us probably carry one or more such genes around with us. But as long as we are lucky enough not to reproduce with someone else carrying one of these genes, the lethal character of our hitch-hiker will not reveal itself. And even if we *do* reproduce with someone carrying the same hitch-hiker, there is still only a one in four chance that any resulting child will be afflicted, because the gene has to be in both the egg and the sperm for the child to suffer. If it is in only one, it will carry the gene into the next generation, without itself being affected.

Incest doesn't increase the chances of the wrong two gametes fusing with each other, but it does greatly increase the likelihood that a reproductive partner will have exactly the same lethal hitch-hiker. And how much the likelihood increases depends on how common the gene is in the population at large.

Suppose that in the scene above the man had carried a gene that would cause his baby to be malformed, and that this gene was present in 1 per cent of people in the population at large. If he had restricted his sexual activities to women from the wider population, his chances of meeting a reproductive partner with the same hitch-hiker gene would have been only one in a hundred. And even if this had happened, as we have noted, there would still have been only a one in four chance that any child they produced would receive two copies of the dangerous gene. So the chances in such circumstances of a baby being malformed because of that gene would have been one in four hundred. However, in the scene, the man did not restrict his activities to women from the population at large – he had sex with a girl he had raised as his daughter. If she *really was* his genetic daughter, she would have a 50:50 chance of containing the gene for malformation. Add to this the one in four chance that their child might inherit the gene from both of them, and we can see that the chances of its being malformed would be one in eight – a massive fifty times greater risk.

Of course, if it had happened that the father didn't carry *any* dangerous hitch-hiker genes, then genetically speaking an incestuous mating with his daughter would have been as safe as any other. On the other hand, if he had carried more than one such gene the chances would have been even higher than we have just calculated. Various studies of genetic disease in children produced by father–daughter and brother–sister incest indicate that about half the children may be afflicted. Studies of the offspring of first cousins in Japan, Brazil, France, India and Britain suggest an increase of around 4 per cent in the children's death rate and in those of uncles and nieces it is about 10 per cent. A little mathematics shows that these figures indicate that people are carrying around, on average, between one and four dangerous hitch-hiker genes. Actual risks from incest, therefore, vary from person to person, but for the purposes of this discussion we shall assume an average risk for father–daughter incest of one in eight (for each dangerous hitch-hiker gene). Mothers and sons would run the same risk as fathers and daughters if they reproduced incestuously. The risk for brothers and sisters, however, is one in sixteen.

When the man and the girl embarked on the sexual acts that produced their child, the man could not decide whether they were running an increased genetic risk or not. If she *was* his daughter the risk was higher, but he didn't know whether she was or not. When the baby seemed normal and healthy, he was reassured – and with some justification. Probably the majority of dangerous hitch-hiker genes would have revealed themselves by the time the baby was born. The foetus might have been malformed, leading in all probability to miscarriage or a still-birth, or a malformation might have been evident when the baby was born. However, if the piece of paper the man flushed down the toilet had told him that his lover really was his genetic daughter, there could still be problems ahead. Some genetic diseases do not show their effects until a child is several years old. One example is VLINCL (variant late infantile neuronal ceroid lipofuscosis), which is more common in Finland than anywhere else. Affected children merely seem clumsy in their first few years but, as time goes on, they suffer from seizures and become blind and paralysed. Usually, they die in young adulthood.

It should be stressed that incest does not *cause* these genetic problems – it simply increases the chances that they might occur. *Any couple*, who are unfortunate enough to carry the same dangerous hitch-hiker gene whether their relationship is incestuous or not, can encounter such problems. In some parts of Finland, for example, where population size is small, mobility limited and choice of mates restricted, genetic diseases such as VLINCL occur quite frequently. Family tree studies in Finland have traced the VLINCL gene back through thirteen generations, to the beginning of the seventeenth century. It has clearly hitch-hiked through over four hundred years of unsuspecting carriers before surfacing in one boy, and the best estimate is that the person in whom the mutation occurred lived about six hundred years ago. By comparison, the person in whom the cystic fibrosis mutation occurred is estimated to have lived about fifty thousand years ago, before the last ice age. Now, one in twenty-five people in England and France carry this hitch-hiker gene, and one in every two thousand five hundred is born with the condition.

So far, our discussion of incest has revealed two opposing factors. On the one hand, as we pointed out earlier, reproducing with a close relative could have genetic benefits because of the number of shared 'good' genes that would be passed on to the child. But against this has to be weighed the risk of unleashing dangerous hitch-hiker genes. Although the trade-off between these two factors is actually a net disadvantage for father–daughter, mother–son and brother–sister couples, it is not so for all levels of relatedness (and mathematically, it would be possible to calculate the level that offers the best trade-off between costs and benefits). There is no single answer, though, because, as we have seen, everything depends on how many dangerous hitch-hiker genes a person is carrying. If he or she is carrying none at all, father–daughter and brother–sister are actually the best trade-offs. With one such gene, the best trade-off will be just about at the level of first cousins, and as the number of dangerous genes increases, so the best level of relatedness retreats.

If humans and other species are behaving in the way that should be most favoured by natural selection, therefore, we should expect to find that they avoid mating with very close relatives but show some preference for more distant ones, if there are any available. And that is what we find. First, incest is as uncommon in other animals as it is in humans. Studies have produced figures ranging from about 1 per cent of matings in a wild bird, the great tit, to about 10 per cent in a feral mammal, the horse, living in the restricted environment of the Camargue in southern France. Second, studies of animals as varied as rats, horses and monkeys have shown that, when they have a free choice, they do show some preference for distant relatives. There are no controlled studies of such a preference in humans. In France, the average degree of genetic relatedness for couples who marry is sixth cousin. In Britain, it is slightly lower. As a matter of interest, Charles Darwin, without knowing the calculations that evolutionary biologists would make in his name a century later, followed his instincts, married his first cousin Emma, and had many children.

These findings lead us to ask how natural selection has managed to engineer such avoidance and preferences. It has done so via three main mechanisms. One is the dispersal of family members before they start to reproduce; another is an aversion to mating with individuals known throughout childhood; and the third is the ability to judge similarities and differences that could indicate kinship.

First, families disperse because natural selection has programmed children, as they reach adolescence, to become restless and to want to travel and explore. These urges eventually take the adolescent away from the family home. This phenomenon is not unique to humans; it is found in all vertebrates. In many species, this restlessness has been fashioned differentially so that *one* of the sexes (usually males in mammals and females in birds) becomes much more stricken than the other with the urge to travel. In a few species, such as some primates – howler monkeys and gibbons, for example – both sexes get almost equal urges to explore during adolescence. Humans fall somewhere between the two. Males either have more motivation to explore, or, in most societies, maybe just more freedom. But females by no means lack such urges, and in industrial societies have much more freedom to follow their inclinations. Whichever the system shown by any particular species, families disperse before the young begin to reproduce. Adolescent exploration is discussed in the discussion following Scene 20; it has several functions, and one of them is to reduce the chances of incest by separating family members during the time that they are searching for a mate.

Second, natural selection has shaped mate selection so that both sexes, but particularly females, have an aversion to mating with other individuals in the family unit. The basic rule is simple: don't mate with anybody you have associated with closely during your childhood, because he or she could be a close relative. Animals, therefore, find greater attraction in strangers than in familiar individuals. This preference has been demonstrated in mammals as diverse as horses, squirrels and red monkeys. Humans seem to be subconsciously programmed to follow the same rule. In one study of Israeli kibbutzim in the 1960s, for example, where children are raised communally, it was found that individuals never married anyone with whom they associated when young. Even though their brains knew that most of their associates were unlikely to be closely related to them, their bodies saw a risk in reproducing with such individuals.

Third, but with more limited success, natural selection has tried to embellish this aversion to mating with close childhood acquaintances with an added aversion to mating with individuals who are so similar that they could be related. Experiments on bees, wasps, frogs, toads, reptiles and mammals such as prairie dogs have demonstrated some ability to distinguish between kin and non-kin, even when raised apart. However, as we noted in the context of fathers being able to judge their paternity, none of these acts of discrimination are absolute. Mistakes are made and the behaviour shown towards kin and non-kin varies only in degree, not in kind. Basically, the yardstick seems to be that the more similar any two individuals are in appearance, smell and behaviour, the more likely they are to be closely related. Thus, animals should preferentially mate with individuals who differ by no less than about the degree expected for first cousins. We do not know whether such yardsticks are part of choosing a mate in humans, but evolutionary biology would predict that they should be.

The way in which these three mechanisms combine to influence the level of incest was neatly demonstrated in a study of the wild horses in the Camargue. In horses, the most successful stallions have a harem of females, most of which are closely related to each other – as mothers, daughters, sisters, aunts and nieces. From time to time, however, these close-knit female groups do allow a new, unrelated mare to join. The stallion who guards the harem and who mates with the adult mares whenever they come into heat is sometimes a cousin to one or more of them, but rarely is he any of his mates' father, brother or son. Most often he is unrelated to any of them.

The mares in the harem raise their sons and daughters to adolescence, at which point the sons become restless and leave to roam around the Camargue, looking for the chance to create a harem of their own. What the adolescent daughters do depends on circumstances. If their father is no longer in charge of the harem, they may stay with their mother and reproduce with the new stallion. If their father *is* still in charge, they leave their mother and go to join a new harem. When they do, they preferentially move to one that is guarded by a stallion who isn't a close relative and that contains one or two females they already know and to whom they may be related. These horses live in tight-knit family units and in the relatively restricted environment of the Camargue. If natural selection had not produced incest avoidance behaviour, many – perhaps the majority – of matings would be incestuous. As it is, only about 10 per cent fall into this category.

Clearly, there is nothing uniquely human about an aversion to incest. But if humans, like these other animals, have evolved a range of mechanisms to avoid it, how is it that it still sometimes occurs? Why do some people, like the couple in the scene above, not feel this aversion and so go ahead with sexual acts that others could not even contemplate? There are two main reasons. First, there is a difference in costs to males and females. Second, there are differences between people as regards how confident they can be that they really are related to the other person.

On the whole, males are much more prepared to risk incest than are females. Fathers are more likely to risk incest than their daughters, and brothers more likely than their sisters. (In the scene above there was just a hint of such a difference.) The reason for this is that although both males and females in these pairings experience similar benefits if all goes well, and a similar chance of things *not* going well, they do not experience similar costs if their incest does produce a child with genetic disease. More often than not, females bear the brunt of parenthood. Not least, they have to endure the risks of pregnancy and labour. Also, because it is men who are much more likely to leave their partner to raise a child single-handedly than vice versa, whatever our scene may have indicated, the female is more likely to end up as a lone parent. This can take its own toll, as we shall see later, and it can only be more problematical if the child has a serious genetic disease.

A child with such a disease, then, is much more likely to reduce its mother's reproductive output than its father's. As a result, daughters and sisters have evolved to be much more resistant to incest than have fathers and brothers. And most resistant of all are mothers. For not only do they run the same risks as just described for sisters and daughters, they face an additional factor – the *certainty* that they are genetically related to their incestuous target.

The risk of genetic disease if mother and son reproduce is therefore as high as it can be – about one in eight – as regards any dangerous hitch-hiker gene the mother might carry. Fathers and daughters and brothers and sisters, on the other hand, cannot be as confident in their relatedness. And it makes a difference. As the man in our scene realised, albeit imprecisely, if the young girl was not really his daughter, there were no particular genetic dangers to their relationship. If she *was* his daughter, the risk was one in eight. A similar principle applies to brothers and sisters. Although siblings can be fairly certain, except in the case of adoption, that they share the same mother, they cannot be as certain that they share the same father. Whereas full siblings have a one in sixteen chance of producing a child with a genetic disease, half-siblings (same mother, different father) have a lower chance on average. If their mother carries a dangerous hitch-hiker gene, the risk is still one in sixteen, as it is for full siblings, but if it is one of their fathers who carries the dangerous gene, their relationship brings no greater danger than if they were simply members of the population at large. Natural selection will have done its best to programme their bodies to judge relatedness, in the way we have described, but inevitably mistakes will often happen.

This is the final irony of incest. If, despite the fact that people *really are* programmed to avoid incestuous relationships, a person's body urges him or her to enter an apparently incestuous relationship, it is probably because it judges that the target is not actually a close relative. If it is correct, of course, the act is not incestuous, but bodies are not infallible when it comes to such subtle judgements. Paradoxically, therefore, 'incest' is most likely to occur when, genetically, the act is least likely to be incestuous. In the scene, the fact that the father felt sexually drawn towards his daughter, and she to him, could well have been an indication that, at least subconsciously, they both suspected they weren't really father and daughter.

The combination of differences in confidence in relatedness and differences between men and women in their levels of aversion probably goes a long way towards explaining why a few people feel drawn to incest whereas the majority do not. On top of this, circumstance and opportunity probably also play a part. The rather extreme family situation portrayed in the scene above, combined with the liberal, bohemian attitudes of the father and daughter, will all have contributed. But the attraction they found in each other will have come from within.

The risk of unleashing hitch-hiker genes is only a risk, not a certainty, and some animals have been pushed, by evolution or by human intervention, into situations in which the advantages of inbreeding outweigh the costs. What is of interest here is not the nature of these situations, but the fact that when incest becomes universal within a species the genetic problems it generates all but disappear. To put it another way, the genetic problems that make incest disadvantageous, something that most animals avoid, *only exist because most animals do avoid it*. It is precisely because two copies of such genes rarely meet each other that they are able to hitch-hike through the generations, always present but hidden. Whenever two copies *do* meet, the individual who inherits them dies, never to reproduce, and both copies of the gene disappear. In the few cases where incest has become universal within a species, such genes have met so often that they have quickly disappeared from the population.

One of the most interesting examples is a mite that infests rats. In this species, the mother gives birth to live young, just like humans. But the sex ratio is heavily biased towards females – only one son but up to twenty daughters. Not only is incest the norm for this species, it happens even before the young are born. While still inside the mother's body, the son roams around, inseminating the daughters. So when the daughters are born, they are already incestuously pregnant! The son dies while still inside his mother.

Far less usual, but nevertheless an illustration of how successful incest can be, is the case of the golden hamster. The whole world-wide population of golden hamsters in laboratories, pet shops and homes is descended from a single litter, captured in Syria in 1930. Only three members of this litter were retained in captivity, and it is the progeny of these that were first imported to the United States in 1938. The matings that took place after the incestuous mating from this original population purged any of the original dangerous hitch-hiker genes that were present in the wild population and allowed that single mother's (and absent father's) descendants to populate the world. New hitch-hiker genes have since arisen through mutation, but even so the hamster population is living testimony to the fact that some animals can thrive on incest.

It is because humans belong to the much more numerous band of species that have evolved an aversion to incest that the behaviour of the man and the girl in the scene is unusual, and that most readers will have found their behaviour distasteful. Yet what if their relationship wasn't, after all, incestuous?

Eventually, the man in the scene found out whether his sexual acts with the young girl were indeed incestuous. The laboratory's written judgement on his paternity would have allowed him to calculate mathematically the risks generated by their sexual liaison. But in all other respects, does it really matter what was on that piece of paper? Whatever it said, they were the same two people, with the same history, the same circumstances and the same feelings. Their bodies if not their brains had decided that, given their situation, a potentially incestuous relationship might well be a route to reproductive success. As far as they could tell from their baby's health and vigour, there had been no unfavourable genetic repercussions from their behaviour, but what would happen if they had further children could be another matter.

In the discussion following Scene 15, it was implied that whenever there were doubts about paternity, men were more likely to show favouritism towards their supposed daughters than towards their supposed sons. We can now see why. If a boy is not a man's son, then he has little further to gain from the youngster in his pursuit of reproductive success, save as a contributor towards the family resources. However, if a girl is a man's daughter, she is his pathway to reproductive success, no matter who fathers her children. If she *is not* his daughter, then she is a potential mate.

We have just seen this principle in action in one guise, and we are about to see it in another. The next scene deals with the sexual abuse of young girls by 'family' members.

SCENE 17
Child Abuse

'Don't go out tonight, Mummy,' the young girl pleaded. 'I hate it when you go out.' The woman sighed. Her daughter was thirteen and on the verge of womanhood.

'I have to,' she said. 'It's an important night for your father and I want to be there with him. Anyway, your brother will look after you – there's no need to worry.'

'He's not my brother and I wish he wasn't here. I hate him!'

'Don't start all that again,' the woman snapped. 'He's nice – and he's *very* nice to *you*. I haven't got time to listen to another of your stories.'

With some difficulty, she stood up and prepared to leave her daughter's bedroom. Pregnant again for the second time in three years, she didn't feel like coping with another sullen mood from her elder daughter.

Pausing in the doorway, she reminded her for the third time that her baby sister was asleep, that her young brother was waiting to have his bedtime story, and that she wouldn't be back until after midnight.

'Now don't stay in your room all night,' she added as an afterthought. 'Go and talk to your brother. He'd like that.'

As she walked gingerly downstairs, the woman wished that her daughter was behaving better. The young girl's dislike of her new partner and his son was the only difficulty at the moment. She could scarcely believe how her life had improved in the past five years, since that day when she had woken to find her partner gone, leaving her to look after their two children. At the time, their daughter was only eight and their son not yet one. For six months the woman had struggled on her own before meeting her current partner. A widower, he had a twelve-year-old son of his own. He was already reasonably well off financially and had excellent career prospects. Within two months of their meeting she was pregnant, and now she was pregnant again.

At first, her new partner had been unable to do enough for her and her children, but then followed three long years during which she wondered if she had made the right decision in moving in with him. The worst period had been from late in her pregnancy until their first child, a girl, was about nine months old. During this time the young son from her previous relationship was going through the 'terrible twos' and spent much of his time crying and throwing temper tantrums. This created a great deal of tension between her and her new partner, which was aggravated by the excessive crying of their baby daughter. Her partner was working particularly hard at the time, and sometimes cracked under the strain. Even in her presence, he would sometimes hit her son distressingly hard when he became impossible to cope with. And she was sure that when she was not around he was hitting him even harder, for she kept finding unexplained bruises on his young body.

Now, however, she felt an optimism about the future that surpassed anything she had experienced since they first met. In a few weeks' time her stepson would be leaving for college, her first two children were doing particularly well at school, her three-year-old was a delight – and she was pregnant again. If it wasn't for her elder daughter's irrational hatred of her stepbrother and stepfather, her whole world would be wonderful.

Just at the moment, anyway, the woman's main concern was to enjoy the coming evening. It was a special event, and she was looking forward to it. She scarcely noticed that her daughter didn't emerge from her room to see them off as she and her partner, resplendently dressed, climbed into the chauffeur-driven limousine that had been sent to collect them. It was a taste of the life that she hoped awaited her in the very near future.

The girl stayed in her room as long as she could, doing her homework, but eventually gave in to her younger brother's demands for her to read him a story. Despite her attempts to read him something different, he insisted that she read him *Hansel and Gretel* – for the fifth night in a row. As she switched off his light and said goodnight, then looked in on her 'baby sister', she could hear her stepbrother moving around downstairs against the background noise of some sporting event on television.

Reassured that he would be occupied for a while, she went to the bathroom for a shower. At least that was one room she could lock. She had been asking for a lock on her bedroom door for over a year, ever since it had started, but neither her mother nor stepfather would agree. It was too dangerous, they said. What would happen if she had an accident and they couldn't get in? Afraid to tell them the real reason why she wanted a lock, she was reluctant to even try to persuade them to change their mind.

Showered, and wrapped in her bath-robe, she ran to her room and wedged a chair against the door even though she knew from past experience that it wouldn't hold if he was really determined. He didn't always insist on coming in when her mother and stepfather were out, but it had happened ten times or so since it first began about a year earlier. She tried to finish her homework, but her apprehension prevented her from concentrating. For an hour or more she lay on her bed, listening to music through her headphones, eyes rarely leaving the door. Despite herself, her attention began to fade and twice she had to wrench herself back from sleep. To her dismay, she realised that it was going to be impossible to last out until her mother returned: she had to go to the toilet. She hung on as long as she could, but she got more and more uncomfortable until she just had to risk it. Moving the chair, she opened the door slowly and listened. The sound of the television drifted upstairs. Clutching her bath-robe around her, she ran to the bathroom, relieved herself as quickly as she could, then dashed back. But she had not been fast enough. No sooner had she entered her bedroom than the door closed quietly behind her. Even before she had time to turn round, her stepbrother had his hand over her mouth, stifling her yelp.

'We're not going to do anything silly, are we?' he said. 'We know what would happen to a little girl who screamed or told stories, don't we?'

She nodded as best she could, fear freezing every muscle. The first time he had done it, he had brought with him a vicious-looking knife. He hadn't brought it since, but had promised her that if she ever told anybody, he would find her and use it. On his second visit, the only time she had tried to resist, he had punched her so hard in the stomach that she had been fighting for breath for minutes on end. Ever since, she had simply done everything he asked. On the first few occasions he had humiliated her but hadn't actually had sex with her. But the last five times he had penetrated her. Tonight, still standing behind her, he took off her bath-robe and made her stand in front of the mirror. Reaching in front and stroking her pubescent body, he remarked that she was rapidly becoming 'quite the little woman'.

At least tonight it was quick. He made her undress him, then fetched the chair that she had wedged uselessly against the door. Making her rest palms-down on the chair while she bent forwards towards the mirror, he entered her from behind – he always entered from behind – so that he could watch his performance in the mirror. When he had finished he said, 'Thank you', told her that one day she would learn to enjoy it, and left her to clean herself up and crawl into bed.

It happened twice more before he went back to college. On the day he left, she felt as if a huge black cloud was lifting. If only she might never have to see him again. Her mother noticed her change in mood, but didn't imagine it was all due to her stepson's departure. In any case, she became far too preoccupied with the last few months of her pregnancy to worry unduly about what she assumed were just the mood swings of a pubescent girl. The last two weeks were marred by complications due to raised blood pressure. She was taken into hospital for observation, and five days later labour was induced to avoid further deterioration of her condition.

The girl was thrilled when she first saw her new half-brother. Mother and baby would have to stay in for a few days longer, but they would soon be home and, despite the imminent return of her stepbrother from college, she was looking forward to having a baby to help look after again. She was in high spirits when she, her stepfather and her young brother and half-sister returned home from their trip to the hospital. Between them, she and her stepfather put the two younger children to bed; then, for once feeling warm towards the man, she sat with him in the lounge instead of retreating into her room. In celebratory mood himself, her stepfather offered her a vodka and orange. She accepted, pleased to be treated as an adult, and quickly drank it. She accepted a second, little appreciating the size of the measures he was giving her. She became rather giggly – everything either of them said seemed hilarious. She had all but finished her fourth large vodka when the room began to spin. Only minutes later, she knew she was going to be sick. Standing up too quickly, her legs buckled and she collapsed on to the floor, then vomited.

When she woke the next morning, suffering the first hangover of her life, she found herself in bed with her stepfather. They were both naked, and the by now familiar stickiness between her legs told her at least part of the story. He was already awake, watching her.

'What would your mother say if she ever found out what you've been up to?' he said, the threat in his voice belying his smile.

When she asked what she *had* 'been up to', he told her a story that she found hard to believe – of how, after she had been sick, she had asked him to take off her clothes and then wash her, before seducing him into having sex with her. And all this, he pointed out, on the day her mother had given birth to her new baby brother. But she mustn't worry. He would never tell her, he promised. It would be their secret – as long as she was a good girl. When she asked what he meant by 'a good girl' he showed her, inseminating her for what he knew, but she didn't, was the fourth time that night.

Never had she had a longer shower than on that morning, as she tried to rid her body of its dirtiness and her mind of the rising guilt and the fear of her mother's wrath. But any cleansing was short-lived, because her stepfather visited her again the following night, and again the night after that. So desperate did she feel about this new ordeal she was suffering that she was almost relieved when his son returned from college for his vacation. Neither would visit her with the other in the house, she assumed.

Two days later, her mother brought the baby home. Despite post-natal soreness and fatigue, she was thrilled to be home, almost as thrilled as she was at her partner's news of promotion. In addition, there was the prospect in a month's time of accompanying him on a business trip to an exotic location; they could take the two youngest children, all expenses paid. Elated by life's prospects, she almost didn't hear her daughter's sobs as she passed by her bedroom on her first night home.

She found her huddled on her bed, distraught. Anticipating nothing more serious than the trauma of a break-up with her boyfriend, she asked what the matter was. The young girl hugged her close, sobbing into her shoulder, but didn't speak for some time. The mother spoke soothingly, stroking her daughter's hair, repeatedly asking her to tell her what was distressing her. In the end she could keep her secret no longer.

'Please stop them from doing it,' she sobbed. 'Please ... please ... it really isn't my fault, it really isn't. Please believe me – please stop them. I can't stand it any more.'

The mother tried to calm her down, and to find out more. Amidst the sobs she caught the name of her stepson, and her heart sank. Since he had been at college she had been spared these tirades, but it seemed she had to listen to her daughter's paranoid dislikes and fears all over again. She really wasn't in the mood.

'Don't start that again,' she said, her soothing tone giving way to irritation. 'He's only been in the house a day and you've started again.'

'But he did it to me again last night – he's been doing it for years. But last night he tied me to the bed. Look at my wrists and ankles. It was horrible. Please stop him. I hate him, I really hate him!'

'Keep your voice down,' the mother warned as she examined the girl. Maybe there were marks on her wrists and ankles, but she couldn't be sure, and what she could see might have been caused by anything. Although she was upset at seeing her daughter so distressed, she was making so much noise that more than anything she was worried her partner might hear. The last thing she wanted was for her children to anger him again.

'Why on earth would he tie you up?' she asked in genuine confusion. 'Was it a game, or are you just making up stories again to get him into trouble?'

The daughter couldn't believe her mother didn't know what she was talking about. 'It wasn't a game! I'm not making it up! He took off my clothes, tied me up and had sex with me! He's been doing it for years! He said he'd kill me if I told you!'

'Don't be silly! What do you mean, he's been having sex with you? For years? Of course he hasn't, you mustn't say things like that.'

'He has, he has. Honestly he has. You must believe me, mum. Please believe me. Please. I'm not lying.'

Suddenly, a deep male voice obliterated her daughter's shrill cries. 'Don't be absurd!' the woman's partner boomed, his voice distorted by fear and anger. He had been listening outside the door. 'How dare you make up such stories about my son?'

Shocked by the intrusion, mother and daughter stared at him, one fearful for her future, the other for her life. The girl edged over to her mother for protection, nestling under her encircling arm. 'Don't let him hurt me,' she whimpered.

The mother pulled her close, but all the time she was speaking she was focusing on her angry partner, trying to reassure him with her eyes while reassuring her daughter with her voice. 'Don't be silly, darling. He won't hurt you. He's on your side. We're all on your side. Nobody's going to hurt you – but you must stop making up these stories. It's not fair. It'll cause trouble.'

'But they're not stories. Honestly they're not . . . and . . . anyway . . .' she hesitated, realising the enormity of what she was about to say, '. . . he's not on my side. He does it too. They both did it last night.'

Her stepfather forced a laugh. 'What?' he exclaimed, feigning an air of amused amazement. 'What? We both did it? How?' Then, resorting to sarcasm, 'Don't tell me – we took it in turns.'

'You did, you know you did,' said the sobbing girl, glaring at him now. She turned back to her mother. 'Honestly, mum, they did take it in turns. He came into the room while it was happening. I thought he was going to help me because he dragged him off and pushed him away. But he didn't help. He didn't even untie me. He just looked at me. Then he got it out and he did it to me too – and he did it so hard, he really hurt me.'

The girl glared again at her stepfather. She was still sobbing, but now in full flow she was angry as well. 'When he'd finished, he told him he could have another go. I couldn't believe it. I was tied to the bed and he was having sex with me too, and he just stood and watched.' She stopped and wiped the tears from her cheeks, trying to catch her breath between her sobs. Suddenly she was afraid again. Her stepfather shook his head.

'She's crazy,' he said to his partner. 'She's sick in the head – and she's dangerous. A story like that could ruin me. It could ruin *us*.'

The mother withdrew her arm from around her daughter's shoulders. She looked briefly at her partner, then stared back into her daughter's eyes as if trying to read her mind. Then, without a word, she slapped her hard across the face.

This scene is every parent's nightmare, second in horror only to the prospect of having a child kidnapped, abused and then murdered. The fear that a child might be physically or sexually abused is ever-present for parents in modern industrial societies – and with good reason, for it is relatively common. In the USA and Europe, as many as one in four girls by the age of fourteen and one in three by the age of eighteen, and one in six boys by the age of sixteen, have been abused in some way, aggressively or sexually. So what *is* child abuse, who are the abusers, and how does the phenomenon fit within the context of evolutionary biology?

It should not be difficult by this point to anticipate how the behaviour of the two men in the scene we have just witnessed will be interpreted by the evolutionary biologist. The stepfather was violent towards his baby stepson when times were hard, and showed simple favouritism towards his own son when circumstances were a little better. Then, when they improved further, he exploited his new partner's dependence on him by sexually abusing her daughter. Similarly, his son took advantage of his and his father's situation by also sexually abusing the girl. By pursuing their own interests in these ways, the man and his son could well have enhanced their reproductive output – in which case, there is every chance that in abuse we are dealing with a phenomenon that has been shaped by natural selection and programmed into human behaviour.

From time to time, evolutionary biology makes itself unpopular by concluding that behaviour thought by most to be unpleasant, immoral, antisocial or dangerous has a biological basis. Usually, just as we are doing, it argues that the behaviour concerned has been favoured by evolution because its perpetrators gain a reproductive advantage from their actions. At this point we begin to tread on dangerous ground. In charting the evolution of such behaviour, and in concluding that it is programmed into a person's psyche by his or her genes, the evolutionary biologist may give the impression of condoning or even encouraging that behaviour. This is not the case. The evolutionary biologist's sole interest is to try to understand behaviour, then to pass on that understanding to society at large to use in the best way it can. There is no point in trying to force on to a phenomenon some politically and socially acceptable interpretation, if this is not the reality of the situation. Child abuse is a problem within modern industrial societies and of major concern to all parents within those societies, and evolutionary biology has a unique part to play in helping to understand it. Without understanding, the problem stands no chance of being solved.

Child abuse has two main elements – violence and sex – either or both of which may be present in any given instance. To many sociologists working in our society, any violent interaction, and almost any sexual interaction, *violent or not*, with a child, is abusive. To the evolutionary biologist, the term 'abuse' is only really appropriate if the victim suffers a reduction in his or her long-term reproductive output as a result of a particular action. We shall return to the definition of abuse later, but this will serve as a starting-point.

If we are using the sociological definition, we can say that we have already encountered abuse in two guises in this book. The first was the neglect, or at worst violence, shown towards individual children in the context of sibling rivalry and parental favouritism. The second was the non-violent incest between father and daughter. Both took place within biological families, but we concluded that both kinds of abuse were more likely to happen when a man's confidence in his paternity is low. It follows that abuse should be most likely when a man is *certain* he is not a girl's father, or an adolescent her brother, and so on, as in the case of a step-relative. This is the situation illustrated in the scene above, and it is also the overwhelming conclusion reached by sociologists and evolutionary biologists alike.

This scene and its interpretation are concerned with abuse, not specifically with step-parents and blended families. (A discussion of the pros and cons of non-nuclear families will follow the next scene.) To avoid misunderstanding, we should stress here that, on average, blended families work to the reproductive advantage of all – or most – of their members. This is why they have been predisposed by natural selection to function as they do. More often than not the children in a blended family *are not* abused by their step-parent – or their foster- or adoptive parent. Even so, the experiences of the girl in the scene illustrate an unfortunate fact: children are *more likely* to be abused by stepfathers and stepbrothers and other male step-relatives than they are by members of their biological family.

Violent and sexual abuse will be considered separately, and we begin with violence. Studies in Canada and Britain show that when a man lives in a blended family he is seven times more likely to abuse his stepchildren than his genetic children, and *one hundred times* more likely to kill them. This increased risk of violence and murder on the part of stepfathers is greatest for young babies up to the age of two. How often does the murder of a child fall under the media spotlight and a full-scale investigation launched, only for it to transpire eventually that the murderer was in fact the child's stepfather or at least a man who has had some sexual contact with the mother?

When biological fathers and stepfathers murder children, their motives and methods differ. Biological fathers tend to kill their children as part of 'family planning', when circumstances deteriorate so badly that the parents can no longer adequately raise the number of children they produced when times were better. In contrast, stepfathers kill their stepchildren in order to avoid having to raise someone else's children. Such differences in motive are reflected in the methods that genetic fathers and stepfathers use. Most children killed by their genetic fathers are killed by non-assaultive means such as smothering, whereas four out of five of the victims of stepfathers are beaten to death.

The murder of a stepchild is the ultimate in step-parental disfavouritism. It is the absolute removal of a child whom, consciously or subconsciously, the murderer sees as a threat to his own reproductive output because that child is a drain on the family's resources. Neglect and violence are less extreme ways of trying to achieve the same thing. Neglect is an attempt to minimise the child's demands on resources. Violence is an attempt to force him or her to leave the family. It is because violent abuse is a reaction to what the perpetrator sees as an avoidable drain on the family resources that, like so many other aspects of family life, it is strongly influenced by the extent of those resources. So it is not surprising that poverty and deteriorating circumstances are two of the most commonly observed triggers for the violent abuse of children.

The mistreatment of stepchildren by stepfathers is not a modern malaise, some by-product of industrialisation. It has a biological basis, shaped by natural selection, and is found both in non-industrial human cultures and in other animals. Studies of the forest-dwelling Ache people in Paraguay, for example, showed that 9 per cent of children raised by a mother and a stepfather were killed before their fifteenth birthday, compared with less than 1 per cent of those raised by two genetic parents. Amongst other animals, the best-known instance of violence towards stepchildren is that of male lions. Lion prides contain two or three males and up to eight females and their young. Wandering over the savanna are bachelor groups of two or three males, each group looking for a pride from which they can oust the current males. If they succeed, the first thing they do is kill the cubs – their stepchildren. The lionesses are brought into heat by the loss of their young, giving the new males an early chance to sire their own offspring. Some monkeys that live in harem groups behave in the same way. If the harem owner is driven out, the new male kills his offspring. Even monkeys that live in much larger groups, consisting of many males and females, show similar behaviour. More often than not, a male acts aggressively towards young which, because he has never had sex with their mother, or because he didn't have sex with her at the relevant time, cannot be his.

In the scene above, and so far in this interpretation, we have concentrated on the violent abuse of children by males – stepfathers and stepbrothers. But step*mothers*, too, are more likely to abuse and kill their stepchildren than their genetic children. However, no study has yet been able to estimate actual rates of abuse and violence because stepmothers are much less common than stepfathers. This in turn is because children, particularly very young children, usually stay with their mother when families split and re-form.

The idea that children risk being abused by step-parents is ingrained in many cultures. As in *Hansel and Gretel,* the image of the 'wicked stepmother' appears in many guises in folk-stories – aimed usually at, of all people, children! Abuse by females, like abuse by males, has a biological basis and is confined neither to modern industrial populations, as studies of tribal foragers have shown, nor even to humans. Here we encounter the possibility of a female, human or otherwise, raising a child who is not her genetic offspring. For obvious reasons, female mammals are not prey to the parental uncertainty that haunts males. Stepmothers, however, knowing that a child is not theirs, are confronted with the same problem as stepfathers. At what point does the cost of raising someone else's child begin to outweigh the benefits that life in a blended family can offer? Because it is at this point that neglect, abuse and even murder may become strategic.

One of the best of the few studies of stepmothers in other species concerns ostriches, which lay enormous eggs in enormous numbers. Not content with incubating just their own eggs, the partnered female ostriches, known as the 'major females', readily stand up to make way for partnerless, wandering females, called the 'minor females', to lay their eggs in the major females' own nests. Some of the eggs thus deposited in a major female's nest contain her stepchildren, sired by her partner. Some, however, contain foster-children – that is, they are unrelated to either her or her partner. Nevertheless, the major female collects the eggs together into one huge pile and incubates them all.

This is no unambiguous act of altruism, for an ostrich step/foster-mother shows favouritism and commits murder. The aim of her strategy is to enhance the success of her own young, using her adoptive charges as decoys and shields. The stepmother can tell the difference between her own eggs and those of any minor females, and pushes the others' eggs to the edge of the pile. These are the ones that occasionally die through poor incubation, and will be eaten by jackals or hyenas. Whereas nearly all of the stepmother's own eggs survive to hatch, only about half of the other females' eggs do. And when the other females' chicks have hatched, they have a further use in the stepmother's pursuit of reproductive success. Since ostrich chicks can feed themselves from the moment they hatch, all their mother has to do is lead them to food and warn them of approaching predators. The presence in her brood of other females' chicks means that when a predator strikes, its prey may not be one of her children, but somebody else's. By having a blended family, and effectively using/abusing other females' offspring, she raises far more of her own to maturity.

Step/foster-parenthood is common in ostriches because there is a small cost and a large benefit. Human step-parents have a much more finely balanced set of costs and benefits, and so blended families in humans are less common than in ostriches. Once again, however, people sometimes find themselves in a situation in which the benefits of step-parenthood only outweigh the costs if they show disfavouritism towards one or more of their stepchildren.

So far, we have discussed only the aggressive side of abuse – neglect, violence and murder. Our conclusion is that such abuse has biological roots and has been designed by natural selection to further the reproductive success of *the abuser*, albeit to the disadvantage of the victim. Even though we may now understand better why abusers behave the way they do, it is clear that even biologically the behaviour we have described is indeed abusive. In other words, biologically as well as sociologically and psychologically, the victim suffers as a result of the abuser's actions. Sexual abuse, however, raises a much more complex set of issues.

Evolutionary biology would argue that the sexual abuse of children also has biological roots. In part, these roots are the same as for violence. The urges that adults sometimes experience to have sexual intercourse with children have been evolved by natural selection to further *the adults'* reproductive success, even when it is to the disadvantage of their victims. However, less serious forms of sexual abuse than intercourse have their biological roots in quite different behaviour, whose role in other primates and in some human societies is the sexual education of youngsters, not their abuse. Nevertheless, such behaviour is still to the child's disadvantage *in modern industrial societies,* and hence nowadays is as abusive biologically as it is sociologically and psychologically.

According to a classic paper published in the journal *Child Abuse and Neglect* in 1984, the sexual abuse of children can be divided into three levels, according to seriousness. The *least serious* is defined as ranging from 'forced kissing, intentional sexual touching of buttocks, thigh, leg or other body part, including contact with clothed breasts or genitals, to attempts at any of the same acts without the use of force'. *Serious* sexual abuse is defined as ranging from 'forced digital penetration of the vagina to non-forceful attempted contact with the unclothed breast or simulated intercourse'. *Very serious* sexual abuse is defined as 'ranging from forced penile–vaginal penetration to non-forceful attempted fellatio, cunnilingus, analingus and anal intercourse'. Contacts wanted by the 'victim' are not considered to be abusive, even if the perpetrator is a relative, as long as he or she is not more than five years older or younger than the 'victim'. This means that all contacts between father and daughter, whether wanted by the daughter or not, qualify as abuse.

We have already encountered, in the context of incest, the biological prediction that intercourse between father and daughter should be more likely if one has, or both have, a low confidence in their genetic relatedness. And just as a putative genetic father may sometimes see a daughter as a long-term object for sexual attention if his paternity confidence is low, even more likely is a stepfather to do so. Males who find themselves in the role of stepfather are not constrained by the biological brakes that have evolved to avoid incest between fathers and their genetic daughters.

There is little direct evidence that biological fathers are more likely to sexually abuse their daughters if their confidence in their paternity is low. But the chances of a father sexually abusing his daughter do increase if the marriage is unstable – and marital instability is often an indication that a man has low confidence in his paternity. On the whole, figures suggest that a girl is about seven times more likely to be abused by a stepfather who helps to raise her through most of her childhood than by her biological father. Girls exposed at some point in their childhood to men who associate with their mother even more transiently – 'short-term stepfathers' – are even more likely to be abused at this level, though by exactly how much has not been assessed. The figures will be higher still as far as older stepbrothers are concerned, as in the scene, though, again, by exactly how much is not known.

In the scene, the girl was inseminated by both her older stepbrother and her stepfather. Again, there are no figures for how often such twofold abuse occurs. We know only that it *does* happen. If, as figures suggest, one in twelve girls who live with a stepfather are inseminated by him, and one in six who live with an elder stepbrother are inseminated by him, we can estimate that about one in seventy girls who live in a blended family containing both will suffer the fate of the girl in our scene.

Both violent abuse and sexual abuse of younger family members thus show similar patterns across nuclear and blended families, and for similar reasons. Step-parents are more likely to neglect, abuse or kill their stepchildren because they have more to gain than biological parents if the children depart prematurely. A stepfather is more likely to have intercourse with his stepdaughter because, on account of the genetic disadvantages of incest, he has more to gain than the biological father if the girl conceives. A somewhat surprising finding from a study of over one thousand women in Canada may be relevant here. On average, a girl who grows up in a household with a stepfather has her first menstrual period about six months earlier than a girl who grows up with both of her biological parents. Evidently, a young girl's body responds to the presence of a stepfather by speeding up its sexual maturation. Perhaps this is most likely to be an adaptation aimed at bringing forward her escape from the household. Alternatively, it could be a way of taking earlier advantage of having unrelated men in the household.

If stepfathers and fathers with low paternity confidence have been programmed to sometimes see their 'daughters' as targets for reproduction, why do they so often inseminate them *before* they reach puberty? Surely such behaviour cannot be reproductive? In fact, it need not be as devoid of potential reproductive benefit for the perpetrator as it might seem. Girls have been recorded as conceiving from the age of five onwards, and can ovulate well before their first menstrual bleed gives the first visible sign that they may be fertile. The reproductive nature of the behaviour is more clearly illustrated, perhaps, by the fact that abuse involving intercourse becomes increasingly likely as a girl approaches puberty, during the phase when she is still naïve and vulnerable, yet increasingly likely to conceive.

Sexual intercourse between a young female and an adult male with a low probability of being her father was socially accepted in some pre-industrial societies. Most of the relevant studies were carried out in the first half of the twentieth century, and many such societies, having been incorporated within the wider industrial world, now behave differently. But the Lepcha of India, for example, used to believe that girls would not develop properly without the benefit of sexual intercourse during childhood. By the time they were eleven or twelve, most girls regularly engaged in full intercourse, both with older men and with their peers. Men occasionally copulated with girls as young as eight, without suffering any social penalty. And in some animals sexual contact between adults and young is rampant. In bonobos – pygmy chimpanzees – for instance, adult males inseminate young females from babyhood onwards. The best studied example of this behaviour in mammals, however, involves the stoat.

Female stoats exhibit delayed implantation. They mate and have their eggs fertilised, but then do not allow the fertilised egg to implant in the womb for up to a year. While containing the eggs fertilised at this first encounter, an adult female moves into the territory of a different male stoat to prepare to reproduce. The new male tolerates her presence and allows her to give birth to the other male's young within his territory. Soon after she has given birth, the new male visits her burrow on a sexual foray. He finds her surrounded by her blind, hairless and helpless young, often attached to her nipples and still unable even to crawl. The mother is then inseminated by this male, who fertilises eggs that will be her next year's litter – and born in another male's territory. Not content with just inseminating the mother, however, the male also inseminates her baby daughters. Grotesque as it may seem, it is normal stoat behaviour for the ferocious adult male to penetrate and inseminate the blind, naked babies, scarcely the size of his head. Furthermore, on sensing the male in the nest, the babies struggle to drag themselves in his direction, attracting his sexual attention with little squeals. Scarcely out of their mother's womb, these females ovulate and their eggs are fertilised by the male's sperm. Again, the eggs will be held in storage for up to a year, at which point each of the now independent adult females will allow the eggs to implant in her womb, eventually giving birth to a litter sired by her mother's paedophile suitor.

The example of the stoat is more instructive about the human situation than it might seem because it gives a biological indication of what is and what is not abusive behaviour. We can clearly see the advantage to the male stoat, but we can also see that, biologically at least, the behaviour is not abusive because it is also advantageous to the baby females. This, after all, is how natural selection has fashioned them to conceive their first litter. They not only cooperate behaviourally with the male, they *also conceive* to him readily. This is in stark contrast to the human situation in which, although young girls very occasionally conceive from forced intercourse by older males, it is far more usual for their bodies to avoid conception.

One of the main features of the sexual behaviour of young children, discussed later, is that rarely do young girls conceive from intercourse, even in the first few years after puberty. Their bodies avoid doing so simply by not ovulating. So we must conclude that more often than not it would be to a young girl's disadvantage to conceive, and they have indeed been programmed by natural selection not to do so. Whereas adult human males are similar to their stoat counterparts in that they sometimes try to exploit young girls as reproductive outlets, it would be difficult to find parallels between young girls and young female stoats. Girls, unable to resist older males physically, nevertheless do so physiologically – by rarely conceiving. This is the clearest biological statement their bodies can make that more often than not it is to a young girl's disadvantage to cooperate with the older male in his reproductive aims. Biologically as well as sociologically, therefore, the behaviour in humans is abusive, unlike in the stoat.

The emphasis so far has been on the most serious level of sexual abuse, particularly that involving intercourse and the risk of conception, as in our scene. When we focus more specifically on the less serious forms – the intimate kissing, touching and fondling of children by peers and adults – the discussion becomes more complex.

When a biologist studies non-human primates, he or she frequently observes intimate sexual contact, without intercourse, both between youngsters and between youngsters and adults. These observed contacts are indistinguishable from contacts a sociologist would describe as abusive. The difference is that, for a young primate, such behaviour is clearly part of sexual education and is reproductively beneficial. Without such intimate sexual activity when young, primates are sexually handicapped in later life. Sexual exploration between young primates is reciprocal, all benefiting from their experiences. Intimate contact with adults of the species is equally beneficial, and often involves parents. The young gain from their experience, and the parents gain from their offspring's enhanced sexual competence in the production of grandchildren.

Education is also the biological role of intimate sexual contact between parents and young in the more permissive human cultures, as we shall describe in the discussion following Scene 19. *Biologically*, therefore, it should also be the role of non-intercourse sexual contacts between parents and children, and between children, in modern industrial cultures.

If the biological interpretation of intimate contact as educational is correct, we should expect such interactions to have the same characteristics as those found in other primates and/or in pre-industrial societies. First, we should expect both parents and children to experience programmed urges to interact sexually, but to avoid incest. Second, although biological parents may never have as great a motivation as step-parents to interact sexually with their 'children', we might expect them to have relatively greater motivation to interact at the levels defined as least serious. Third, we should expect such interactions to peak in the years preceding puberty, before the child needs to put its knowledge about sex into reproductive action. Fourth, we should expect boys to be educated in this way as well as girls, and women to be educators as well as men. Finally, we should expect children who experience such intimate contacts to be reproductively more successful in later life.

Unfortunately, there is no really good evidence by which to evaluate these biological predictions. Much more high-quality research is needed before any reliable picture can emerge. In the following paragraphs, therefore, we simply present some of the generally relevant information.

A study of nearly one thousand women in San Francisco revealed that one in forty of those raised in a household containing their biological father, as opposed to one in six of those raised in a blended family, were sexually abused at some level by their 'father'. And three-quarters of those abused by their biological father were abused at the less serious levels, compared with half of those abused by their stepfather.

Ninety per cent of abusers are male, and half of those women who abuse do so either in collaboration with a man or as a member of a poly-incestuous group. When she *is* involved, however, a woman plays just as active a role in the abuse as does a man. Women abuse girls and boys more or less equally, whereas men are most likely to abuse girls. Usually the women who abuse, like the men who abuse, are family members, the remainder invariably being caretakers of some sort, such as baby-sitters. Another feature of abuse by women is the young age of the victim. Women are more likely to abuse younger children (average age about six) than are men (average age about nine). But both are most likely to abuse children before they reach puberty.

Over the whole of the abuse range, boys are perhaps half as likely to be targets as girls. However, relatively few boys – perhaps fewer than one in a hundred – have experienced abusive (anal) intercourse by the age of fourteen, even when living in a blended family. This represents about a tenth of the risk of intercourse (vaginal or anal), experienced by girls. Less serious sexual abuse, however, is only a little less likely for boys than for girls, and violent abuse is equally likely.

Children who are abused by adults during their childhood are likely to experience a variety of negative psychological consequences, ranging from lowered self-esteem to depression. The important question to an evolutionary biologist, of course, is whether such psychological responses influence reproductive success. There is an indication from studies in the United States that children who experience genital contact with peers or elders during childhood have more lifetime partners than those who don't. Girls who have been abused before puberty are more than twice as likely to conceive before the age of eighteen. This is not because they have their first voluntary intercourse any younger, or because they have intercourse more often, or are less skilled in their use of contraception, but because they are two to three times more likely *to try* to conceive while still young. They are more likely to have an older partner than girls who were not abused. Perhaps because he is older, the partner is also more likely to urge them to conceive. Moreover, once they have conceived, they are three times *less likely* than girls who were not abused to deliberately abort the baby. To a biologist, though not to a sociologist or a psychologist, these are all positive reproductive repercussions which could perhaps indicate a greater eventual level of reproductive success.

The available evidence does not allow us to claim firmly that modern sexual abuse has its biological roots in the process of sexual education found in some non-industrial human societies and in all primates. Neither, though, does it allow such a hypothesis to be refuted and, on balance, the evidence is biologically positive rather than negative. But the fact that some children may gain reproductively from their 'educational' experiences does not stop the behaviour from being abusive in the context of the modern industrial society – even biologically.

There is one very important consequence of sexual abuse that we haven't yet mentioned, and that changes the whole picture: children who are sexually abused are at far greater risk of contracting diseases that may threaten their long-term health or fertility, or even their life.

When a couple interact sexually, even if their contact does not involve intercourse, the younger partner is on average at greater risk of contracting a new disease than the older. And when the younger partner is a child, the risks are very one-sided. Two studies of sexually abused children in North America found that by the age of fourteen about one in ten had contracted at least one sexually transmitted disease, such as gonorrhoea, and some had more than one. This is far higher than the rate for children who have not been sexually abused. The conclusion is clear. In modern industrial societies, whatever educational elements there may be to the behaviour, sexual contact between adults and children is on average disadvantageous to the children because of the high risk of disease. In general, therefore, such contact in modern industrial societies is abusive – biologically as well as sociologically, psychologically and legally. There will be more to say on this subject when we discuss the more conventional sexual education of children, as understood in our own society.

There is one other feature of step-parental, or even parental, abuse that was illustrated in our scene but that has not yet been mentioned: namely, that a child cannot rely on getting support from its biological parent. In a blended family, for example, the biological parent is presented with an enormous conflict of interest. On the one hand, if he or she protects the child and successfully raises it through to independence, he or she may enhance his or her reproductive output. On the other hand, the new partner can also offer a road to enhanced reproductive output via further children, but perhaps only if previous children are neglected. Often the parent is faced with a finely balanced trade-off between these conflicting pressures if he or she is to safeguard his or her long-term reproductive success. As a result the parent may vacillate between protecting and abandoning the confused child. In the scene, the mother clearly had great expectations of her new relationship and, if forced to choose, seemed likely to favour her partner rather than her unfortunate daughter. Sadly, this seems to be a common response and can very often lead to the abused child leaving home prematurely. We shall look at this in the discussion following Scene 20.

Because blended families predispose to abuse, much of our discussion here has concerned such families. But they are not the only alternative to the standard nuclear family. Another alternative is the subject of the next scene.

SCENE 18
Lone Parenthood

The woman gently replaced the receiver for the third time in a minute. She picked at the nail of her index finger for a second or two, then snapped up the handset again. Yes, she would phone her.

On the other side of town, the phone rang four or five times in the sitting-room of a modest ground-floor flat, and was answered by a thin, youngish woman with long hair scraped back in a pony-tail. On her hip sat an eighteen-month-old baby girl sucking noisily from her trainer mug. Before bending down to reach for the phone, buried beneath a pile of old TV magazines on the coffee table, she hitched the toddler higher up. 'Hello,' she said, in a slightly agitated voice.

'Hello love, it's me, Mum. I was just wondering how she is. Did you manage to take her to the doctor's?'

'Oh, hi. Yes I did, I took her before work. I was only half an hour late, nobody seemed to mind that much.'

'Before work?' Her mother sounded puzzled. 'You mean you went to work? . . . but surely you didn't send her to school? She wasn't fit for school. If you'd rung me I could have come over and stayed with her for the day.' Her mounting frustration was barely disguised.

'Hang on, Mum,' interrupted the young woman, sounding tired. 'I left her with a friend for the day. She was fine, honestly.'

'Oh,' said her mother, crestfallen. 'You know I really wouldn't have minded coming over.' At that moment the baby began to squirm, straining to reach a toy that had caught her eye. Stepping sideways towards the desired object, the young woman stretched the cable enough to pull the phone off the table. She swore under her breath. 'Mum, I'm sorry, I've got to go. I'll phone tomorrow, I promise. Don't worry about us, we're all fine honestly. Bye!' Without waiting for a reply, she retrieved the phone base and slammed down the receiver.

Their conversation had left both women feeling agitated – the younger because yet again she had lied to her mother, and the elder because yet again her daughter had brushed aside her offers of help.

The young woman put the baby down. Watching her toddle off towards the toy she had been after, she sat down on the floor, willing herself to calm down. These days the slightest thing seemed to make her anxious. She looked at the mess around her, and determined to do some tidying up later when the kids were in bed. Then she remembered the pile of ironing in the kitchen. She also had to wash her hair that night. Earlier in the day she had caught sight of herself in a shop window during her lunch break. Appalled at how jaded she looked and at the state of her hair and clothes, she had resolved to make more of an effort with her appearance.

Dishevelled and sweaty, the five-year-old on the sofa coughed and sat up. At the same moment a loud crash came from the kitchen, followed by two more. 'Just a second, darling, mummy won't be a minute,' the young woman reassured her, then moved swiftly across the sitting-room in the direction of the din, her heart beating fast, her head buzzing with a dozen dreadful scenarios. She took in the scene. The fridge door was wide open. Various food items lay scattered on the floor, two broken plates amongst them. The toddler was standing on a chair, still exploring the inner depths of the fridge. Her mother raced over, just managing to whisk her off the chair before another plate crashed to the floor. The child screamed in protest at having her game spoilt. Fighting the urge to shout back at her, the young woman carried her into the lounge and sat her down on the sofa next to her sister. She blamed herself, of course – she always did whenever anything bad happened to the kids. It was at times like this, but only at times like this, that she wished she had a partner again, if only to be an extra pair of hands and eyes.

The toddler immediately made to move off the sofa, in the process leaning heavily on her sister, who whimpered in response. The young woman felt panic rising within her. She looked at her sick child, now slumped against a cushion. Maybe her mother was right. Maybe she should have taken her to the doctor's. What if she was really ill? If her daughter still had a temperature in the morning, she decided, she would take her to the doctor's. She wouldn't be popular at work, though, if she took the morning off.

It was another four hours before she could finally sit down and read the paper. Having made the children's tea, bathed them and read them a story, washed up, put the washing in the machine, done the ironing and got things ready for the morning – and all after a full day's work – she was exhausted. Certainly too exhausted to read. She put the paper aside. She was also annoyed – annoyed with herself that once again she hadn't managed to fit in washing her hair.

Maybe she should go back on her resolve and try to find another partner. But how was she to meet someone? And, anyway, she had no time for relationships. It was a year since the father of her two daughters had walked out on her – to her relief. He had been a liability as a father, and she had vowed never to put herself in the same position again. Her feelings hadn't changed, but days like today did shake her self-confidence. There was always her mother, of course, who would help if she needed her to, but rarely did she feel like taking her up on her offers. In the early days they had argued so much about her determination to stay single that she always felt it was some sort of defeat to call on her for help.

She was just beginning to nod off when the sitting-room door opened and her elder daughter appeared, looking frightened and ashen.

'Mummy, I think I'm going to . . .' she began. Before the young woman could move, her daughter was violently sick.

Women can find themselves raising a family single-handed, if only briefly, for a variety of reasons. Rape, a one-night stand, the break up of a short- or a long-term relationship, or the death of a partner, can all leave a woman pregnant or with children, and alone. The relative importance of death and separation in generating lone-parent families has varied throughout history, and there will undoubtedly have been times when death was the more common cause – as it is, for example, in India even now. At present, however, in both industrial and many pre-industrial cultures, parental separation is the usual cause of lone-parenthood, and this is likely to have been the case throughout most of human evolution. In the scene we have just witnessed, the lone parent was the mother, and since this is the case for the majority of lone-parent families we shall concentrate on this scenario, commenting briefly on lone-father families later.

Only ten industrialised nations have recent statistics on the number of children growing up without a father in the home. At the bottom of the list is Italy, with only one in twenty-three children in homes without a father. At the top is the United States, with one in five. Of those born since 1980 in the US, as many as half of white children, and eight out of ten black, will spend some part of their childhood in a lone-parent family.

It is important to remember that lone-parenthood as it is experienced today is a relatively recent phenomenon. Even now, throughout south Asia, lone parents are simply absorbed within the extended family and are not really lone parents as we understand the term in the industrialised world. Even in developed countries, the degree of lone-parenthood is relatively recent; a steep rise began in the 1960s, reflecting major changes in economic life. In the days when most families lived and worked on the land in tightly knit communities separation was socially and economically difficult, and extended – multigenerational – families relatively common. With increasing industrialisation, urbanisation and mobility, the move of more and more people to the cities and the rise in paid employment for women weakened the economic and social barriers to separation and independent life. Today, both men and women can leave their homes and families while keeping their jobs and incomes. In the first half of the 1990s, in both Britain and the United States, lone mothers and their children comprised about one in five families with dependent children – slightly under in Britain, slightly over in the US. In both, the figure had almost trebled since 1970. The rise has been particularly steep since 1987, increasing in the USA from 14 to 23 per cent in seven years.

Studies of cultures as different and as far apart as the Ache forest-dwellers in Paraguay in the 1980s and the inhabitants of Ostfriesland, Germany, in the eighteenth century have shown that the loss of a father has a significant influence on a child's survival. The father's contribution becomes increasingly important once the youngster is past the age of two, though at all ages the loss of a father is less damaging than the loss of a mother. In contrast, among the Kipsigi of Kenya in the 1970s and 80s, the presence or absence of a father had no influence on child survival. But even for these people, having a partner still influenced the mother's long-term reproductive output, since she would have more grandchildren via each son and daughter if the father was present.

The advantages to a woman of having a man to help raise her children range from the most direct – having an extra pair of eyes and hands – to having someone to provide, or help to provide, the money, food or space that her children need for healthy development. With a man to help, a woman's children are more likely to escape accident and disease and to grow into healthy, fertile adults. As a result, a woman can often manage to raise more children and hence have more grandchildren. But even though it is clear that a partner can make a significant difference to a woman's reproductive success, we should not lose sight of the actual level of a man's contribution to child-care. As fathers, men are by no means in the top division compared with some other primate males. They may look very caring alongside the average orang-utan or chimpanzee, but they fare badly in comparison with the tamarin monkey or Barbary macaque.

In the wider primate perspective, humans are classed as 'affiliaters' rather than 'intensive caretakers'. Rates of interaction with infants are generally low. In 20 per cent of the eighty human cultures included in one world survey of paternal relationships, fathers were rarely or never near their infants, and in only 4 per cent was there a close father–infant relationship. Even in these latter societies, such as the !Kung San bush people of south-west Africa, fathers spent only 14 per cent of their time interacting with their children. This is about the same as the three hours a day recorded for the most active of fathers in industrial societies. However, some modern fathers spend as little as forty-five minutes *each week* interacting with their children.

Human fathers rarely assume major responsibility for child-care, and actual caretaking is rare. !Kung San fathers in the survey contributed no more than 6 per cent of infant caretaking, even though for at least half of their time they had nothing else to do for the family. Instead, in both industrial and non-industrial societies, the major form of male–infant interaction is play. Only in their provision of food do human males resemble the most active fathers among other primates. But even here the food is typically given to the mother, who then feeds it to the offspring.

In an even wider biological perspective, humans are unusual, though by no means unique, in showing biparental care – the raising of children by *two* parents. Most animals show no parental care at all, the young being left to fend for themselves from the moment they are born. In a considerable range of species, mainly animals with backbones, parental care does occur, but *lone-parenthood is the rule*, not the exception. In fish, frogs and toads the lone parent is usually the father, and the mother leaves. In birds and mammals, it is usually the other way round. It is only in a very few species apart from humans that we find biparental care: it happens most often in birds, but also in a few fish and mammals.

This pattern of parenthood in the animal kingdom has led to a common misconception: that biparental care is *the ultimate* system, and that evolution has really been striving to get all animals to do this but with most of them has failed. In fact, biparental care is not some pinnacle of evolutionary success from which most animals have been barred as a result of physical or mental shortcomings. On the contrary, there are very few situations in which parental care by both parents actually enhances reproductive output. It just happens that the human situation is one. For most animals, it would actually be counterproductive if both parents stayed to help. Two examples will illustrate this – ducks and black bears.

Most ducks are exceptional amongst birds in that the male does not help to raise the young. He stays with his partner just long enough to see the last of her eggs fertilised, then disappears, leaving her to raise the young single-handed. This may seem hard, but the female is in fact better off without him. First, her ducklings can feed themselves from the moment they are born, needing only to dip their heads into the water or dive – rather like living in a bowl of soup. All the mother has to do as a parent is keep her offspring together, stop them from getting lost, and teach them how to avoid being eaten by predators. Not only does she need no help, her partner would actually be a liability. As most male ducks are brightly coloured, the father might attract predators to the family's vicinity. So it is better for everybody that he leaves.

The same is true for black bears. The females conceive in autumn, give birth and breast-feed their two cubs during hibernation, and then emerge emaciated in spring needing to feed up over the summer to regain their strength. The mother's and cubs' survival over the winter depends on how many berries the mother has managed to eat during the previous autumn and hence how much in the way of fat reserves she has laid down. If the lumbering father had stayed in her territory after she had conceived, there would have been less food for her and less chance of both cubs surviving. So her reproductive output, too, is enhanced by lone-parenthood.

Occasionally, the same may be true for women, as we shall see later, but usually it probably is not. Unfortunately, our discussion is hampered by the fact that most sociological studies of the consequences of lone-parenthood do not measure reproductive success. They concentrate on social measures such as high-school drop-out rate, teenage pregnancies and employment potential. Only the examples already given – the Ache, Kipsigi and eighteenth-century Germans – show directly that, even when the mother is absorbed within an extended family, there is a *reproductive* disadvantage to absence of fathers and lone-motherhood. All other studies simply show that the children in lone-parent families are socially disadvantaged. So the only measures are indirect. Thus, mortality rates may be higher for lone mothers than for mothers in couples, and the children of lone mothers are likely to be in poorer health than those in nuclear families. Both factors are likely to decrease the mother's long-term reproductive success, and hence support the conclusion reached from the more direct studies.

Even though there is widespread evidence that it is a disadvantage to a woman to be a lone parent, it is by no means clear what causes this disadvantage. Most of the studies that have been able to unravel the relative importance of the different factors suggest that, more often than not, the cause is financial. The nature of the parenting is at most only a secondary factor, and in many cases is not a factor at all.

A lone-parent family is more sensitive to deteriorating circumstances than a nuclear or blended family. If times get hard as a result of low income and poor health, the children of lone parents are particularly vulnerable to accident, disease and abuse – and in lone-parent families such circumstances are more likely. In all industrialised nations for which 1990s information is available, children in lone-mother families are at greater risk of poverty. In Australia, Canada and the United States, over 50 per cent of children in lone-mother families are living below the poverty line. In Australia, Norway and the US, such children account for over half the children in poverty. In other countries, government policies mitigate the effects. For instance, Denmark, Finland and Sweden also have a high percentage of children in solo-mother families, but fewer than 10 per cent live below the poverty line.

For many lone mothers it is the harsh economics of lone-parenthood that influence their reproductive success, rather than the quality of their parental care. Apart from the consequences for their own and their children's survival, health and fertility, there are other, social, consequences. For example, the children of lone mothers tend to behave in ways that are more common in lower socioeconomic groups, which means that lone-parent families *on average* produce children who perform less well at school and show higher rates of delinquency. They are also associated with a decline in the mental health of both mother and children. And since the daughters in such families are also more likely to conceive in their early-teenage years, they often create a new generation of lone-parent families. (We discuss early-teenage pregnancies further in the discussion following Scene 19.)

The association between lone-parenthood and poverty is not only a factor of the reduced earning power of the lone-parent family itself: poverty is associated with the formation of lone-parent families in the first place. Divorce studies in the USA have shown that unemployment and low pay are significant factors in creating hostility between husbands and wives. An analysis of divorce during the three recessions between 1970 and 1982 estimated that recession accounted for about half of the increase in the number of divorced or separated mother-only families between 1968 and 1988. In the USA, even in families not living below the poverty line before parental separation, the decline in income after separation is 50 per cent. But although lone parents are more likely to crop up in impoverished situations, they are not confined to the lower socioeconomic groups. For example, during the second week of December 1992, all six of the Queen of England's grandchildren were living in lone-mother families!

Difference in income between lone parents and nuclear families accounts for at least half, and perhaps as much as 80 per cent, of the reduced social and psychological performance of lone-parent families. Some studies show that performance is often more sensitive to how much the income declines after separation than to absolute income. This explains why children from *widowed* lone-parent families, which suffer much less of a reduction in income, often do just as well as their peers in nuclear families. In contrast, children who have experienced lone-parenthood as a result of parental separation do worse socially and psychologically, on average. The measured differences between these children and those from intact nuclear families, however, to a large extent obtain even before parental separation, and do not necessarily worsen afterwards. It is the quality of the family relationships, of which separation is only a part, that seems to be most influential. This does not mean, of course, that lone-parenthood has no problems in its own right. Some of the reduced social performance – 20 per cent is one estimate – is due to the quality of parenting itself. But it is not a question of differences in maternal ability – a woman who finds herself a lone parent is no less competent a mother than one who does not. It has more to do with the situation she finds herself in. It is an inevitable consequence of having only one pair of hands and eyes, as we saw in the scene above.

Apart from accident, as illustrated by the incident with the refrigerator in our scene, ill-health and the consequences of reduced income, there is no indication that children suffer in any other major way from having just one parent. In particular, much as traditionalists might prefer it to be otherwise, the absence of a live-in male role model seems to have little influence on the child's performance in later life. In modern societies, children perform no better, either socially or psychologically, if they are raised by both parents than if they are raised by a widowed mother (as opposed to a separated mother) or by a mother and a grandmother. Other studies show that how long a child is without a live-in male also makes no difference. Biologically, this is probably what we should expect. In the majority of primates, the young are raised by a group of females, all cooperating in the reciprocal raising of children. Often these females are related – sisters, aunts, nieces, grandmothers. The same is true for many human societies. Both in humans and in other primates, males float in and out of these female groups, offering occasional 'paternal' care but most often simply going about their business of collecting food and trying to inseminate females. There is no reason, therefore, for children in industrial societies suddenly to have evolved with a need for a *live-in* male role model. There are plenty of males in the wider environment from whom children can learn what they need to learn.

At first sight, it would seem that a woman who finds herself with a child or children but no man is in a Catch 22 situation, because she then has to decide which is the best of two undesirable options – to expose her children to the dangers either of a blended family, or of a lone-parent family. Which course of action will most enhance, or least disfavour, her reproductive success will depend in part on her circumstances and in part on the range of stepfathers available.

Because Scene 17 was primarily concerned with abuse, a decidedly negative picture of blended families will have emerged. As we pointed out, however, here is the potential for two lone parents to benefit considerably from merging their families. Both could benefit from the increase in total resources that may result from doing so – not only the obvious resources, such as income and space, but also the less obvious ones, such as the increase in parental energy, time and watchfulness. In addition, both parents have the opportunity to increase their reproductive output by having further children with their new partner. We have also acknowledged that men may gain reproductively from sexual access, for themselves and their sons, to any daughters their new partner may have. Finally, the partner who will gain even more from the blended family is the one who manages to make it *his or her* children who gain the major share of the total family resources. To achieve this, he or she may need only to show favouritism to his or her own children, but under more extreme conditions he or she may begin to abuse his or her stepchildren.

There are no useful data to help us decide the best course of action for any woman who finds herself in the position of a lone parent. But we might guess that the more constrained she is in her ability to support herself and her children, the more likely she is to enhance her reproductive success by running the gauntlet of a blended family. In the United States, half of white women and one-third of black remarry. Others cohabit for varying periods of time. The woman with the abused daughter in Scene 17 followed just such a course, and despite the undoubted costs to her daughter, looked as though she was going to benefit reproductively as a result. However, under the right circumstances, a woman may sometimes be better off, reproductively, on her own than if she risks family life with a partner who is more of a liability than a help. Nutrition data from the Northern Province of Zambia, for example, show that children under five years old in female-headed households are less likely to be malnourished than children in slightly better-off households where both parents are resident, because more of the, albeit smaller, household resources are devoted to the children if the father is not present. Increasingly, therefore, with ever more favourable child-support legislation in industrial societies and with more and more women of independent means, we might expect increasingly more women to opt for lone-parenthood – and benefit as a result.

As mentioned earlier, in humans, unlike fish or frogs, over 90 per cent of lone parents are female: it is men who are more likely to desert their children, and who are more likely to die while their children are young. Also, men are immune to the dangers of being left with a child from a one-night stand or rape. When men do find themselves in the role of lone parent – as in Scene 16 – the considerations we have discussed here in the context of the lone mother apply as forcefully to them as they do to women.

On balance, children seem to do better with a lone father than with a lone mother. This is a reflection not of better parenting, but of higher income and of the ability to afford day-care. Actual measures show that children are healthier when with lone fathers than with lone mothers, but do only equally well in terms of social development. On the negative side, daughters are more likely to conceive in their teens and lone fathers seem to have a higher mortality rate. When allowance for their higher income is made, men emerge as less competent lone parents than women. Studies in Ghana in the 1980s and 90s show that resources under the control of women are more likely to be devoted to children than are resources controlled by men. Similarly in Brazil, income in the hands of a woman improved a child's health almost twenty times more than income controlled by a father – and also increased the child's survival prospects. Presumably, the reduced competence of men as lone parents is due once more to the spectre of paternal uncertainty. We might expect that, combined with the urge to find new women to inseminate, this factor will lead men to take greater risks with their children's health and safety.

CHAPTER SEVEN

The Road to Grandparenthood

SCENE 19
Preparing the Ground

The mother woke from her brief sleep. Shielding her eyes from the sun, she turned to look around the garden. Her seven-year-old daughter was crouching in one corner, in the shade of a tree, taking an intense interest in something on the ground.

'What is it?' she asked, above the sound of the radio beside her on the grass.

'It's a big bee,' replied her daughter. 'I think it's dying.' She prodded it with the stick she was holding, then, taking advantage of her mother being awake, ran over to her sun-bed. The girl was bored, irritated that her mother kept falling asleep in the sun – and hot. 'Do I have to keep my clothes on, mummy? I'm all itchy.'

The mother felt sorry for her. Normally, neither of them would wear anything in their secluded garden on a day like this, but her eight-year-old son had a friend round to play for the afternoon. She found him odd at the best of times and something told her it would be a bad idea for him to see her or her daughter naked.

'I'm sorry, darling,' she said, sitting up. 'You can't take them off while your brother's got his friend here ... where *are* the pair of them, anyway?'

Sulkily, the girl said they had gone upstairs to play with her brother's trains. The woman peered at the upstairs window, then turned down the radio for a moment to listen for sounds of mayhem, but all was quiet. She turned the radio up again, rolled on to her front and reached behind her back to unclasp the top of her bikini. Before closing her eyes, she asked

217

her daughter to run upstairs and see what the boys were doing. She had about ten more minutes before needing to make their tea and wanted to catch the last of the day's sun. Unknown to her, she would probably have derived more entertainment from listening to the conversation that was going on in the upstairs room.

The visitor, nine years old but young for his age, was incredulous.

'You mean you and your sister take off all your clothes and get in the bath together? You mean she sees your ... thing ... and you can see hers?'

The young host carried on playing with his train set, making steam noises as he pushed it up a steep hill. The set was electric but wasn't working and so far he'd been unable to persuade his father to fix it.

'Don't you get embarrassed?' the visitor persevered. 'Doesn't it get all hard and stick up? Mine would if a girl looked at it. Doesn't it make you feel all funny?'

'But she's only my sister. She's only seven,' he said, as his train reached the top of the hill. He let go so that it free-wheeled down the other side. 'Anyway, it does stick up sometimes, especially if she touches it. My Dad say's that's all right – his sticks up sometimes. It's supposed to stick up, sometimes.'

There was a pause while they both wondered what to say next. Then the younger boy continued, 'My sister thinks my Dad's is really funny. She likes to pat it and make it swing from side to side.'

Apparently finding this even more difficult to believe, the older boy had to know more. 'You mean you've seen your Dad's thing? And your sister's seen it – and she's touched it? What does it look like? Does it look like ours?'

'Not really,' his friend replied, puzzled by the other's interest. 'It's ever so big with this funny purple knob at the end and blue veiny things. There's all this hair everywhere, and his balls are big too – it's horrible, really.' He paused for a moment, then looked up at his friend for only the second time in the conversation. 'Why? Haven't you seen *your* Dad's?'

The elder boy shook his head, recoiling at the prospect. His parents had told him that only naughty boys and nasty grown-ups let other people see their 'private parts'. Never having seen either of his parents naked, he was intensely curious. 'And your Dad lets your sister *touch* it? Doesn't he mind?'

'I don't know,' the other one said, marginally embarrassed. Then he laughed. 'Sometimes she hurts him. She slaps it so hard, or pulls it, that he shouts at her. He tells her she's got to be gentle with men's bits.' He hesitated for a second, as if unsure that he should carry on. 'Anyway, I've touched it, too – and I've touched my mum.' He put his hand over his mouth, as if to prevent what he was going to say from being heard. 'Do you know what I do, sometimes?'

He giggled at what he was going to say. 'Sometimes my mum lets me stroke the hair on her tummy. It's ever so soft. I like it best when she's just had a bath. It smells really nice then.' Breaking off to retrieve his train, he didn't notice the expression on his friend's face.

'You mean – your mum has got hair on her tummy?' The thought appalled him. He was sure *his* mum wouldn't have hair on her tummy.

'Don't you know *anything*?' the eight-year-old sighed. His parents spent so much of their time around the house naked – he had been used to seeing their bodies since the day he was born. He couldn't believe that somebody a year older than himself didn't know such things. 'It's just here, lots of it. Really black and thick,' he said, pointing at his own body.

'Has your sister got hair there?' his friend asked, almost afraid to hear the answer.

The younger boy couldn't believe his friend's naïveté. Just then, his sister came into the room. 'He thinks you've got hair on your tummy, like mum,' he laughed, pointing at his friend.

'I will have, one day,' she said indignantly, 'mummy said so.' She felt embarrassed and annoyed, but just a tiny bit excited, that the two boys had been talking about her. She had a bit of a crush on this big boy, two years older than her.

She picked the pillow up off her brother's bed and hit out at him with it. 'What have you been saying about me?' she asked aggressively.

'Nothing,' he said, giggling and dodging her attempts with the pillow as she chased him round the room. The older boy looked on enviously. He was an only child and would have given anything to have a sister or a brother to play with.

The girl pinned her brother in a corner and tried to smother his face with the pillow, showing off in front of the older boy. Still laughing, her brother tried to tickle her and the pair of them collapsed on the floor. Despite the twenty months between them, she was not much smaller than her brother and their rough-and-tumble play was pretty evenly matched. They spent a lot of time rolling around on the floor together, in mock fights, sometimes naked after their bath.

The nine-year-old watched the brother and sister wrestling on the floor, legs tangled, and stared as the girl's short, loose dress rode up round her waist. Clumsily, he threw himself on to the pair of them. This was his first ever physical contact with a girl, and it excited him. He was determined to make the most of it, but he had no idea what he could and couldn't do. It seemed to him reasonable to assume that if the girl didn't mind wearing nothing with her brother she wouldn't mind doing so with him. Announcing that he was going to pull off her knickers, he asked her brother to help. Excited himself, and eager to impress the older boy, he sat astride his sister's chest while the other tried to contain her thrashing legs for long enough to pull her knickers down. Screaming and flailing, she kicked him in the face, but he didn't care. Triumphantly pinning down both her legs, he felt his excitement mounting. He was just moments away from seeing his first ever fanny.

And he did — briefly. But when he'd pulled her pants down to her knees, and saw what, moments earlier, had seemed so important, he felt a rush of remorse. So did her brother. Getting off her chest, he told the other boy to stop and let his sister go. The older boy complied, keeping his eyes fixed on the girl's pre-pubescent groin in the seconds it took her to cover herself, confused rather than excited by what he saw.

The girl swore at the pair of them in language that surprised the nine-year-old. Her brother was used to it — and could be as coarse himself. She sat there for a few moments, glowering, while the boys fidgeted uneasily. Then she picked up the pillow again and lamely tossed it at the older boy, threatening to tell her mother what the pair of them had done. He hadn't needed to do that, she told him sulkily. She would have shown him if he'd asked — as long as he'd shown her his, too. But she wasn't ever going to let him see it again, after what he'd done.

Taking his cue from her and eager to make amends, the brother suggested they pull down the other boy's trousers. In fact more excited than upset by what had happened, the girl wanted more rough-and-tumble, and before the visitor knew what was happening, it was his turn to be set upon. But before the brother and sister could get stuck in, their game was interrupted. Wondering why her daughter was taking so long, the woman had come indoors to investigate. What was all that noise? she shouted up the stairs. But without waiting for an answer, she told them to come down for tea.

This was nearly the last time the boy visited the brother's and sister's house. The girl soon tired of his attempts to lift her skirt and grab at her knickers. It was all he seemed to want to do when she was around. At first, she had amused herself by teasing him, nearly letting him see her and then changing her mind at the last minute. Once, without warning, during one of these sessions, he had whipped down his trousers to reveal a stiff little pink thing – rather like a baby carrot, she thought, unimpressed. She *had* to show him hers now, the boy asserted. But she never did. The brief glimpse he had forced with her brother's help was to be the only image of female genitals he would take with him on his journey to manhood.

The boy also lost interest in his friend's company, wanting someone to share his interest in football and trains rather than someone so preoccupied with snatching glimpses of girls – to him they were an everyday experience. And they remained an everyday experience until he was twelve and his sister eleven. Then, gradually, despite their parents' example, they each became more and more secretive about their bodies and the changes that were taking place. They remained close, but communal baths and naked romps became a thing of the past. Nevertheless, they saw each other naked often enough to keep track of what was happening to them as they each approached puberty. In contrast, their parents, disappointed by the effect that age was having on their own bodies, became increasingly disinclined to appear naked in front of their children.

All the same, they felt satisfied by the way they had handled their children's early sexual education. As far as they could tell, both had a healthy understanding and respect for their own and each other's bodies. They hoped they had prepared them well for the excitements and disappointments of the next few years. In the meantime, they would do their best to steer them through puberty, though like most parents they would only ever be told a small part of their children's experiences.

Within the space of a month, beginning soon after the daughter turned eleven, two things happened. She had her first period, which triggered a lengthy discussion between herself and her mother. And the son had his first ejaculation – which triggered no discussion at all, because nobody ever knew. He had been standing naked in front of a full-length mirror and innocently playing with himself, as he had done many times before, when the tingle in his groin suddenly erupted. The first spurt hit the mirror, the rest went on the floor. Half an hour after his initial panic and a desperate attempt to clean up the mess, he found that he could make the same thing happen all over again, only this time he caught it in a tissue. Having thus discovered masturbation, there would sometimes be whole weeks when he would ejaculate every day, sometimes twice. On one occasion he wanted to see how many times he could do it in succession, but it took him two hours to manage it three times, and then lost interest in the challenge.

In the year that followed he spent many solitary hours in his bedroom, trying to conjure up ever more erotic images and to simulate sexual positions and sensations with the imaginative use of pillows and toilet-roll holders. Then, playground gossip led him to worry that perhaps he would hurt himself, grow warts or go blind. So he tried to stop doing it. But the effort didn't last long. If he abstained, he had wet dreams – it was better to risk blindness and warts than risk having his mother find out what he was doing, he decided.

She actually felt a little surge of pride when she saw the first tell-tale marks on his sheets. Her little boy was becoming a man, and everything was working as it should. She had suspected that he had started masturbating from the way he kept disappearing into his room and locking the door for an hour at a time, but she couldn't quite believe he could ejaculate until she saw the evidence of it. They had talked openly about masturbation with their children whenever there was a natural opportunity, usually prompted by scenes on the television. Even so, she now urged her partner to talk to their son, just to make sure he hadn't been fed any misinformation by his friends.

Despite their habit of mutual frankness, both were acutely embarrassed when at last the father found the opening he needed. The conversation was disjointed, oblique, and very brief. Nevertheless, the boy got the message. His parents knew what he was doing, they didn't mind – and it was safe. The one thing he couldn't believe was his father's claim that *he* still did it. He tried a few times to imagine his father masturbating, but he just couldn't, and soon he shut the thought from his mind altogether. Also, he wasn't sure that he quite believed him when he said that it was harmless. His father thought *everything* to do with sex was OK, so he wasn't convinced he was totally reliable on the subject.

However much or little he owed to the conversation with his father he could never really work out, but from then on he had a full and active sex life with himself. More and more he yearned to sample the real thing, but for a long time he had no real success in getting a date with any of the girls at school. As much as anything, he wanted reassurance; he knew from what he saw every week in the shower-room that he was not the best endowed. He needed to know what girls thought of him, wanted confirmation that they would be as impressed by his penis and what it could do as he was.

Failing to get any further with the girls he knew, he turned his attention to his sister. Not that he was attracted to her – on the contrary, the thought of touching any of *her* bits made him feel peculiar. But she was female, so she should be able to give him the reaction he needed. For a few months, he tried to contrive situations in which she might see him with an erection. When his parents were out he would leave his bedroom door unlocked, or even partly ajar, while he wandered around with nothing on taking ages to get changed or prepare for a shower. Then, one day soon after he had turned fourteen, his sister walked in just as he had got himself as hard as he had ever been. With no more than a passing glance at his manhood, she asked him to disentangle a zip in the back of her dress, then left. Dismayed that she had been so totally unimpressed, apparently, by what was rapidly becoming the most important feature of his life, he had consoled himself with the thought that she was probably too young to judge anything, anyway. After all, she was only thirteen.

What he didn't know was that his sister had seen him erect before, just as he had intended, through his open door. But she had assumed that by now his body was as much a fact of life to him as it was to her, and it had never occurred to her to comment. Anyway, she had known about male genitals for as long as she could remember. By the time she had last seen her father naked, when she was about eleven, her brother's body was beginning to metamorphose into something similar. She hadn't seen her father with an erection since she was nine, and the last time she had touched him was two years before that, but the subliminal memories of the sight and feel were still there. The male body held no threat or mystery for her.

The only reaction to maleness she had registered recently, after a glimpse of her brother through his bedroom door, had been mild panic. How would she ever be able to accommodate such an object? However, a conversation with one of her friends at school, the one who claimed not to be a virgin, had reassured her.

As the parents watched their children emerge into adulthood, they noted with growing satisfaction how easily they seemed to form friendships. Both seemed popular – not least, they thought, because they were clearly at ease with the opposite sex, appearing to treat 'dates' like only slightly more exciting versions of each other. They would have loved to know how their children's sexual education was progressing, but their subtle enquiries never elicited the things they most wanted to know.

In fact, both were learning fast. Within a few months of his fourteenth birthday, one of his sister's friends allowed the boy to put his hand inside her blouse, and he had slid his fingertips on to her nipples. Just a few weeks later, his sister let one of his friends do the same to her. Soon afterwards came his first faltering attempts at putting a finger inside a girl's vagina, and his sister's equivalent experience. Standing on the back doorstep after an evening out, she parted her legs just enough to let her eager young companion feel inside her knickers. She guided his hand to the right place, let him enjoy his success for a few seconds, then pushed him away with an admonition.

None of this was ever revealed to the parents, who simply stayed alert and kept their fingers crossed. They knew that both children were regularly alone with friends of the opposite sex, and more often than not they were told *something* about how the date had gone. The father, in particular, began wondering if his son was still a virgin and, despite himself, found himself hoping that he wasn't. But he never questioned that his daughter was still a virgin.

In the long hot summer when the brother was sixteen and the sister fifteen, both took a major step forward in their sexual education. The son had been asked round by the friend of his sister's who – he had never forgotten his sister telling him – had lost her virginity at thirteen. Arriving early in the afternoon, he found her alone, in the garden sunbathing. After a while they went to her room to listen to music. As the sound blasted out through the open window, he found himself in a state of high excitement, so that when she invited him to remove her bikini while he was still fully clothed, he ejaculated at the sight of her pubic hair. She watched in amused fascination while, with acute embarrassment, he cleaned himself up. Then she invited him to stroke her naked body. In the fifteen minutes it took him to regain his potency, she slowly educated him in the finer details of the female body, things he had certainly never gleaned from seeing his sister and mother. Then, at last, he lost his virginity. It was the first of several trips he made to her bedroom that summer, ending only when she got together with the drummer in the school's rock group, who had a car.

It was a car that also led to his sister's first major step in her pursuit of sexual experience. Lured by the prospect of a drive into the country, she accepted an invitation from the lad who, all those years earlier, had pulled down her knickers in her brother's bedroom. No more exciting to be with than when he was nine, he had nonetheless achieved a little status amongst her circle of girlfriends when his parents had given him a car for his seventeenth birthday. He drove her to a place he knew by a river, that could be reached only via a steeply sloping field. As they made their way gingerly between the cows, he asked her for a kiss.

The weather was hot and she was enjoying being out in the country. She thought he deserved a kiss for bringing her there, but he certainly didn't deserve to put his hand up her dress which, within seconds of their lips meeting, is what he tried to do. Nor did she think the kiss should have brought on the erection she could feel through his shorts as he pressed against her. He grumbled when she pushed him away, but didn't try to stop her moving on down the field.

He caught up with her just before she reached the river bank, and asked her for another kiss. One was enough for now, she told him, but if he was good he could have another back in the car. With that, she ran the last few yards down to the river and gazed into the water. A movement caught her eye. 'Look,' she called, 'there are some trout or something in here.'

'No, *you* look,' she heard him say behind her. 'Look at me.'

A strangeness in his voice, as if the words were catching in his throat, made her turn round straight away. Before she could stop herself, she laughed. He was standing, naked apart from his shoes and socks, a few yards up the slope. His erection was certainly more striking than the puny little object he had shown her that day in her brother's room, but it did as little for her now as it had then.

'Don't be silly,' she said sharply, turning her back on him again. 'Get dressed, you look ridiculous. Somebody might see you – come and look at the fish.'

A second later she was face down on the ground, the breath knocked out of her by a rugby tackle from behind. Pressing down with his full weight and with his knee on her back, he had pulled her skirt up and her knickers down almost before she knew what was happening. But as he struggled to pull her knickers over her shoes, she began to fight free. Suddenly, she was seven again, engaged in rough-and-tumble with her brother. All of the old tricks came back to her and before long she could feel her assailant losing his grip. In desperation, realising he couldn't hold her, he gave up trying to remove her knickers and put all his effort into pinning her down. Throwing his full weight on top of her again, he tried to force himself between her thighs. But her knickers were still round her ankles, and he couldn't open her legs. He realised he was rapidly getting nowhere. In the end, his urgency defeated him and he ejaculated over her buttocks.

Cursing him furiously, she wriggled free, wiped herself clean with a handful of grass, threw it at him, then pulled up her knickers. Deaf to his apologies and his pleas for her to stay, she took off angrily up the hill, cows scattering before her. When he was dressed he could drive her home, she shouted over her shoulder – and if he so much as touched her again she would cut short his manhood.

The girl never told her parents, or even her brother, about the young man's attempt to rape her.

Several times during this book, we have pointed out that a person's reproductive output does not end with his or her production of children: it is the reproductive rate of their descendants that matters to natural selection. Rarely can people significantly influence the conception and raising of their great-grandchildren, and beyond that generation the chances of doing so are infinitesimal. They can, however, exert a considerable influence on the production of their grandchildren; and as we saw in the previous chapter, in many ways the production of grandchildren is even more important than the production of children. It is only a slight exaggeration to say that, as far as natural selection is concerned, people have and raise children as an avenue to grandchildren.

Each of the three scenes in this chapter illustrates an aspect of the road to grandparenthood as seen in an evolutionary perspective. All involve the same characters, at different stages along that road. They illustrate the ways in which parents can influence their offspring to become successful parents in their own right. We follow the interaction between parents and offspring as the latter go through the process of development from childhood, through adolescence and into adulthood.

The more, and better-quality, grandchildren a person gains, the more is he or she favoured by natural selection. There are subtleties involved in maximising the number of grandchildren, as we have already seen in the context of parental favouritism, family planning and family size. But, by and large, once parents have given birth to the optimal number of children for their circumstances, the challenge is then to raise those children to be as healthy, fertile and attractive as they can. Then, the parents will gain the optimal number of grandchildren.

Usually, parents are in little doubt as to what will maximise their children's potential for success, and their conscious decisions will match very closely the subconscious decisions that have been shaped by natural selection. Parents usually strive to create the best living conditions and the best opportunities for their children. But there is one aspect of child-raising that is not so clear-cut, and this is the aspect illustrated in the scene above. What is the best way to educate children sexually? Should parents be as liberal as possible, as those in the scene aspired to be but didn't really manage? Or is it best to protect children from their and other people's sexuality for as long as possible, like the parents of the childhood friend in our scene? *Or* is there some preferable middle road?

In an anthropological context, every extreme is found. As we shall see later, there are some cultures in which open sexual exploration and contact between young children and between adults and children are normal and encouraged. There are other cultures in which the full weight of the law prohibits all sexual acts involving young children. And, of course, there are many that occupy various levels of middle ground, some acts being acceptable and others not. Whereas Western industrial nations have in the past occupied a slightly conservative middle ground, they are rapidly moving towards prohibiting any form of sexual contact with children, even by other children. So why? Why is there so much variation between cultures? Which *is* best for parents and their children? And why does natural selection seem to have left the question open, instead of programming a 'best answer' into our behaviour as it has with many other aspects of parenthood?

The answer to all of these questions is that, although it might not be obvious, natural selection *has* programmed the best answer into our behaviour. It isn't as obvious as the answers to many of the other questions we have considered because, as we found when discussing birth order, the best answer is a conditional one: in one situation, do this; in another, do that. The variation we see between cultures, and between people within cultures, comes about partly because different people find themselves in different circumstances.

The problem faced by natural selection is that there are both costs and benefits associated with the sexual behaviour of children – costs and benefits to both them and to their parents. On the one hand, children gain from early sexual experience for reasons we shall discuss in a moment. On the other the earlier they begin their sexual exploration, the more likely they are to encounter and succumb to sexually transmitted diseases, as we saw when discussing child abuse. As with most other conditional responses, therefore, natural selection has programmed into people rules for behaviour that begin with monitoring their situation and subconsciously judging the costs and benefits. The problem is that, since children, particularly young ones, have little experience of the world in which they find themselves, they are in a poor position to judge the pros and cons of their behaviour. So the solution that evolution seems to have adopted is to programme children to seek as much sexual experience as they can get, and to programme parents to encourage or restrain their children's urges according to their (the parents') perception of the circumstances. Thus, if parents judge the benefits of early sexual exploration to be high and the risks low, they should adopt a permissive attitude towards their children's sexual education. On the other hand, if they judge the risks to be high and the benefits low, they should be more repressive.

The fact that children are programmed to seek sexual experience from an early age is clearly illustrated by their behaviour under both permissive and repressive regimes, whether parental or social. The children with liberal parents in our scene took full advantage of the prevailing permissiveness to explore from an early age both their own and their parents' bodies. The child with repressive parents disobeyed their wishes when given the opportunity, and followed his natural urge to see and learn. The kind of behaviour illustrated in the scene is mirrored in much wider social contexts.

In early-twentieth-century societies that used to allow their children not only free sex play but also the opportunity to observe adult sexual behaviour and to participate in discussions of sexual matters, children took full advantage of their situation and learned from an early age. According to a survey published in 1952, the children of the Alorese Islanders of Oceania, for example, were well informed on all details of the reproductive act by the age of five. Sexual life began in earnest for the Trobriand Islanders of Oceania at six to eight years for girls and ten to twelve for boys. Both sexes received explicit instruction from older companions whom they would imitate in sexual activities. Sex play included masturbation, oral stimulation of the genitals of the same and opposite sex, and heterosexual copulation. At any time, a couple could retire to a convenient place and there engage in prolonged sexual play with the full approval of their parents.

In early-twentieth-century repressive societies, despite the threat of punishment, young children still took what opportunity they could to engage in secret sexual activity. The children of the Truk Islands in the North Pacific used to play at having intercourse from an early age, even though their parents beat them whenever they were caught. Among the Native American Apinaye, both boys and girls masturbated frequently even though such play was punished whenever observed. Moreover, it occurred despite the fact that at a ceremony conducted when they were half grown, the children's genitalia were examined and they were flogged if there appeared to be any evidence of masturbation. Today in North America which, like all modern industrial societies, is restrictive, brother–sister incest appears to be more common in households with puritanical and repressive parents. The suggestion is that, unable to explore sexuality elsewhere, brothers and sisters turn to each other.

So wherever we look, we see evidence of a programmed urge in children to explore sexually from an early age. How often they succeed depends on the restraint applied by their parents, once they have assessed the potential costs and benefits for their children of early sexual experience.

Most of the costs of early sexual exploration (which we shall come to in a moment) are obvious. What might be less obvious are its benefits. Surely, with something as important as repro-duction, natural selection should have worked out every aspect of the reproductive process down to the last detail, leaving nothing to chance? Well, it didn't – and for good reason. Of course, certain basic reactions were programmed into us – the chemistry of interest, attraction and arousal, for instance, along with the physics of lubrication and the mechanics of penile and clitoral erection – but not the subtleties of courtship, stimulation, intercourse and relationships. Natural selection left these for people to learn, just as it did with other primates, because, throughout the evolution of all these species, learning as they went along allowed programmed urges to be tempered by the precise requirements of local circumstances.

Male primates, for example, have to learn how to copulate. Erection comes gratis, as does the urge to thrust, but where to put the penis has to be learned. Even as intelligent an animal as an adult male chimpanzee is totally inept if denied sexual experiences during childhood and adolescence, when most sexual learning occurs. In one study of the sexual development of a pair of chimpanzees in captivity observations began when they were the equivalent of about seven years old in human terms. By then the young male would have erections in front of the female and she would hold his penis and play with it, often for minutes at a time. On the ground, he would sometimes lie on top of her and rub his penis against her body. When they were a little older, with each other's assistance, penetrations began. They also started to experiment with the adult copulatory position which, for chimpanzees, is usually rear entry. Some time before puberty, penetration and thrusting reached adult efficiency.

An adult male chimpanzee deprived of early sexual experiences such as these becomes aroused and erect in the company of a female but has no idea what else to do. He even has trouble knowing which end of the female to approach with his penis, and rarely succeeds in copulating on his first or even next few encounters.

In the scene above, the eighteen-year-old in the field was equally inept. With a more liberal sex education during his childhood, and more direct experience of girls, female psychology and the female body, his afternoon on the river-bank might have gone very differently. Had he had the same experiences as her brother, he might even have been able to court and seduce the girl into being a willing sexual partner instead of feeling his only course was to force her. He would certainly have known that showing her his erection was not the best way to impress her; and when the moment came he might have succeeded in inseminating her instead of ejaculating over her buttocks.

Young females, of course, have far less to learn about the basics of intercourse than have young males. Nevertheless, girls do benefit from learning the subtleties of self-presentation and seduction. They also have to learn how to test males for status, strength, experience and potential fidelity. In other words, they have to learn how to collect all of the information they need to select as good a mate as possible, someone to help them raise their children and maybe also to be those children's genetic father. Moreover, they have to learn how to do this without unwittingly exposing themselves to the risk of a forced insemination by a male they would not otherwise choose to be the genetic father of their next child.

Young girls are driven at an early age by their genetic programming to begin testing males. When the girl in our scene was only seven years old, she was already becoming adept at teasing and provoking. She was also learning when it was, and when it was not, safe to be provocative. In her rough-and-tumble play with her brother and his friend, she found out that she was unable to prevent them from physically overcoming her, but she learned the techniques and manoeuvres necessary to avoid being easily overcome when wrestling. Buried in her memory, such experiences surfaced when she needed them, and helped her to avoid an unwanted insemination nine years later on a picturesque river-bank.

The very good reason, then, why natural selection has programmed children of both sexes to seek sexual experiences, is so that they can instinctively test and hone the crude genetic strategies with which they are born. And this they do in many different ways, starting with a fascination with each other's bodies. Both sexes are preoccupied with testing their ability to persuade and resist, boys tending to rely on strength and bluster, girls on teasing and agility. Both sexes also have to learn how to judge and compare potential mates, how to court and seduce him or her once selected, and how to avoid unwanted sexual attention. Eventually, both also have to learn the strategic subtleties of both short- and long-term relationships, including infidelity and the prevention of infidelity.

The earlier both boys and girls begin to learn all of these things, the less likely they are to make mistakes or to miss opportunities when they reach puberty and adulthood. For girls in particular, learning while they are too young to conceive is an obvious advantage. It should be no surprise, therefore, to find that evolution has programmed even the youngest of children to explore their own and others' sexuality. Such exploration is a vital step in each individual's pursuit of reproductive success. And for the majority, the most accessible targets – and the safest, as we shall see later – for investigation during childhood are their parents and siblings.

In many pre-industrial cultures where people go naked, children have nothing to learn about what bodies look like, including the way they change as they age, for it is obvious to all from birth. In the South Pacific, for example, all members of the Pukapukan households used to sleep in one room under one mosquito net. Many sleep with their parents, or even with other families, and see their parents and other adults having intercourse. As they seek to emulate their parents, their exploration centres on the way bodies respond to touch and stimulation, and the way potential mates and competitors respond during courtship and seduction. There are frequent opportunities for youngsters to observe adult sexual activities, and sexual matters are often discussed.

In permissive pre-industrial societies, children gradually increased their sexual activities as they approached puberty and during adolescence. In some societies, the enforcement of the local incest laws was the only major restriction on adolescent sexual activity. Their sex play would first include self- and then mutual masturbation with members of the same and opposite sex, but as they grew older it was characterised more by attempts at heterosexual copulation. By puberty in most of these societies, expressions of sexuality were more or less fully adult, then persisted unchanged throughout people's sexually active years.

Some of these societies consciously acknowledged the educational nature of their permissiveness. Among the Chewa of East Africa, for example, people believed that unless children began their sexual activity early, they would never produce offspring.

Older children built little huts some distance from the village and there, with the approval of their parents, would play at being husband and wife. Many of these pairings extended well into adolescence, with periodic exchanges of partners until marriage occurred. The only check on promiscuity was that imposed by the children themselves. Most industrial societies, however, now discourage intimate sexual exploration by children. Even so, the repressive environment of the young boy in the scene who had never seen his parents naked is probably an extreme, as is the liberal sexual environment of the brother and sister. The majority of modern families probably fall somewhere between the two.

It is tempting to compare naked societies with modern ones and conclude that industrialised cultures have in some way strayed from the natural human condition, as if evolution had produced a naked, permissive society which culture then condemned and repressed. Such a conclusion paints the sexually oppressive milieu of the average modern family as a social artefact, a victory of culture over evolution. But human behaviour is not so easily separated into natural and cultural: there is another, more likely, interpretation. Perhaps the truth is that in some societies parents enhance their reproductive success by giving their children sexual freedom, but in others they do so by repressing their children's sexuality. Natural selection has allowed for both extremes of parental reaction, as well as every intermediate one, but as each society adopts its evolved behaviour it deludes itself into believing that culture thought of it first.

For the argument that cultural differences are really evolutionarily dictated differences in disguise to be correct, there has to be some reason why in some cultures reproductive success might be enhanced by sexual permissiveness but in others by sexual repression. We have already answered this in principle – the best attitude depends on the balance of costs and benefits in each situation. But why should costs and benefits differ between societies?

As we have seen, in the absence of costs, children *and* their parents gain from their acquiring sexual experience as soon as possible. But the picture changes when there are prices to be paid, and the main biological price to be paid for early sexual experience is the risk of disease, as we have already seen in the context of child abuse. So is there any evidence that whether a society becomes permissive or restrictive depends largely on the risk of its children contracting infectious diseases? Before answering this question, we first need to consider why societies differ in their vulnerability to disease.

Because they lived in small, isolated communities with *relatively* little mobility between them, and had a healthy, protein-rich diet, our hunter-gatherer ancestors ran a relatively low risk of death or infertility due to infectious diseases, sexual or otherwise. Such communities, now as well as then, have been relatively disease-free for two reasons. First, any persistent diseases from the past are now benign, because they will have killed off the vulnerable, leaving only the immune to survive. Second, new and virulent diseases are rarely encountered, because there are too few people for such diseases to arise often via mutation, and too little mobility for them to arrive often via migration.

Diseases are not a scourge unless people live in large, settled communities with considerable interpopulation mobility; then, mutation often generates new diseases. For example, according to the World Health Organisation, thirty new and dangerous infectious diseases have arisen around the world in the last twenty years alone, and people are forever encountering new ones because of their and other people's mobility. Our agriculturist ancestors, with their unhealthy carbohydrate-rich diet but without the benefits of modern medicine, suffered particularly badly from infectious diseases. In the modern world, people live in even larger populations and have even greater worldwide mobility, and as a result they run an even greater risk of *encountering* novel infectious diseases than our ancestors did – although thanks to modern medicine they rarely die of them. Nevertheless, the high incidence of infertility is one of the prices we have to pay for our modern way of life, and the earlier our children begin their sexual adventures the greater the risk they run of infertility or even death.

So societies do differ in their vulnerability to disease. But does the risk of disease show any sign of involvement in the shaping of sexual permissiveness and repressiveness? The evidence from pre-industrial cultures, studied by anthropologists in the first half of this century, seems clear. In one survey, published in 1952, of

234

the seventeen small and relatively isolated human societies that dotted the Pacific Ocean, which in their recent past will have been relatively disease-free, twelve (71 per cent) were totally permissive and only one, the Trukese, was repressive. By comparison, of the societies living in the band that stretches from North West Africa across to the Indian Ocean, an area of high disease risk, not one was permissive, and 70 per cent were highly repressive. In between these two extremes, in terms both of disease risk and of permissiveness, were the small societies of continental South America and North America, Eurasia and southern Africa, which were, respectively, 20, 17, 29 and 45 per cent fully permissive.

Modern industrial societies, the largest and most mobile in which humans have ever lived, have continued this trend. When such societies are permissive, children are exposed to a high risk of disease. As we have already seen, one in ten children who have sexual contact with adults contract a sexually transmitted disease. The street children of Brazil provide a graphic example of the dangers of giving children free rein in a modern industrial setting. These children are particularly vulnerable to exploitation by adults. Sexual initiation happens at about eleven for boys and twelve for girls. Over one in three eventually contract a sexually transmitted disease. With such dangers, it is perhaps not surprising that modern societies are, or are rapidly becoming, probably the most puritanical and repressive of all.

Early sexual behaviour in modern society also generates additional costs of its own. One such cost to the child is early-teenage pregnancy. In Britain in 1994, for example, although less than one per cent of girls conceived before they were fourteen (and 61 per cent of those legally aborted the child), 4 per cent conceived before the age of sixteen (and 40 per cent aborted). In the industrialised world, the United States has the highest rate of early-teenage births and Japan has the lowest, closely followed by Switzerland and the Netherlands. Although early-teenage pregnancy is usually costly in the modern environment, in our evolutionary past it was *sometimes* to a young girl's, and hence also to her parents', advantage. Nonetheless there will always have been costs attached to early pregnancies, for both the girl and her baby. Even now, such mothers face higher risks of complications in childbirth, and their infants are at greater risk of prematurity, low birth weight, death in the first year of life and developmental problems. Early-teenage mothers may also end up with fewer children when their family is completed. Occasionally, however, such potential disadvantages may be offset by compensations, such as the shortening of the generation interval or conceiving to a particularly desirable male (which we discuss in other chapters).

It was to allow for these costs and benefits that natural selection designed fertility at different stages in a woman's life in the way that we have already discussed. In the years immediately following puberty, a few cycles *are* fertile but the majority are not. Even in the most permissive of societies, girls have seldom conceived in the years after puberty, even when having intercourse frequently. So a young girl could sometimes take advantage of her earliest reproductive opportunities while most of the time remaining protected from pregnancies that her body judged to be unwise. Essentially, if she conceived it would be because her body judged conception to be advantageous.

In the modern world, however, there are other factors, such as education, social prospects and wealth, that influence a girl's long-term reproductive prospects and that may suffer if she embarks on motherhood at too early an age. The protection and opportunism that natural selection afforded girls in the ancestral environment is imperfect in today's environment, so that very often those pregnancies that a teenage girl's body does allow may actually reduce, rather than enhance, her long-term reproductive success. Parents do their best to restrain and protect their teenage daughters. They are working, though, against a young female body that natural selection has predisposed to sometimes allow or even seek conception.

Another new risk to the modern child arises from the link between sexual contact with adults and the risk of being killed. How often in Western civilisations are child murders linked with sexual contact? And how often is the murder committed because, having been driven to commit the particular sexual act, the perpetrator tries to avoid retribution by killing the only witness? Such murders would be far less likely in a permissive society because there would be no penal repercussions for adults arising from sexual contact with children. But sexual contacts would be much more common.

Such considerations are irrelevant to the average parent in modern Western society. Disease (particularly the spectre of HIV), murder (particularly paedophilia-linked) and early-teenage pregnancies all *appear* to be on the increase because they are more and more in the media spotlight. Whether they are *really* proliferating is a matter for interesting debate but is not germane to this discussion. Natural selection has programmed parents to respond to any *apparent* increase in risk by restraining even more rigorously their children's urge for sexual exploration. In the 1990s, this is what seems to be happening throughout Western societies.

At a social level, rigorous restraint involves categorising as abusive any behaviour perceived to be dangerous. As we noted in the discussion following Scene 17, the definition of child abuse has become so wide in some countries that it now includes forms of parental behaviour that would never previously have qualified. Even behaviours that in the past many would have seen as good parenting – extended breast-feeding, access to the family bed and nudity – now all hover precariously on the abuse/education borderline. The family in our scene could well have been a target for scrutiny if their form of parenting had ever come to the attention of a zealous social worker. Such families will always exist because parents have been programmed to weigh up the costs and benefits of their and their children's sexual behaviour and restrain or give rein to their children accordingly. No matter what the legal strictures, different individuals within any society will perceive the risks and benefits of their children's sexual exploration differently.

SCENE 20

Rebellion, Exploration and Fledging

'I've just found a cigarette end in the garden,' said the puzzled father. 'You don't think he's started smoking, as well as everything else, do you?'

The mother had been dreading this moment, but hadn't imagined it would begin with a cigarette end in the garden. She knew their son had started smoking. Despite the ever-open window in his room, she had picked up the smell on more than one occasion, but she hadn't dared tell her partner. There was bound to be yet another scene, yet another reason for father and son to argue. There was already tension in the air. Upstairs, the drone and thud-thud of their son's latest taste in music was making the whole house shake. She decided not to tell her partner what she knew, at least not yet.

'It could have come from anywhere,' she lied. 'He knows how strongly you ... we ... feel about it. I don't think he's likely to smoke, at least not while he's in the house. Maybe it blew there, or maybe the window-cleaner dropped it.'

The frown remained on the man's face. 'It's not the first I've found just there,' he said. 'And it's just under his window.' He paused and his gaze shifted in the direction of the sound. 'Anyway, I'm going to move it. Maybe it *was* the window-cleaner.'

The mother breathed a sigh of relief as her partner went back into the garden. If he only knew — not only had his sixteen-year-old son started smoking, but so had his daughter.

Her partner had never smoked. As a country-born seven-year-old, he had once refused to smoke with some older boys he'd become friendly with. So incensed had they been at his nonconformity that they had chased him across the fields, eventually to catch him, pin him to the ground and stuff half a packet of cigarettes into his mouth. Ever since, he had recoiled at the thought of a cigarette between his lips. She had once smoked, and still did when drunk and in social situations, especially if her partner was elsewhere, but all the same she considered herself a non-smoker. She didn't like the thought of her children doing it, but family relationships were so strained at present that she preferred to turn a blind eye rather than risk any further confrontation. Her partner, she knew, would not see it the same way.

She made herself a coffee, then went into the lounge, picked up a magazine and flopped down in a chair. At least during these long summer evenings one or the other of them was usually outside — her partner pottering in the garden or her son out with friends. The less time the pair of them spent in each other's company, the more peaceful her life.

There were three main areas of contention. One was the amount of time their son spent listening to his music, which neither parent could stand. Another was how little time he spent on his school work. And the third was his choice of friends and how much time he spent with them. Both parents suspected that, as a gang, they were quite capable of experimenting with drugs. They certainly drank. One of his friends was older than the rest and had his own flat. Often their son would stay there for weekends. Hearing nothing from him for forty-eight hours or more, they would have visions of him stretched out on the floor in a drunken or drug-induced slumber.

The most recent confrontation had concerned the gang's proposal to go travelling around Europe during the summer vacation, living rough and getting work where they could. Their son wanted his parents to finance his trip. Of course, he would pay them back . . . They had refused and he had been sullen ever since, unwilling to talk or cooperate with them. Now they had to ask him three or four times to turn his music down, whereas before twice would have been enough. The previous night he had informed them that he was going anyway. One of his wealthier friends had offered to lend him the money. He could easily get casual labour as they went along, he was sure, and would soon be able to repay him.

Every day her son and her partner had three or four minor skirmishes, and hardly a week went by without a major row. She had to admit that, although she tried to keep out of it, she was so worried by her son's behaviour that she often joined in the arguments, in an effort to persuade him to change his ways and his plans.

She was also worried about the effects of the family fights on her daughter. The girl worshipped her big brother, and only wished she could go with him on his travels. At fifteen she already looked adult, especially when she made herself up. Friction was growing between mother and daughter over the girl's makeup, as well as over the revealing clothes that had begun to appear in her wardrobe. The woman knew her daughter was buying alcoholic drinks when she went out with her friends. She also knew she was being pursued by older boys, and seriously worried about the influences she was coming under. Even this afternoon she had gone off for a drive with a boy three years older than she was. She didn't know whether it was her son or one of her daughter's boyfriends who was to blame for *her* starting to smoke, but she could already see the problems that lay ahead. Her partner was so possessive about his daughter: if he knew she was smoking, drinking and probably being mauled by boys he would probably ban her from leaving the house. They had once prided themselves on how liberal they were, but in the last year they had found their permissive principles slipping away.

She turned the pages of the magazine without really looking at them.

239

Her heart sank when she heard the back door open and her partner come back into the house. Going straight to the foot of the stairs, he bellowed, '*Will* you turn that bloody music down! One of the neighbours has just complained.'

The change was subtle, but she was sure that within seconds of her son being asked to turn the sound down he had turned it up instead. She sighed. If only her daughter would return from her trip, she could serve the dinner.

W e might think that there should be no need for adolescent rebellion. In the interests of eventually producing grand-children, parents' and offspring's aims should surely coincide. It is in both their interests for a child to behave in the way that affords it the best out of life, and for it to live in the best possible environment before it begins to reproduce. Surely, then, natural selection should have fashioned adolescence, the transitional phase between dependence on parents and independence, as a time of peaceful cooperation, of teaching and learning. So why is adolescence such a tempestuous stage in the lives of so many families?

In part, adolescence seems so difficult because it follows a phase of ten to fifteen years or so during which children more or less do as their parents request, sibling rivalry and parental favouritism notwithstanding. Such compliance is in a child's own interests, because by and large the parents will know how best to survive and succeed in the place where they all live. Children have no choice over where they are born and raised, so that while they are growing they can do no more than make the most of the environment their parents have provided for them. And on the whole the best way to do this will be to adopt their parents' codes of behaviour. It is from their parents, and from the world around them, that children learn. And the behavioural and social code that they learn is usually well suited to the environment into which they have been born, because it was the code their parents learned and *they* have been reproductively successful. Inevitably, therefore, children have been programmed to copy parental behaviour and to adopt parental values and attitudes in their early years.

So after having their example followed and their views heeded for so long, parents like those in our scene may find their child's adolescence a great shock. Suddenly, he or she begins to question their values and to experiment with activities of which they disapprove, or even abhor. Gradually they gain the impression that the child feels an ever-increasing disregard for them, their home and everything they stand for. Associated with this dissatisfaction, as illustrated in the scene, may be an increasing displeasure with the home territory or a restlessness and urge to travel to new places.

Inevitably, a child's questioning of everything its parents hold dear generates argument, conflict and concern. Parents are convinced that the child, by deviating from the behaviour and ethics that worked for them, is going to be less successful in its own life. Although few parents would rationalise their feelings in this way, an evolutionary biologist would argue that parents subconsciously see adolescent rebellion as a threat to long-term reproductive success. Unless their children unquestioningly obey their wishes they will not have as many grandchildren as they could. So why don't children follow their parents' example?

The principle is simple. People differ and environments change. Simply because a particular location and behavioural code were the best for the parents does not make them the best for their child born twenty or thirty years later. Quite possibly someone with the child's characteristics, not the parents', could now find a better place to live and a better way to behave. But how can a child best discover what opportunities are open to it that weren't open to its parents? There is only one way – to explore and experiment, both geographically and behaviourally. The child already knows how to behave like its parents. And having lived and possibly travelled with them for years, it already knows the places they know. All that remains, before it finds its own best place to live and its own best way to behave, is to visit places that they have never seen and to behave in ways that they would never behave.

To most parents, this looks like rebellion. They decided, during their own adolescence, where they should live and how they should behave. And because their decisions worked for them, they tend to make the assumption that it will also work for their children. And so it might – but it might not, and children who do not explore as many avenues as possible before they in their turn begin to reproduce run the risk of missing opportunities to maximise their own reproductive output. Having experimented, they may well decide that what was best for their parents remains best for them, and after a phase of rebellion and exploration they may re-adopt their parents' codes of practice. But they may not.

Being of different generations and having experienced different environments, parents and children disagree over how their long-term aim of maximising reproductive output is to be realised. In a stable, slowly changing environment there is in fact a very good chance that, after its rebellious phase, a child will return to live near its parents and adopt traditional values. In a rapidly changing environment, however, such as confronts today's adolescent, this is less likely. Also, it is not equally unlikely for all of the children in a family. Much will depend on sibling rivalry, parental favouritism and birth order, as we have already seen. On the whole, it will be later-born children who are most likely to rebel and reject parental values permanently.

Why has natural selection designed the urges to rebel and explore to peak during adolescence rather than earlier or later in a child's life? There are two main factors. First, it is important that by the time a person settles down to reproduce he (or she) has explored enough of his environment to have found a good – the best available – place to live. Moreover, before beginning the difficult job of reproduction and parenthood, he (or she) needs to have found, learned, practised and perfected a consistent code of ethics and behaviour that will allow him to succeed in his chosen home and environment. Second, because leaving home and becoming independent constitute a leap into the unknown, it can be a dangerous phase in a person's life. It cannot, therefore, be done safely until he is both experienced and physically strong enough to look after himself. Rebellion and exploration are thus too dangerous for children, but too important to leave until adulthood. An additional advantage of exploring during adolescence is that it provides the opportunity of meeting a succession of potential mates. Moreover, because all this happens away from the parents' home, incest can be avoided, as we discussed earlier.

Although rebellion and exploration peak during adolescence, they have their roots much earlier in a child's life. Something as important as the process of becoming independent cannot happen efficiently overnight – it needs practice. We can trace its beginnings as far back as the second year of a child's life – the 'terrible twos'. This is the time when a child first begins to test its ability to oppose its parents, learning the principles of threat, defiance and bargaining. The process continues throughout childhood, of course, as part of the continual cut and thrust of sibling rivalry and parental favouritism, as each child tries to further its own interests. But to the parents the terrible twos can seem so much worse than any conflicts they may have with infants or juniors, because the subtle pressures and bribery that can be used on older children via language do not work as effectively with a two-year-old. Equally, a two-year-old cannot convey the subtleties of its needs, so it is forced to resort to crying, yelling, kicking and running. Add to this its total lack of both social embarrassment and sense of personal danger, and a rebellious two-year-old can make life just as difficult for parents as a rebellious adolescent – but fortunately it lasts for nowhere near as long.

The whole process of adolescent rebellion and exploration and the adoption of ways to behave and places to live might seem to be a very cerebral one. But the urge to travel and to collect the necessary information is programmed by the genes and mediated by the hormones, and there have been a whole range of experiments that prove that this is the case.

Humans are not the only animals to go through an exploratory phase during adolescence. All vertebrates do. If a gorilla turns up in a village in equatorial Africa, miles from the nearest gorilla habitat, it's sure to be an adolescent. If a bear turns up in a garden in North America, it will be an adolescent. These young animals are not lost – they are exploring. A radio tag placed on any one of them from birth will show that as the individual enters adolescence, it begins a phase of wandering. It will leave the place where it was born and travel, sometimes long distances – a radio-tagged male black bear in North America was once followed on an exploration of two hundred kilometres. These wanderings are not random: they follow an efficient search pattern. Often the prodigal will briefly return to its home area before eventually settling down, there or elsewhere, in the best of the areas discovered during its travels. Studies like this have been replicated for fish, frogs, reptiles, birds and many mammals.

The most intensive study of this adolescent urge has been on rats and mice. Even when the adolescent rodents are caged, their strong urge to explore can be seen in a massive increase in the amount of time they spend running in a wheel. The activity begins at puberty, when the testes first begin producing sperm or the ovaries produce the first eggs, reaches a peak soon after puberty, then starts to decline at the age when the rat or mouse would normally begin to reproduce. When it does start to reproduce, its exploratory activity subsides to the normal, relatively low, level typical of adults.

The urge to explore is part of a lifetime's schedule rigorously programmed into a mouse's body by its genes, as demonstrated by breeding experiments. Selective breeding can produce some strains of mice that are chronic explorers, and others that take no interest in exploring. Other studies have shown that the 'exploration genes' exert their effect via sex hormones. Castrate a male or remove the ovaries of a female, and the urge disappears. Many pet-owners have done this experiment for themselves. A neutered dog or cat stops travelling long distances and settles for a contented life at home just as surely as a castrated rodent. And they can all have their exploratory urge restored by the injection of the appropriate hormones. What all of these experiments show is that adolescent behaviour is programmed into mammals, humans included, by their genes and orchestrated via sex hormones.

In many human societies, adolescent males go through a culturally embraced phase of exploration and discovery. The best-known is the walkabout that used to be such a part of central Australian aboriginal culture. At puberty, young male aborigines would leave their parental territory – thereby abandoning parental influence – to set off on journeys of exploration and discovery that could last for several years. At first, they wouldn't go far – they would walk a little way, then come back. But as they became more familiar with their surrounding area and more able to fend for themselves, they travelled further and stayed away longer. Eventually, they could travel hundreds of kilometres. And like the black bears and gorillas mentioned earlier, they were not lost. At any time they could find their way back, either to their parental territory or to the best of the places they had discovered during their travels, there to make their home. In modern industrial societies, the walkabout urge is transformed into an acute restlessness, reflected in a dissatisfaction with home, an urge to see new places, meet new people and have new experiences. We do not know if the eunuchs of past cultures, like castrated cats and dogs, had less of an urge to explore or rebel, but we may suspect that they did. What we do know is that a person who takes steroids becomes more restless and more quarrelsome, as well as more sexually motivated, just as do rats and mice who are injected with them. Adolescent restlessness and rebellion in humans, no matter how cerebral they may seem, are as much a genetically programmed, hormonally mediated part of the human life-plan as are puberty, the menopause and senility.

Thanks to the precision with which natural selection has shaped their genetic and hence hormonal programme, the majority of adolescents will time their rebellions and explorations according to their own best interests, and will eventually metamorphose unscathed into adulthood. A few, perhaps with a faulty genetic programme, may stay with their parents too long and miss out on many opportunities. A more unfortunate few may leave parental care too soon and live homeless, vulnerable, miserable and sometimes short lives on the streets of the industrial world's cities. Occasionally, such premature departure from home may also be due to a faulty genetic programme, one that triggers the child into restlessness and rebellion before its experience and physical development are adequate. But more often than not, such children are escaping parental or step-parental abuse or disfavouritism for any of the reasons we have already discussed; they have decided, wisely or not, that their uncertain prospects in a distant city are likely to be better than their more certain prospects if they stay at home.

Of course, even though adolescent rebellion and restlessness are driven by an evolved genetic and hormonal programme, and run by the body, the brain has an important part to play in their success. Driven by the body's urge to test and evaluate the environment, the brain has the vital job of collecting and remembering all the information gathered. In addition, it is the brain's responsibility to monitor and remember the consequences of behaving in this way in this place, as opposed to in that way in that place. It is also – or it was, in the past – responsible for collecting the information needed to navigate: to know not only where the body is at the moment and where it is best for it to go next, but also to know how to get there. Lastly, it is the body that eventually says, 'I've had enough. It's time to start thinking about settling down. So which was the best place we found, how do we get there and how do we re-establish contact with parents?' All the brain has to do is sift through the information it has collected and stored and come up with the answers.

For once, parents may not need much convincing that their child's behaviour is driven by his or her body, as opposed to his or her mind. Often the rebellion of adolescence will seem to them irrational, rebellion for rebellion's sake. Yet, as we have seen, it is a very important part of their child's pursuit of reproductive success. Adolescents do sometimes contract diseases, fall prey to drugs or die during the trial and error of exploration, but most will emerge better equipped for their own world than if they had simply listened to their parents. On average, a child enhances its own and its parents' reproductive output by its behaviour. Disconcerting, distressing and tumultuous as it may be, a child's behaviour during adolescence is a vital leg on the parents' road to successful grandparenthood.

SCENE 21
Mate Selection

Slamming the car door, the young girl walked up the path to the house, oblivious of the sheepish expression on the driver's face. With dried semen on her buttocks and cow dung on her shoes, she was not in the best of moods. She wanted a shower and she wanted it now. As she opened the front door, she was greeted by the familiar blaring of her brother's music and her parents' raised voices. On hearing the door close, her mother broke off their heated discussion to call out that dinner would soon be ready. The girl hesitated at the foot of the stairs, then shouted back that she wanted a shower and that she wasn't hungry yet anyway.

The mother looked in her direction as she heard her run up the stairs. Something in her voice made her suspect that all was not well. She guessed that the afternoon drive had not been a success. Her daughter was only fifteen, but the thought flitted through her mind that perhaps it was time to talk about contraception.

The young girl was beginning to feel ambivalent about sex. On the one hand, she worried about getting pregnant. On the other, she was fretting a little about being left behind and about still being a virgin. It felt as if soon she would be the only one, even though she knew, really, that she was still in the majority. Her brother had had sex, though. She knew this because both her best friend and he himself had told her, soon after it had happened. And some of her other friends, too, were beginning to have their first experiences of intercourse. Every so often, one or another of them would become the focus of a giggling, eagerly questioning audience huddled in the toilets. Few actually recommended the experience, but whatever tale of discomfort or disappointment they told, their story did nothing to discourage the rest from wanting to find out for themselves. As for her best friend, she seemed to be on a crusade. After her fling first with the girl's brother and then with the drummer, she had moved on, and within twelve months she had reached double figures. Then she met a twenty-year-old with an apartment, and settled into a year-long relationship based on their mutual interest in drinking, dancing and sex.

By sixteen, the girl herself had had little success with boys. Since the incident in the field with her brother's old playmate, several nice but boring boys had invited her out on dates, but rarely did she go out with anybody more than once or twice. Mostly, they just sat around on park benches or stood on street corners while the boy would find excuses to grope her. Sometimes she felt like cooperating, but more often than not she fought them off. She couldn't contemplate sex with any of them, not least because she was becoming infatuated with the recently appointed biology teacher. Soon it was he who began to take centre-stage in her fantasies. Every time she saw him, and every time he stood near, her whole body tingled. She never felt anything comparable with her fumbling contemporaries. She used to look for excuses to walk past his classroom and to ask him questions during lessons. Most of all, she worked hard to excel at biology, hoping to force him to notice her. In practical classes she would draw his attention to this or that specimen, so that he would have to bend over her to see, and she would then contrive to brush against him. Her friends noticed and began to tease her, but this pleased rather than upset her. She was happy that, in her friends' minds at least, the two of them were linked. She soon convinced herself that he was beginning to respond and going out of his way to bump into her.

Then, one afternoon at the beginning of her last year at school, she got the evidence she needed. Driving past as she made her way home, he stopped and offered her a lift. As she walked the hundred yards or so from where he had dropped her off, however, her earlier excitement had turned to misery. She had been completely unable to say anything sensible, she reflected. The ghost of that afternoon was not laid until a week later when he offered her a lift again – and this time she managed to string a few sensible sentences together. That day, she walked the rest of the way home on air. The lifts became increasingly frequent until, one wet afternoon, he dropped her right outside her house. Getting out of the car in full view of her mother who was watching from an upstairs window, she walked out of one storm and straight into another.

For over a month, now, the woman had been putting her daughter under increasing pressure. She wanted her to go out with a boy whose wealthy parents had once confided that their son thought her daughter was wonderful. The mother was so enamoured of the idea of her daughter going out with the son of one of the highest-status couples in town that she would grasp every opportunity to sing his praises, and to criticise any other male in whom she might show an interest. The sight of her stepping out of the rusting car of a struggling young teacher was something she could not let pass without comment.

Despite protesting that all her teacher had done was give her a lift on a wet afternoon – strategically forgetting the nine earlier fair-weather occasions – the girl had to endure a lengthy tirade consisting mainly of a list of the dangers of accepting lifts from men. The brain of even teachers resided in their groin, the woman asserted, then proceeded to ask her daughter whether he had ever touched her, made sexual suggestions, or harassed her in any way. If she became pregnant while so young her life could be ruined, she pointed out, and she needn't expect *her* to look after the baby for her. Cruellest of all her comments – it was also her own fear – her mother told her not to fool herself that the teacher was actually interested in *her*. Like all men he was only after one thing, and once he'd been inside her knickers he would be off like a shot to the next starry-eyed virgin without giving her a second thought.

There was one good thing that emerged from the episode, though, as far she was concerned. Her mother suggested, almost insisted, that it was time for her to go to the family planning centre and get herself prescribed contraceptive pills, 'just in case'. This was a relief, because it meant that she would no longer need to hide the supply she had already acquired. She had decided months earlier that, if the situation arose, she would go all the way – if only so that she could stop thinking of herself as a virgin. And whatever her mother might say, the girl could think of no better person to take her virginity than her teacher. Ten years older than she was, he should know all there was to know about sex. She fantasised about long hours naked in his arms, about the kisses, caresses and compliments he would shower on her as he showed her every inch of her body's potential. She had even decided when it would happen. Early in the New Year, she and the rest of the senior biology class were to go away on a field experience week. In the meantime, while she waited patiently but with mounting excitement for her fantasy to materialise, she contented herself with occasional class-room contact and the once-weekly excitement of a lift home, though never again to her door.

She also endured a couple of dates at the local cinema with boys of her own age. One squeezed her breasts so hard they were tender for hours afterwards. The other – her mother's choice – spent the first half of the film trying to force her hand down the front of his trousers. Grudgingly, she complied, then remembered her father's warning that men's bits needed gentle handling. So she yanked the boy's foreskin back so hard that his barely stifled yelp made several people in the row in front turn round. He disappeared into the toilet to check the damage, and when he returned showed more interest in pop-corn than sex.

The following morning, her mother was eager to know how the evening had gone. When the girl told her how he had kept wanting her to touch him, to her surprise, she simply said that boys were like that and she would soon learn how to handle them. He would probably behave better next time. But there was no next time. To her relief and her mother's disappointment he didn't ask her out again.

On the second night of the field course, the girl slipped away to the biology teacher's room equipped with a flimsy pretext, a racing heart and damp knickers, to find him just out of his shower and wearing a towel. When, after minimal discussion on the ostensible subject of her visit, he offered her the use of his shower so that she could avoid queuing with the other students, she accepted, and went and undressed behind the half-open bathroom door. Drawn irresistibly by the sight of her body, he offered to join her in the shower. She again accepted, then removed his towel with a single deft tug. Slippery with soap, she wrapped her arms round his neck, hitched her legs around his waist and offered him her vagina. But he could barely keep his balance, and in the tight confines of the shower cubicle they couldn't quite make it. Maybe they would have transferred to the bed, but an urgent knock on the door had them both frantically searching for something to put on.

He was to spend the next two hours in hospital with her best friend, who had drunk herself into a coma.

On the third night of the course, she made it into his bed. Three times she thought her fantasy was about to be realised, but although he stroked and nuzzled her, his heart didn't seem to be in it. Each time, she had hardly begun to focus on the sensations she had dreamt about for so long than he was clambering on to her, then entering her and thrusting so hard that she couldn't wait for him to relieve himself and stop. In between, he dozed. After the third intercourse, he suggested she should go back to her room to prevent her room-mates from becoming suspicious, and so that they could both get some sleep. When she arrived at his door on the fourth night, hoping that this time he would live up to her expectations, just as she was about to knock she heard the muffled but unmistakable sounds of intercourse. Equally unmistakable was the voice of the girl – fully recovered, clearly, from her coma.

At the end of the week, she returned home disappointed and chastened. Not only had she been dissatisfied with the sexual act itself, she was annoyed – though she didn't tell her – that her mother had been right. After the field trip, she avoided all extracurricular contact with the biology teacher, and for a while had nothing further to do with men.

Eight months later she left for college, two hundred miles away. In spite of her mother's warnings about men and her own experiences with her teacher, she felt such a release at being away from home that she fell for the first attractive man who told her they were made for each other. Meeting him at a welcoming party for new students, she allowed him to drive her into the dark countryside where, after a few more drinks and promises, she let him satisfy his urgent needs. She remembered little of the drive home, and wasn't to see him again for a long while.

Over the next few months, two other good-looking men made intercourse seem worth while, only to leave her bed and disappear into the early-morning light. Despairing of anybody ever wanting a relationship with her, when she had been at college for nearly a year she met her first real boyfriend. Less attractive than those who had gone before and certainly less well off, he was nevertheless kind and considerate. During that first summer vacation, she invited him home. Her parents were disappointed in her choice and made little attempt to hide their feelings. She didn't need to ask whether the two of them could share her bed – she knew too well what the answer would be. True to form, her mother gave him the spare bedroom on the other side of the house from hers. This didn't, of course, stop them: he would creep past her parents' room and into hers in the early hours, then return before first light. Although this was better than nothing, they never really felt comfortable having sex there. What particularly annoyed her was that although, like her, her brother wasn't allowed to share a room with his girlfriend when they came to stay, they were at least given adjacent rooms. The episode confirmed for her something that she had known for years – that, unlike her brother, she never had her mother's approval over anything.

The girl and her boyfriend remained together for a while, sharing a flat for a few months. But as time went on and more and more of her friends hinted that they couldn't understand what she saw in him, she became bored and disappointed with the relationship. Just after they had begun to live together, she was unfaithful to him. From then on, she increasingly found excuses not to accompany him on his trips home or on his nights out with friends. On three further occasions while her partner was away she found herself accepting the invitations of more exciting men, only to wake feeling guilty and alone the following morning.

Then, quite by chance, a few weeks before the end of her second year she ran into the confident young man with the sports car who had whisked her off in her first week at college. He, too, was living with someone, but out of nostalgia and a sense of mischief they re-enacted their first encounter. This time, however, he asked to see her again. She quickly began to enjoy being with somebody with money and a car, as well as the freedom of being able, on a moment's whim, to drive off into the country for a few hours in an expensive hotel. In the end, however, she began to feel guilty about the fact that they were deceiving their partners. She also felt vulnerable, fearing that she might still be only his second choice. Eventually, she pressured him into choosing between her and his partner – he couldn't have both. Her gamble worked. At the end of term after their exams, they both finished with their partners.

The best moment of their new-found relationship came, for her, the first time they visited her parents. Their approval was unequivocal. It was a completely novel experience for her to be the centre of her parents' attention, as they made every effort to impress her boyfriend and to make them both welcome. She even half-suspected her mother of fancying him herself. And her father was particularly impressed when her boyfriend solved a long-standing problem with his car. Neither parent raised any objection when told that they were going abroad together for the summer, nor later when they informed them that they were going to live together for their last year at college.

Throughout that year, the girl grew increasingly amused by her mother's concern with her boyfriend's health, exam preparations and prospects. Sometimes she thought both parents were more interested in *his* progress than her own. And if she ever hinted that they were anything other than ecstatically happy, her mother would double the frequency of her phone calls. On two occasions she and her boyfriend arranged to visit her parents at weekends when her brother and his girlfriend were also invited. It was another new experience for her, the six of them sitting around as one big family, discussing their plans for the future.

After graduation, the girl and her boyfriend found good jobs in locations close enough for them to continue living together. Four years after leaving college, she conceived their first child. When, a few hours after giving birth to a baby boy, she watched her mother's face while holding her first grandchild in her arms, she knew that at last she had done something absolutely right.

Scenes 19 and 20 each illustrated an arena for conflict between parents and offspring on the road to grandparenthood. This scene has illustrated a third: the selection of a mate. Why has natural selection predisposed parents to take such a keen interest in their offspring's choice of boyfriends and girlfriends?

The answer is, as noted earlier, that the number and quality of a person's grandchildren are directly influenced by the quality of mate or mates acquired by their offspring. Often, as in the scene above, parents' interest and concern lead them to try to influence the choosing process, to the extent of encouraging or even occasionally forcing their child to choose a particular person. The most extreme manifestation of such parental influence is the phenomenon of arranged marriages. But even in the most liberal societies such pressure still occurs.

We might think that mate choice should be an area of relatively little conflict between parents and offspring. After all, it is in everybody's interests that the son or daughter maximises his or her reproductive output. Nevertheless, it can often be a major trigger for disagreement – one of the last arenas for grown-up baby wars. The girl in our scene probably wouldn't agree, but in fact she suffered relatively little parental interference as she sampled the men around her. Choosing a mate entails shopping around for genes and resources, then trying to strike the best compromise between the best, most suitable person available and the best, most suitable person that can be attracted to form a relationship. The 'sampling' behaviour of the girl in the scene illustrates this process clearly. But why should parents and children so often disagree over who is a suitable mate and who is not? There are two main reasons. First, each generation has a different experience of the process of mate choice. Second, parents and their children have different priorities.

Let's consider the first point. Some things never change from one generation to the next and, having already experienced or witnessed many of the strategic mistakes that can be made when seeking a partner, in these respects parents are likely to be the better informed. In the scene, for example, the mother was better able than her naïve daughter to guess the schoolteacher's intentions. Some things do change, though, over the generations. As we discussed in relation to adolescent rebellion, behaviour that may have indicated the best partner in one generation may not do so in the next. It is the children not their parents who are at the cutting edge of their generation's requirements, and they learn by direct experience which of the people available is best suited to them. Whichever – parent or offspring – is correct in any given instance, there is almost bound to be friction.

Second, we must consider the much more complex and important role of the differing priorities of the two generations. The parents' preference is for each child to become as independent as it can. The less they *have* to support any one of their offspring, the more freedom they have to apportion support across their entire family in their own best interests. In order to maximise the number and quality of their grandchildren, and perhaps even their great-grandchildren, parents need all of their children to avoid choosing a mate who turns them into a liability. A daughter who becomes pregnant with no help from the father, or a son who lays himself open to claims for support for a child who may not be his and hence not his parents' grandchild, can jeopardise the parents' plans to apportion support in their own best interests. On the other hand, as we noted when discussing sibling rivalry, each child is seeking to further its own reproductive success, even if at the cost of its parents' and siblings'. One way that it can do this is by exploiting its parents' pre-programmed inclination to help it if it gets into difficulties. For example, if the girl in our scene had become pregnant by her teacher, her mother would probably not have left her to fend for herself, despite her statement to the contrary. Only when family resources cannot stretch any further might a daughter find herself empty-handed after calling her parents' bluff.

The net result of these differences in priorities between parents and offspring is that children tend to take more risks than suits their parents. Both sons and daughters may use intercourse to test potential partners more extensively than their parents would consider ideal. As a son or daughter shops around for a partner, he or she does so in the confidence, albeit subconscious, that even if he or she does produce a child that he or she cannot support, help may yet be extracted from grudging parents who might otherwise have given none. This feeling of security allows a daughter to risk placing more emphasis on a male's genes and less emphasis on his wealth and ability to support her than her parents might wish. A son may pay more attention to a girl's genetic qualities – her physical attractiveness – than his parents might wish and less to how good a mother she might make. He may also place more emphasis on the number of girls he inseminates and less on whether he can support any children he sires.

There is scope, then, for parents to cross swords with both sons and daughters over their pursuit and choice of mates, and some of the conflicts are greater with sons than with daughters, and vice versa. For instance, parents are less likely to be called on to support an errant son's child than that of an errant daughter. As a result, a son's sexual activities while sampling potential mates may produce grandchildren who will be much less of a liability – if any at all – than any produced by a daughter at the same stage. Generally, therefore, parents tend to have a more cavalier attitude towards their sons' behaviour in this respect than towards their daughters'. Furthermore, on the whole both fathers and mothers should take a closer interest in their daughters' choice of mate than in their sons', because they can be certain a daughter's children are in fact hers, whereas they cannot be certain about a son's. For this reason, they may also take a close interest in how faithful a son's chosen partner is likely to be. If she shows signs of promiscuity, they may well be tricked into helping to raise someone else's grandchildren. Any concern over the likely fidelity of a daughter's chosen partner will be different, because any child she produces is their grandchild whether or not her partner is the father. Their concern is more likely to be over his ability and disposition to care for their daughter and any children: if he shows signs of promiscuity, then some time in the future he may desert their daughter and grandchildren for someone else. They may then be left *having* to help out, instead of doing so only if it suits their own plans.

A son's or daughter's quest for a partner may cause conflicts beyond those between themselves and their parents. Although this didn't happen in the scene above, mother and father can often disagree between themselves when assessing their offspring's choice. Why? What factors influence the father's long-term reproductive output differently from the mother's, given that they are going to share their success via grandchildren? Apart from the often mentioned one that men have a lower certainty of their parenthood and so should take generally less interest in their offspring's pursuit of partners, there are other considerations.

The mother, for example, because she will take the brunt of grandparental care, as we shall see in the next chapter, will be more concerned than the father about whether her son's choice will be a good and self-sufficient mother. Then, any help she gives in the raising of her grandchildren will be a bonus, not a necessity. Partly for this reason, the mother will also show particular concern over how compatible she and the girl might be in their cooperative care of any children.

The father's interest, however, may be slightly different. It is by no means unheard of – and has been fodder for many a tabloid –

for a young woman initially to be attracted to a young man only to discover when they meet that she prefers his father. So for a father the succession of young women brought home by his son are potential mates, and for many men old enough to have a grown-up son this is one of the few ways that they can meet younger women. A father, therefore, has an interest in the women his son brings home that is not shared by the mother; in fact, the more a son's choice appeals to the father, the less she may appeal to the mother and the more she may seem like a threat. Occasionally, a mother may take a sexual interest in her daughter's choice – but probably less often than the father finds himself attracted to his son's.

A father's main concern over his daughter's choice – and it will have been the same in the past – will be the extent to which the pair can complement each other and work together to increase the extended family's total resources. In the scene, the girl's final choice of partner was an immediate hit with her father when he fixed the latter's car! Shared and complementary interests will be important to their mutual reproductive output, whereas they will be less important to the mother.

In an ideal world, there will be minimal conflict between parents and offspring and between the parents themselves if an offspring's choice of partner satisfies everybody's priorities. Few potential mates, however, will be able to satisfy *all* requirements. Despite the parents' many shared priorities as they move towards grandparenthood, there are enough differences between them for an offspring's choice of partner sometimes to delight the father but disappoint the mother, and vice versa.

CHAPTER EIGHT

Grandparenthood

SCENE 22
Extended Help

The woman paused in the bedroom doorway and looked back at her handiwork, finger poised on the light-switch. Now in her late fifties, she had never been houseproud, but she had made a real effort for this weekend. Two of her grandchildren were coming to stay – for the first time she was going to have them all to herself for two whole days. Looking at the two beds – side by side because they liked to sleep next to each other – a flicker of grandparental emotion brought a tear to her eyes. She and her partner had bought the bedding only that week – pillowcases and duvet covers sporting trains for their grandson and teddies and rabbits for their granddaughter. She could just picture their beaming little faces as they said goodnight, tucked up in their new beds. She switched off the light and closed the door. Tomorrow night – she could hardly wait.

Nearly two hundred miles away, the woman's daughter was chasing her two children with a towel, trying to dry their hair, but they were having none of it. They were always excitable after their bath but tonight, with the prospect of staying at their grandmother's, they were irrepressible. Her parents were really good with them, and the children loved the wholehearted attention and the treats they received. Until now, though, the woman had felt reluctant to leave them with her parents. She just hadn't been able to face the thought of not having them with her, of not knowing what they were doing, of not knowing that they were safe. But now, though still somewhat reluctantly, she had agreed to a weekend away, on their own. They were going to stay in an expensive hotel on the coast, and she was looking forward to the prospect of a sauna and a cordon bleu menu.

As she watched her offspring rolling around on the floor tickling each other, still naked from their bath, she was reminded of herself and her brother when they were the same age. Her daughter was just five and her son six, going on seven, and getting an obvious thrill from the rough-and-tumble, just like her brother used to.

'Come on, you two,' she said, beginning to lose patience. 'I want you in bed. We've got an early start tomorrow if you want to see Grandma, and you can't go to bed with wet hair.' Even so, it was another half-hour before she had them settled enough to say goodnight. Then she turned her attention to packing the mass of clothes and toys that she felt they had to have if they were to get through a whole two days away from home.

It was still dark, and raining, when they set off the following morning, and the last hour before departure had been fraught. The children were excited, she and her partner were tired and irritable, and in spite of all her preparations the night before they were still late leaving. She had phoned her mother just before getting into the car to warn her they might be a bit late, while her partner complained that all she was doing was delaying them still further. Each blamed the other for not helping as much as they could and by the time they backed out of the drive they were no longer talking to each other. Usually, their mood would have quickly recovered, but this morning the weather conditions combined with her muttered disapproval when he took a corner faster than she would have done caused extra friction. Both shouted at the children in the back of the car, but they were too excited to take notice of their parents' mood.

Nearly four hours later, as they turned into the road that would take them on the last fifteen minutes of their journey, it was still raining. The children were asleep, heads tilted and resting awkwardly on their seat belts, but a friendly, if still not quite tranquil, atmosphere had returned. Any detectable tension was due to the fact that it was nearly an hour past their projected arrival time. For the last half-hour they had vacillated between speeding on or stopping to phone to say they would be even later than anticipated. In the end, they had decided not to stop. Now with the long, straight road ahead of them, her partner put his foot down.

A few minutes later, the low winter sun broke through the cloud ahead of them, reflecting off the glistening road. The man pulled down his sun shield and, as he did so, saw in his rear-view mirror a rainbow against the wall of dark cloud behind them. 'Look!' he said, and she turned, wishing the children were awake to share the spectacle.

As she turned back, a pulse of light in the distance in front of her caught her eye: the sun was glinting off the roof of a car that had just appeared far away to her left – like a jewel set in the dark hillside, she thought. She idly watched it appearing and disappearing, as distant trees and dips in the road briefly hid it from view. The road the distant car was travelling on snaked down to cross theirs at a junction about half a mile ahead. They would reach the junction first, she reckoned – but the next instant she wasn't so sure. The other car was travelling faster than she'd thought. Out of the corner of her eye, she saw her partner sneak another look at the rainbow through the rear-view mirror. She drew breath to direct his attention to the other car, then hesitated. He always snapped at her if she pointed out something he'd already seen. When, at the last moment, she realised that the other car was actually speeding up, she tried to shout a warning, but no words came.

In the split second that it took to shoot across the road in front of them, she registered inside the other car two laughing boys, one of them punching the air with his fist. Her partner braked instinctively, but clipped the rear of the other car just enough to catapult them into the side of the road. As it hit the lamp-post, the front of the car on her partner's side caved in, and in the second before her head struck the dashboard she saw him caught amongst a mass of crumpling metal and shattered glass.

Just five minutes down the road, the woman's mother was getting rather annoyed. 'They're an hour late,' she said for the third time. 'They're never on time. I hope they don't think they can just fly straight in and out. There are things I need to know about looking after the children.' She got up out of her chair again and went to the window.

As another hour passed, her irritation gradually turned to fear. Something had to be wrong, she was sure. Her daughter would have phoned by now if they were simply late or had broken down. Her partner tried to reassure her that maybe they had broken down a long way from a phone. But it was no good. She couldn't just sit there any longer. Who should she contact – police or hospitals? Hospitals. She began with the nearest one. If she drew a blank there she'd try further afield. *Then* the police. But there was no need – the third hospital she rang had just received unidentified accident victims answering the description she had given. To her anguish, they would give her no further information. But would she come in as quickly as possible, they asked.

Her nightmare came true when she saw her daughter and grandchildren lying there. To her relief, she was told that the children just had scratches and bruises; but her daughter was in a much more serious condition and hadn't yet regained consciousness. She wasn't allowed to see her daughter's partner. He had been killed instantly.

Three days after the accident, she was allowed to take her grandchildren home with her, but her daughter was still in a coma — she was fighting what seemed to be a losing battle. That night, as she looked at her grandchildren tucked up in bed under their brand-new duvets, faces still tear-stained, she thought back to the night before the accident. If only she could turn back the clock. She had been so happy then, so full of anticipation at the prospect of having her grandchildren with her for a couple of days. Now, it seemed, she might be looking after them for a long time to come.

The tragic circumstances illustrated in the scene above generate a situation that is fairly uncommon in the modern industrial world — that of children being raised by their grandparents. To our ancestors — and in many of the more tribal cultures even today — a comparable situation was the rule rather than the exception: it was not so much that children were raised by their grandparents *instead of* their parents, but that they were raised by their grandparents *as well as* their parents. Throughout most of human evolution, the normal environment for a child has been an extended family. People have been programmed by natural selection to look after their grandchildren almost as rigorously as they have been programmed to look after their children.

The influence an individual has on his or her reproductive success does not end with the production and raising of children: a recurring theme throughout this book has been that success is measured also by the number of grandchildren, great-grandchildren and future descendants that he or she has. It is because of this that reproductive success can be increased by having fewer children but, by making a greater investment in each, producing more grandchildren. Of course, the question of 'quality or quantity' can be extended beyond the first generation: a person's child may also have fewer children in order to concentrate on quality. But somewhere along the line of his or her descendants a person must reap the benefit of this emphasis on quality and gain a pay-off in terms of quantity. We saw this in Scene 12, when a woman received her pay-off via a grandson who was so successful that she eventually out-reproduced her main childhood rival, despite having had fewer children.

Each of the three scenes in this chapter illustrates an aspect of human behaviour that has evolved to further reproductive output via the successful raising of grandchildren. Scenes 23 and 24 are concerned with more specific aspects and apply only to some families, while in this first discussion we concentrate on some of the generalities of grandparental care.

We begin by considering the factors that were important during the evolution of human grandparenting. More often than not the extended family was patriarchal, revolving around the father's family. For example, among New Guinea highlanders a young man would wander off during adolescence, find a partner in some neighbouring or even distant tribe, and then bring her back to live in his extended family. In matriarchal families – for example, among various African pastoralists and agriculturists – although it was still the adolescent male who did the wandering, a newly formed couple would settle down with the woman's family. In some extreme conditions, such as those lived in by the Yumbri in the rain-forests of Thailand, men and women spent much of the year apart, the young being raised primarily by an extended family of related women.

Just as parents can influence the survival, health and success of their children by the quality of the care that they give them, so too can grandparents who live with them influence their grandchildren by the quality of *their* care. All the same factors of favouritism and rivalry apply as with parental care, and the most successful grandparents are those who apportion their help and investment in the best way possible. But there are two factors that are more relevant to grandparental care than to parental.

First, grandparents can sometimes improve their reproductive rate by helping to raise, or by raising as their own for a few years, a grandchild born to a son or daughter at an age when he or she is too young to take on full parental care. In this way they can reduce the generation interval, thus increasing their reproductive rate. Second, grandparents face the challenge of apportioning their investment across two generations, and strategically there is a danger that too much investment in a favoured grandchild at the cost of their children may reduce the total number of grandchildren. Of course, even this might be advantageous if the greater success of the favoured grandchild eventually made up for the reduced total number of grandchildren – but the strategy has to be carefully balanced.

The contribution of grandparents to the success of their grand-children can be direct, in the sense of extra pairs of hands and eyes to help feed and carry or prevent accident. It can also be indirect, in the sense of provision or defence of space, and provision of resources and passed-on experience. However, as we saw in connection with mate choice, experience is a double-edged sword. In a slowly changing environment, the grandparental experience of previous decades can be invaluable, but in a rapidly changing one it can be a hindrance. Parents are forever piggy-in-the-middle, sifting out from the steady stream of grandparental advice and help what is relevant to their child's generation. The most successful grandparents and parents are those who successfully negotiate this conflict to complement each other as a reproductive unit. This again emphasises the importance to potential grandparents of trying to influence their son's or daughter's choice of long-term partner, as discussed in Scene 21.

The grandparent-plus-parent unit – in other words, the extended family – evolved in ancestral environments that changed relatively slowly. Moreover, a child lived with one of its sets of grandparents in their home area, an environment with which they had a lifetime's familiarity. Information, skills and techniques learned by one generation of hunter-gatherers and, to a lesser extent, agriculturists, will have been useful for generations. It will have been largely to reap the benefits of grandparental care in the furtherance of reproductive success that early human cultures, in both hunter-gatherer and agricultural societies, will have lived in extended families. Most long-lived social animals, such as lions, horses, sheep and primates, also show grandparental care. Males, though, play relatively little part. Social groups usually consist of related females – mothers, daughters, granddaughters, sisters, aunts and nieces. Any male who associates with the group, siring the children and perhaps offering protection, is usually unrelated to the females, as mentioned in connection with incest. The result is that males rarely contact their grandchildren and, even when they do, as in some of the primates who live in large and extended groups, they take relatively little interest in them compared with the interest that females take.

The explanation is once again the probability of parenthood or, in this case, grandparenthood: a female can be absolutely confident that a daughter's child is her grandchild, but has to be less confident about a son's child. In humans, much depends on how confident a woman is of the fidelity of her son's partner – one of the reasons why she takes such a close interest in her son's choice of mate. In contrast, a male cannot be totally confident about his grandpaternity of his putative daughter's child, let alone of his putative son's putative child!

The absolute confidence a female can have in her grandparenthood of her daughter's offspring is probably the main reason that social groups in non-human species tend to form around a nucleus of related females. We would have expected the same to occur in humans, newly formed couples living with the woman's parents rather than the man's, but as we have seen, more often than not they tend to live within the influence of the man's parents. Nevertheless, there does appear to be a pattern to this otherwise surprising behaviour. Couples seem most likely to live within groups of related men in circumstances in which physical defence of the group is of critical importance. New Guinea highlanders in the first half of the twentieth century, for instance, and even in the 1980s the Yanomamo living in South American forests, have provided graphic examples. In such tribes, the survival of extended families depended crucially on the ability of the males to defend them against marauding warriors from neighbouring areas, intent on rape and murder. Under such circumstances, the stability that kinship imparts to the fighting unit outweighs other considerations.

Whatever the structure of the extended family, however, it is almost universally true, in humans as in other animals, that females take a much greater interest in helping their grandchildren than do males because their certainty in their grandmaternity gives them a much greater chance that their grandparental activities will further their own reproductive success. And it is probably partly for this reason that women have gone a step further than men in their preparation for grandparenthood. For not only does their behaviour shift from parental to grandparental, their body chemistry changes in such a way that they can never again become parents. They pass through the menopause.

The menopause – the cessation of periods – is the physiological stage of a woman's life when her body chemistry transforms itself. It switches off the complex cycles that were so important as she pursued her reproductive life, replacing them with a body chemistry better suited to avoiding reproduction and being a better grandmother. The age at which the menopause occurs – between the mid-forties and mid-fifties – has been chosen by evolution as the best time for a woman to maximise her reproductive output. It is the age by which she should already have had the optimal number of children, the eldest of which are beginning to reproduce in their own right, and at which her reproductive effort is best served by concentrating her time and effort on raising any younger children she may have while helping her older children with her grandchildren. If she continued to be capable of conceiving, she might end up with fewer grandchildren, not more, for all the reasons we have already discussed.

There are two main reasons why males do not have a menopause – at least, not in any physiological sense: first, the lower confidence that they must inevitably have of being a given child's grandparent; second, the fact that no matter how old a man may be, further children need not involve any great cost to himself. Men do not suffer the strains and stresses of pregnancy and caretaking. They can continue to father children without inflicting hardship on themselves for as long as they can get younger women to be interested in their genes, wealth or status. If all they have to do is inseminate a young and able woman, particularly if they can cuckold a young and able man in the process, then they can further enhance their reproductive output right up to the moment they die.

In many other species, from primates to cows and horses, females cease to be reproductive earlier in life than do the males. And in most of these there is contact and influence not only between mothers and children but also between grandmothers and grandchildren.

Among our hunter-gatherer ancestors, post-menopausal women made an invaluable contribution to their children's, and hence their own, reproductive success. As a result, the approaching menopause was by no means the spectre that it is to the modern woman. In the confusion of media and other pressure, women can often suffer psychological stress as they approach and experience it. Many are led to think of it as an end to the most important and desirable phase of their life, rather than the beginning of an equally important one. In large part, this attitude towards the menopause has been exacerbated by the recent decline of the extended family. Over the past few generations in the modern world, technological advance and the scope for travel, leading as they both do to increased contact between people from different parts of the world, have led to rapid social and other environmental changes. Consequently, the contribution of grandparental knowledge to the success of their grandchildren has been devalued in all the ways we discussed at the end of the last chapter. Such devaluation creates greater intergenerational conflict, as parents reject more and more of what they see as outdated advice – and the best way to avoid such conflict is to live separately. The result is that grandmothers get increasingly less opportunity to behave in the ways for which they have been programmed by natural selection.

Few women, of course, would want to find themselves in the position of the woman in our scene; no amount of access to grand-children would make up for the loss of a daughter. Nevertheless, having been forced by circumstances to raise her grandchildren herself, the woman will probably find her post-menopausal life more rewarding than that of the majority of her contemporaries. For most grandmothers, their hands-on contribution tends to be limited to occasional baby-sitting. Other contributions they can make, such as gifts and financial help, although valuable, afford much less satisfaction to their programmed urges.

There is an irony, then, to modern industrial society. On the one hand, it has provided everybody with the potential to live much longer and thus to influence their children and grandchildren for many more years than was usual in the past. On the other, because society has changed so rapidly, the value of the grandparental contribution has been greatly reduced. In that sense, therefore, the menopause may well be ill-adapted to the modern setting. Maybe the modern woman, waiting until her late thirties in order to build up wealth, status and experience before starting a family, would actually achieve a greater reproductive success if the menopause came much later in life. If so, then in the generations to come a later menopause should be what evolves.

SCENE 23
Beyond Reproduction?

'What a cliché!' thought the man as he studied himself in the mirror. 'Under the station clock at four, with a red carnation in my lapel. What a cliché!'

Even so, he was pleased with his suggestion, and even more importantly she had seemed to appreciate it as well. That could be a good sign. Maybe they would get on. Never had he imagined himself acting out the lonely hearts scenario. Yet here he was, on the verge of a date with a woman he had never met and had spoken to only once on the telephone. Despite himself, he was excited. He knew the chances of anything developing from the meeting were slim, but at least there *was* a chance where before there had been none.

The ring on the door-bell told him his taxi had arrived. Taking a last quick look at himself in the mirror, he straightened his collar, then tipped back his head to look up his nostrils. With one last smile at his reflection to make sure there were no bits of food between his teeth, he hurried to the door.

On the other side of town, waiting at a bus stop, the woman felt decidedly conspicuous. She seemed to have spent most of the morning ironing, bathing and dressing. She had toyed with the idea of treating herself to a taxi, but that seemed to be making too many assumptions, as if this afternoon really *was* something special. It was, of course, but she knew that having taken the lonely hearts plunge she would probably have to re-enact this scene many times before she met someone suitable – and she certainly couldn't afford a taxi every time. It was a relief when her bus appeared around the corner, promising the warmth and anonymity of a bus-seat.

In his taxi, stuck fast in a traffic jam, as he felt the beginnings of an erection the man told his body not to be ridiculous. The meeting was not about sex, his brain told him, but his body wouldn't listen. Since arranging it three days earlier he had masturbated twice as his fantasies took him backwards and forwards in time, feeding on both precious memories and hopeful anticipation.

He had arranged everything down to the last detail, even taking care that their rendez-vous should be near to the bus stop as well as the taxi rank so that she wouldn't have far to walk.

Stepping carefully off the bus, the woman made her way towards the clock. She spotted him almost immediately. He looked smart but stood slightly bent. Motionless for a few moments, she watched as he turned in expectation towards almost every woman who walked by. A sudden urge to run for it gradually subsided and, almost with a will of their own, her feet started to take her slowly in his direction. When his gaze focused on her, she half raised her hand in confirmation that she was indeed the person he was waiting for.

Within minutes, they were sitting at a table ordering drinks, immediately at ease in each other's company as they joked about the way they had met. They were in a large room, with tables around the sides and half a dozen elderly couples fox-trotting on the dance-floor. Their respective ages had been no surprise to either of them. They had each put in their adverts not only that they were in their mid-sixties but that they were also seeking a companion of similar age.

They gave each other a résumé of their lives so far, or at least a nicely edited version that each felt suited the occasion. He had had a college education and had run his own small but moderately successful business. His wife had died just over a year earlier, scarcely a week after hearing that their youngest child, a daughter, had given birth to their sixth grandchild. She had never seen this latest addition to their family because their daughter, in fact both of their daughters, lived on the other side of the world. However, their eldest child, a son, had taken over the family business and lived nearby, and they used to see him and his three children fairly regularly. Unlike when his wife was alive, though, the family only ever popped in briefly. They never came to stay any more.

The woman and her husband had both been schoolteachers. They had lived together for thirty years, until the day he caused a local scandal by running away to live with one of his pupils, forty years younger than himself. The woman couldn't suppress a wry smile as she told the man that her ex-husband had died of a heart attack less than a year after leaving her, though not before he had made his young lover pregnant.

As a graceful couple, younger than all the others, swept past on the dance-floor, the woman broke off from her story and watched. The couple reminded her of her son and his partner, she told her companion. He was her only child, but she had four wonderful grandchildren. They used always to be staying with her but, since she had been on her own, she had found them too much of a handful, even for just a weekend. They were expensive, too, and although she could manage perfectly well herself on her pension, she couldn't indulge her grandchildren as much as she would have liked to.

Now the first few bars of a new tune prompted them to say, almost simultaneously, 'Let's dance.' They had both mentioned in their adverts that dancing was a passion, as well as requesting somebody who liked children.

As late afternoon turned into early evening, the slight awkwardness of their first dance had become smooth elegance as, belying their years, they glided over the floor. At first they held each other a little formally, but with growing confidence they relaxed enough for their bodies occasionally to touch. She was the first woman he had held so close for three years, since before his wife had become bed-ridden. To his embarrassment, another erection began. He had immediately liked this woman, and the last thing he wanted was that she should think he was looking only for sex. But she gave no hint that she had noticed his excitement. She felt a momentary worry about his motives, but was more flattered than offended – and not displeased that he could still respond.

When the dancing was over, they took a taxi. He dropped her at her house and they arranged to meet again later in the week. Soon, their dance dates were regular twice-weekly affairs. Six months after their first meeting, they found themselves in bed together and nearly naked, discovering that sex was neither quite as easy as they remembered nor anywhere near as difficult as they had feared.

Within the year, she had sold her bungalow and they were living together in his much larger house. At first, *his* children in particular were suspicious of her motives and unnerved by the apparent shortness of their romance. Before long, though, grandchildren from both sides were coming to stay with them, enjoying treats they had missed during the previous year or two. Gradually, each new step-grandparent was finding a place in their affections. It was the trip of a lifetime for them both when the elderly couple flew to the other side of the world to meet the man's two daughters and their children.

But the equanimity of their new-found blended family was shattered when, after they had lived together for nearly ten years, the man died suddenly from a heart attack. His son, though neither of his daughters, objected to the size of their stepmother's inheritance. Two years later he complained again when, on his stepmother's death, much of his father's wealth passed to her grandchildren.

The couple in this scene are by no means unusual. People are programmed to retain an interest in relationships – and in sex – long after the age at which the ability to have children normally ceases. Why should this be, and how can it have been shaped by natural selection?

Most people would say, of course, that the reason elderly people seek to retain, or find, a partner has nothing to do with evolution and natural selection. What drives people like the couple in our scene, they would maintain, is the need for companionship, not for reproductive success. But although this is a good description of people's motivation, it is not an explanation for their behaviour. It is no more elucidating than to say that people eat because they are hungry – the statement is true, of course, but it is not an explanation. People eat because they need energy, protein and vitamins to maximise their reproductive output, and that is why their bodies have been programmed by natural selection to generate the hunger that drives them to seek food. Similarly, in terms of enhanced reproductive output there will be a benefit to elderly people living with a member of the opposite sex, and this is why their bodies generate the need for companionship, which drives them to seek a partner. The evolutionary biologist's job is to identify the benefit of post-reproductive relationships, including the involvement of sex.

There is one apparent problem, however. The *average* life expectancy of our ancestors during long periods of our evolution was probably no greater than forty to fifty years. Even now the world's lowest average life expectancy at birth – in Sierra Leone – is just forty, and in at least eighteen other countries in Africa it is still fifty or less. One of the advantages of life in a modern industrial society is that more and more people can expect to live into their sixties, seventies, eighties or beyond than could ever have done so in the past. Average life expectancy at birth globally in 1995 was more than sixty-five years, an increase of about three years since 1985; it was over seventy-five in developed countries and the world's highest, that of Japan, was 79.7 years.

It could be argued, therefore, that natural selection *could not* have influenced post-reproductive behaviour because nobody lived long enough in the distant past to be exposed to such selection. In which case, the interest in sex and relationships shown by post-reproductive people nowadays could simply be a charade, meaningless actions driven by bodies that mistakenly think they are still young and reproductive. However, such a view is unlikely to be correct. As long as *some* of those ancestors – about 1 per cent would probably have been enough – survived beyond, say, sixty, then natural selection will have shaped modern post-reproductive behaviour just as surely as it has shaped people's behaviour in the early and middle phases of their lives.

There are three key factors in the action of evolution on the behaviour of older people, all of which have already been mentioned. First, old people enhance their reproductive success via their influence on the number and quality of grandchildren. Second a pair of grandparents, as in an established couple, are likely to have a greater influence than a single grandparent, just as two parents are usually better than one. Third, genetic grandparents are likely to have a more positive influence than step-grandparents, just as genetic parents are usually better than step-parents.

It follows from these three factors that people gain some advantage from staying in established relationships with the genetic parent of their children beyond the point at which they, as a couple, stop having children. But if their partner leaves them or dies, or if they leave their partner, they may behave like the two in our scene and seek a new partner to help them in their grandparental role. There is little doubt that, overall, both the man and the woman enhanced their reproductive successes by their actions, largely because their new relationship afforded them greater opportunity to interact with their grandchildren again. As a result, difficult though it would be to measure, all of those grandchildren in their turn may well have become reproductively more successful.

It is relatively easy, therefore, to see why people should be driven to continue with established relationships, or to seek new or better ones, beyond the normal age of producing children, and why they should try to apportion their combined time and resources optimally between children and grandchildren. Of course, the sibling and other conflicts that we have discussed in relation to blended families may surface if step-grandparents attempt to favour their own grandchildren. In the scene, no such conflicts emerged until the man died and much of the wealth that would otherwise have gone to his descendants went to his partner, then to her grandchildren. Although both the man and the woman probably enhanced their reproductive success via their relationship, of the two the woman probably gained more, simply because she was initially poorer than him but lived longer.

And now we get to the aspect that is more difficult to understand – namely, why sex should be part of such relationships. Again, most people wouldn't see a problem here: it's obvious, they would say, that elderly people don't have sex to reproduce – everybody knows a woman can't conceive after the menopause – so it must simply be that they have sex because they want to. Again, though, the evolutionary biologist would say that this is not an explanation. There has to be some pay-off from post-reproductive sex – and a pay-off, moreover, in terms of reproductive success. So what *is* that pay-off?

It is important to keep a historical perspective here. Some of the knowledge that we, in our modern world, take for granted was simply not available to our ancestors. For instance, in the absence of official records, a person's opinion as to his or her own age was unreliable. And just as our ancestors were very uncertain as to how babies were conceived, they will have been equally uncertain as to when conception ceased to be possible for a woman. By contrast, the links between ovulation and conception on the one hand and between the menopause and the cessation of ovulation on the other are obvious to us, thanks to biomedical research. It is important to keep these differences between modern and ancient knowledge in mind.

In figuring out the reproductive benefit of sex to elderly people, we have to distinguish between men and women. As we have noted, men are never really post-reproductive. Although the

271

average age of last reproduction for men is little different from that for women, it is due to ever-decreasing opportunity rather than ever-decreasing ability. A man does produce fewer sperm as he ages. He also ejaculates less often and has less frequent, more flaccid and shorter-lasting erections. Periods of impotence become more common. Nevertheless, the majority of men are still potentially capable of fathering children even beyond the stage at which physical infirmity renders intercourse difficult. A man's only problem is an increasing difficulty in attracting a young and fertile woman as his sexual partner. Surveys show that beyond the age of fifty he has to be increasingly rich to attract young women, but that a very rich man can do so well into his seventies and beyond. It is not surprising, therefore, that men retain an interest in young women, in sex, and in accumulating wealth and status, throughout their lives. But although the vast majority have to settle for partners who are much nearer their own age, many retain an interest in sex with these aged partners. Why? What is the reproductive pay-off, to a man, of sex with a woman who is too old to reproduce?

The explanation has three parts. First, as we have just established, even an old man retains the potential to sire further children. Second, an older woman gains from preventing her partner from leaving her for a younger, still fertile woman, because if he left she would lose his help in the grandparental role. Third, strange though it may seen, it is very difficult to know when a woman is too old to reproduce.

Take the last point first. Even if a man knows a woman's age, he can rarely be absolutely certain she is post-reproductive. Records show that some have conceived up to the age of fifty-nine, and up to seventy if some undocumented cases are to be believed. We must remember, too, that our male ancestors will never really have known the age of a given woman. Moreover, the woman herself may not have known it and even if she did, she could always have lied. The reason why the records of seventy-year-old women conceiving are questionable is because, even in the twentieth century, not everybody knows how old they really are – and anyway, *they* may have lied.

So all a man can do is try to judge a woman's fertility from her appearance. If he knew when she last menstruated, he might gain a clue. However, a post-menopausal woman so often gets decoy vaginal bleeds that, denied the benefits of modern medical investigation, our male ancestors would have found it very difficult to know which was his partner's last real period. In any case, women have conceived up to two years after their last apparent period. Because of all this uncertainty, men's bodies seem to have been programmed to assume that as long as a woman retains an interest in intercourse, sex with her may not be reproductively fruitless. This gives the post-menopausal woman's body an ideal way to hide its infertility – by allowing, or even soliciting, sex. By this means, an older woman can gain some leverage in trying to prevent her partner from running off with the first young woman who takes an interest in him. It doesn't always work, as the woman in our scene discovered when her schoolteacher husband ran off with his pupil, but it is often enough to satisfy an older man's subconscious drive to pursue any possibility of further children.

In a sense, therefore, the sexual behaviour of people between their fifties and eighties really is a continuation of the sexual conflict and cooperation pattern that formed part of their reproductive lives. What it is not is a meaningless charade, untouched by natural selection. People's behaviour may have less and less influence on their reproductive success as they age, but it always has *some*. It will have been fashioned by natural selection via the successes and failures of our elderly ancestors just as surely as has sexual and parental behaviour in the first forty years of life.

SCENE 24
The Family Helper

Panicking at the sound of the door-bell, the old woman grabbed the hand-grip on her living-room wall. With great effort, she tried to pull her arthritic body out of the chair in which she spent most of her waking hours. Normally, her daughter would answer the door, but she was out shopping and the old woman was alone in the house.

At the third attempt, she managed to get to her feet. Then, leaning on her walking-frame, she began to shuffle out of the living-room towards the front door. Her heart was racing, partly from the exertion and pain of moving and partly from fear. There were so many stories on television and in the papers about women of her age being attacked in their homes. When she reached the door, she tried to look through the window at the side of it to see who was there. However, with her failing eyesight all she could tell was that there were two people outside, maybe a man and a woman.

As her stiff fingers struggled with the door-lock, she called out as loud as her thin voice would allow that she was coming. There was a chain on the door, and at first she opened it only enough to be able to peer through the crack. Then, relieved and elated to see that the couple were her brother and his daughter, she fumbled excitedly to release the chain.

When at last she opened the door, she apologised for taking so long and embarked on a tortuous explanation. Her niece reassured her that none was needed. The old woman's brother, just as infirm – and from the same family affliction – was also leaning on a walking-frame. Behind him stood his daughter, now in her sixties. She had brought her father to visit, she said to the old woman. She had some shopping to do, and would return in an hour or so to collect him. Then, almost as an afterthought, she asked her where her own daughter was. On hearing that her cousin was out she hesitated, not too happy to leave the aged couple on their own but equally reluctant to change her plans and stay with them. She had relied on her cousin being there, knowing how much she liked to fuss around and do things for people on those rare occasions when anybody visited. Reassured by the old woman that her cousin would not be long and that they would be all right until then, she offered to accompany them into the house and settle them down in the sitting-room. Used as she was to old people, she could not help but smile as she patiently followed her father and his sister slowly moving in single file down the narrow hallway, heads bent over their walking-frames.

Left to themselves, the old couple expressed their delight at seeing each other. The brother, now a widower and with his children scattered around the country, lived in an old people's home. He was totally dependent on family members to take him to visit his sister and his rapidly dwindling circle of friends, and much of the time between their visits and phone calls he spent sleeping. She, however, could still manage to live in her own home, and he envied her that. Although most of her family had dispersed, his niece – conceived when his sister was in her mid-forties – had lived with her mother all her life. And as his sister had become increasingly infirm, the younger woman had taken on more and more of the household chores. Now she was his sister's lifeline, an umbilical cord in reverse, without whom the old woman simply would not manage.

He asked after his niece. Was she well? Now that she was in her late thirties, he knew that she could no longer be sure of good health. Relieved to hear that, although increasingly forgetful, she was as well and happy as ever, he began to reminisce with his sister. They touched only fleetingly on the shock of his niece's birth, recalled the joy of how happy and loving she had been as a child and the way she had helped look after her nephews and nieces when they were little. One of the things he had always enjoyed about visiting his sister, the man said, was the wonderful hugs he used to get from his niece, not only when he arrived and left but also every so often during the visit. How well she now looked after her mother, and how happy she was to do so. He knew, as they both did, of friends with daughters who had devoted their lives to looking after their ageing parent, but they had found it a great strain and the relationship had often become bitter.

There was a pause in the conversation. The man glanced at the clock on the mantelpiece, his long vision still as sharp as ever, and mused over how much longer his niece might be. He had been so much looking forward to seeing her, but if she was much longer his own daughter would be back before she was and they'd have to be off.

No sooner had he voiced the possibility than the door-bell rang. He volunteered to go and answer it, being marginally the more active of the two. It *was* his daughter. He felt a tinge of disappointment at seeing her because it meant he was going to have to say goodbye to his sister for a few more weeks or even months, and nowadays every time he did so he worried that it might be for the last time. But he needn't have worried about not seeing his niece. Scarcely had he let his daughter in than the younger woman appeared at the front gate. As soon as she saw him, her face broke into a broad smile. Despite being laden with shopping, she hurried as fast as she could – she wasn't built for speed – down the path towards him. Cheerfully greeting her cousin as she swept past her, on reaching her uncle she put down her shopping. Then, beaming up at him, she gave him a kiss and a big hug, nearly separating him from his walking-frame in her excitement.

At the end of this scene we meet a woman who makes no attempt to reproduce. Instead of seeking a partner and trying to raise children of her own, she devotes her life to her mother, enriching not only *her* life but also, during their childhood, the lives of her siblings and her nephews and nieces – her mother's grandchildren. Why should natural selection have programmed anybody to give up their own chance of reproducing in order to help others?

The answer to this question is very instructive, telling us a great deal about the workings of natural selection. Before any of the arguments can make sense, however, we need to know more about the woman in question, the *helper*, in the scene. For once, there is absolutely no question that her behaviour, as well as her chemistry, are under the control of her genes, for she is a genetic type, a Down's syndrome person.

The general public still have a very negative view of individuals with Down's syndrome. They are often considered 'mistakes', genetic errors: if a foetus is found to have Down's syndrome following routine amniocentesis during pregnancy, more often than not it will be aborted. Even *The Cambridge Encyclopaedia of Human Evolution*, published in 1992, describes the syndrome as 'a form of mental subnormality' and as the 'commonest cause of severe mental retardation'.

Evolutionary biology has a problem with such a negative view. First, unlike other syndromes with similar genetic bases, it is too common an occurrence to be dismissed as a simple mistake. Over 2 per cent of women who conceive after the age of forty-five produce a Down's syndrome baby. In addition, Down's syndrome people have a number of very positive characteristics that can give them a valuable role within the extended family. Let's concentrate on those positive characteristics and consider the possibility that the Down's syndrome phenomenon has been shaped by natural selection. It should be stressed that this discussion is no more than the exploration of a hypothesis, an attempt to stretch biological theory in order to find a positive explanation for a phenomenon that is usually viewed negatively. The evidence needed to evaluate the hypothesis is not available, and may never be so.

Individuals with Down's syndrome are found in all human

populations, and wherever they occur they have the same features. They are shorter than average and have distinctively shaped heads, eyes, eyelids and faces. The condition is not confined to humans, a similar syndrome having been reported in chimpanzees. But despite its universal occurrence in humans, it was not described scientifically until 1866. The vast majority of Down's syndrome individuals are infertile. This does not mean, however, that they have no interest in sex, and occasionally *females* are fertile and reproduce. When they do, half of their offspring have Down's. More often than not, Down's syndrome individuals take pleasure in doing things for other people rather than trying to reproduce.

But if Down's syndrome people have a minimal reproductive output, and if evolution works by favouring people with characteristics that enhance reproductive success, how can it be claimed that Down's people have been shaped by natural selection? The principle behind the answer is important: evolution has produced the phenomenon of sterility combined with the urge to help, by acting not on the helper *but on the mother.*

There is only one key element to this interpretation: namely, that a woman may produce more grandchildren in total by recruiting one of her children to help rather than to reproduce. If this seems paradoxical, consider these two scenarios for a woman who produces three children; in both scenarios, as in all of our discussions of grandparenthood and related matters, we have to imagine an ancestral situation in which people are living in an extended family.

In the first scenario, all three of the children reproduce. Suppose that the strain on parental and later grandparental resources is so great that each child succeeds in raising only one child of his or her own to adulthood. In this situation, the woman achieves a total of three grandchildren. In the second scenario, suppose that instead of allowing them all to reproduce, the woman engineers it so that one of her offspring throws all of his or her energy into helping the rest of the family. One of the most important things the chosen offspring will have to do is give up the distraction and drain on family resources that come from trying to reproduce. As a result of the help they all receive from this non-reproductive offspring, the other two manage to raise two children each to adulthood. In this scenario, therefore, the woman achieves a total of four grandchildren, and her reproductive output has actually been increased by one-third by having one of her children help, not reproduce.

Clearly, in principle the potential is there for a woman to increase her reproductive output in this way. Her needs are straightforward: that she should give birth to someone who is more interested in helping than reproducing, and that the help should begin at about the time that her eldest children are beginning to produce her first grandchildren. On the other hand, raising a helper can be costly and under some circumstances can be something of a luxury. In particular, until the helper reaches the age of at least six or seven, he or she is more of a drain on family resources than a help. During the period from conception to the point at which he or she becomes helpful, from the viewpoint of the evolutionary biologist the mother gains from the helper having a pre-programmed vulnerability, because if conditions for the family become difficult, the helper, not the reproductives, will be the first to succumb. At the other end of helpers' lives, their role declines when the last of their nephews and nieces, their mothers' grandchildren, become adult and independent. On average, therefore, their greatest contribution will be while their mothers are between the ages of forty and eighty.

Individuals with Down's syndrome fit these requirements so precisely that it is difficult not to interpret their characteristics as a product of natural selection. First, they are born at just the right stage in a mother's life. Second, their skills and aptitudes are just the ones needed to be helpers. Third, they have a built-in vulnerability from conception to the age of about five and a relatively short life expectancy (forty to fifty years) – undoubtedly, the cruellest aspect of the way natural selection has designed them. The details of these three sets of characteristics are not generally known, and merit more attention.

Irrespective of the age of their partner, women become increasingly likely to produce a Down's syndrome baby as they grow older. More often than not, they are born to women who already have children. Women under twenty have only a 1 in 2300 chance of producing a Down's syndrome baby. Between the ages of twenty-five and thirty the chances double to 1 in 1200. They then increase to 1 in 880 between the ages of thirty and thirty-five,

1 in 290 between thirty-five and forty, 1 in 100 between forty and forty-five and 1 in 46 between forty-five and fifty. So how do women increase the probability of having a Down's syndrome baby at the appropriate age?

Unlike the subtle genetic differences that we have discussed elsewhere in this book, the genetic basis of the syndrome is obvious, even under a microscope. In the vast majority of instances, it is the result of the baby having an extra chromosome (forty-seven instead of forty-six). This extra, small, chromosome is an extra copy of a chromosome called chromosome-21. Normally, people have only two copies of it, one from their father and one from their mother, but Down's syndrome babies have three. This extra chromosome-21 usually comes from the mother, and is most often the result of an unusual cell division inside her during the early stages of egg production. Instead of each of the newly formed cells receiving one copy of chromosome-21, one receives two and the other, none. The critical event in this process may occur while the mother herself is a baby, or even while she is still a foetus, because this is when she produces the primary follicles which are her future eggs.

When the mother is a foetus, her ovaries contain about seven million primary follicles. By the time she is born, her body has got rid of most of them, leaving her with about four hundred thousand. Only about four hundred of these will develop further during her lifetime, and the number that actually develop into eggs is only about sixty. So most of the primary follicles that a woman has when she is born are destined to produce eggs with just one copy of chromosome-21 and therefore to produce babies capable of reproduction. Those that will produce eggs with *two* copies of chromosome-21 are potential Down's syndrome babies. An equal number will produce eggs with no chromosome-21, and if these are ever fertilised by a sperm they are spontaneously aborted by the mother.

During each menstrual cycle, between six and twelve of the mother's primary follicles begin to grow, but one nearly always outgrows the rest and gives rise to the egg produced at ovulation. The remaining follicles stop growing and eventually disintegrate. Throughout most of a woman's reproductive life, her body grows an egg from a primary follicle with only one copy of chromosome-21. As she passes forty years of age, however, her body becomes more and more likely to select one of the follicles that will produce an egg containing two copies.

In what ways do the abilities and aptitudes of Down's individuals suit them to the helper role? Typically, their mental aptitudes are adequate for them to learn the skills necessary for life within a close-knit extended family, but they find it difficult or impossible to learn the skills needed for an *independent* existence. Usually, their social skills are much more developed than their intellectual ones. In particular, they are happy, affectionate and caring. The woman in our scene was fortunate in that she had been given the opportunity to fulfil the helping role for which she was genetically programmed. Many Down's syndrome children in modern societies find no such outlet.

That helpers should have a built-in vulnerability that comes into operation when times are hard is precisely the pattern that we would expect for a child born to be its mother's helper. About 60 per cent of Down's foetuses are spontaneously aborted and, as in all forms of spontaneous abortion, the figure will be higher when the mother is stressed. About 20 per cent of Down's foetuses are stillborn. Of the rest, 15 to 20 per cent die before the age of five, usually as a result of severe congenital and inoperable heart disease. Again, the prediction would be that such deaths will be most likely when the mother's and child's situation is most stressful. As we noted earlier, those that survive beyond the age of five have a life expectancy of forty to fifty years. Beyond forty, they begin to age rapidly.

If giving birth to a Down's syndrome baby can be advantageous to a woman for her long-term reproductive success, why don't all women produce them? The answer is probably that there is a very fine trade-off for a woman in her late thirties to mid-forties with regard to the costs and benefits of reproduction. On the one hand, she may benefit most by not reproducing at all and concentrating all her effort on doing the best for the children she already has. On the other she may benefit by producing another fully reproductive child, despite condemning herself to another eighteen years or so of parental investment. Somewhere between these two options there is likely to be a very narrow range of situations in which the best option is for the woman to produce a helper, someone who will need about half as many years of parental investment but who will then be a benefit, not a further drain.

It will be because the range of situations in which a helper is the best option is so narrow that often, having conceived a Down's baby, the mother's body changes its strategy and aborts, undernourishes, or even kills the child. Even when a Down's child survives beyond birth, it is only if circumstances for the first five years or so continue to favour the mother raising a helper that he or she survives to fulfil his or her helper role. If circumstances are unfavourable, the mother either conceives another reproductive child or avoids further conception altogether, depending on the direction in which circumstances have changed. The hypothesis that Down's syndrome has been shaped by natural selection now needs testing by further research into the circumstances in which Down's children are conceived, survive and die. Most needed is information – ideally from societies still living in extended families as well as from those in modern industrial societies – on the impact of Down's on their parents' reproductive output in terms of grandchildren.

A whole range of other species, too, have evolved helpers in their quest for greater reproductive output. Not all other species' helpers are sterile, like the majority of Down's syndrome humans, but many are. The best known examples are the sterile worker castes of ants, bees, wasps and termites. Some birds, such as the acorn woodpecker of America, and some mammals, such as the naked mole rat of Africa, also live in social groups containing non-reproductive helpers. The situation is not so very different in some carnivorous mammals, such as wolves and hunting dogs in which only one pair in the pack reproduce, the others helping them to raise their young. In these species, the helpers are usually the *earlier* offspring of the reproductive pair, not the later as in humans. But this is because their role is to help their parent(s) produce more children rather than more grandchildren. The principle remains the same.

There is some indication that humans, too, sometimes use an older child as a helper in their production and raising of further children rather than of grandchildren. In these cases, however, the helpers are not genetically different, nor are they usually physically sterile. They look no different from offspring who do reproduce, but they differ behaviourally in that they are susceptible to being inveigled by their parents into staying at home and helping rather than leaving and reproducing.

The best study is perhaps that of reproduction and movement patterns in nineteenth-century Sweden, which showed that women who stayed in their village of birth, probably with their parents, had a higher likelihood of remaining childless. In contrast, those women who stayed in their village of birth but did have children appear to have had, on average, more children than those who emigrated. We do not know if there was really a direct link between these two findings, but it is possible that some of the women who remained at home assumed the role of 'sterile helpers' to their parents and siblings, thus enhancing their parents' production and raising of children and grandchildren. Various anthropologists, particularly in East Africa, have also reported the possibility of such behaviour in pre-industrial cultures.

There is a final sad postscript to this interpretation of the role of human helpers. With the disintegration of the extended family, the role has been increasingly devalued. It may well be that in modern societies Down's syndrome offspring can make less of a contribution to a woman's reproductive success than has been anticipated by natural selection.

CHAPTER NINE

The End

SCENE 25
Final Commitment

'I wish she would die, I really do. I love her very much and she's been a wonderful mother, but now she's ruining my life – all our lives – and I really don't think I can take any more. I shall go mad if she hangs on much longer.'

The distraught woman looked hard at her friend, wondering if she had shocked her. She had been bottling up her feelings for so long that once she had started to voice them she couldn't stop. She hadn't meant to say that she wished her mother would die, but it was the truth. Her friend reached out and patted her hand, nearly spilling her half-empty cup of coffee as she did so.

'It must be terrible,' she said. 'At least when my mother died it was sudden. One minute she was part of the family, cheerful and busy, the next she was gone. It was a real shock – the children were upset for weeks. I'm glad it happened that way, though. I should hate to go through what you're going through.'

'It's not just the money,' said the woman, wiping away tears, 'though it really is costing a fortune to keep her in that home. She didn't have much in the way of savings, and if she lives much longer it'll all be gone and we'll either have to move her or start paying. The cost is bad enough, but it's the time and the disruption that are really getting me down. Nearly every day I go in there, just to talk to her – they say she might be able to hear what I'm saying – and I can't just leave her with no visitors. But the children don't like going. It upsets them to see her just lying there, dribbling and twitching and not saying anything, just staring.'

She paused to fumble for a tissue.

'I'm neglecting them, I know I am. I just haven't the time and energy to visit her – and worry about her – *and* be a proper mother to them. I'm not feeding them properly. I'm not helping them with their homework. It's just not fair on them.'

Her friend drank the last of her coffee, then put the cup on the table with a briskness that said she was about to go.

'Well,' she said, trying to find something reassuring to say, '. . . maybe it won't be for much longer. Anyway, I'm sorry, I really must go. It's my turn to meet the children from school today.'

She stood up and adjusted her clothes.

'She used to be so active, before her stroke,' the woman went on, looking up at her friend, unable to stop the flow. 'She used to give me so much help with the children.'

Without responding, her friend began to walk towards the door, forcing her host to take her need to leave seriously.

'I'm sorry about my outburst,' the other said, as she caught up with her friend at the door. 'But all I can think about is that my life is being ruined and there is absolutely nothing I can do about it.'

The visitor tried to smile reassuringly. 'It's all right,' she said. 'I'm sorry I can't stay any longer.'

The woman closed the door. She was taking the children straight from school to the nursing home this afternoon – their complaints were ringing in her ears already. She hated herself for thinking it, but she really did wish her mother would put them all out of their misery.

D eath is an emotive issue, and difficult to discuss objectively with equanimity. So for once we shall start by considering non-human species, then examine the relevance of our conclusions to people. The central principle is that there comes a point in an animal's life at which its long-term reproductive success is most enhanced not by trying to stay alive in order to reproduce later, but by throwing everything into reproduction *now*. It is often difficult to see how this works for species like humans, with no clearly defined point at which this strategic decision has to be made. But some species – Pacific salmon, for example – illustrate the situation clearly.

Pacific salmon migrate thousands of kilometres from the rivers in which they are born to the Pacific Ocean, in which they feed, grow, and mature into adults. Then, a year or more later, they migrate back to spawn in those same rivers. When the adult salmon returns to its home river, it has a strategic choice. Either it can guard its health and vitality so as to be able to perform its exhausting migration all over again, and spawn again in a couple of years' time. Or it can throw all caution to the wind, exert itself to the point of exhaustion, and reproduce to its limit at its first attempt. In doing so, however, it will forgo any possibility of ever migrating or reproducing again.

Natural selection, of course, has programmed Pacific salmon to make the decision that leads to greater reproductive success – and that is to reproduce, then die. Modern Pacific salmon, on their return to the stream of their birth, throw everything into reproduction. So programmed are they to maximise their reproductive effort that every part of their body – even their stomach and guts – that is not needed for either swimming or sex, degenerates. This degeneration releases the energy that is then used to enhance their once-in-a-lifetime reproductive effort. Having used all of that energy, however, there is no going back; there is no chance of repair or regrowth once reproduction is over, and the spent salmon rapidly decline, through senility, to death.

There are two reasons why this programmed death is the best way for a salmon to maximise its reproductive output. First, if a female salmon chose not to reproduce to her maximum when she arrived at her home river but instead tried to stay alive, she would have less energy and hence would produce fewer eggs. Similarly, a male would fertilise fewer eggs because he had less energy to expend on winning fights and manufacturing sperm. Second, even if either sex did stay alive by restraining their reproductive effort in one year, their chances of surviving another exhausting and dangerous migration would be so low that they wouldn't reproduce in a later year, anyway. All they would have achieved would be a reduction in their reproductive output.

Obviously, humans, and most other species, are not programmed to die in the furtherance of their reproductive success in quite such a spectacular way as Pacific salmon. Nevertheless, a similar process is at work. Again, as in all of the discussions of the last two chapters, we have to think in terms of natural selection acting within the context of an ancestral extended family. The key principle is that beyond a certain point, a person's continued presence within that extended family begins to have a negative influence on her (or his) reproductive output. When that point is reached, the only course of action open to the individual if she is to avoid undoing all the good work she has done so far is to remove herself. One way would be to leave. Another is to die. On the face of it, leaving would seem a more sensible option than dying. And so it would be, if it weren't for the years of senescence that would precede it. As it is, senility and frailty have usually progressed to such an extent that leaving to begin an independent life is not an option. Why, then, does ageing in humans involve becoming increasingly frail and senile, a process which begins almost imperceptibly in the fifties and ends in the seventies or later with death?

There are two main theories which attempt to explain the existence of the old-age syndrome and death. One postulates that they are simply the result of accumulated mutations and chemical mistakes over the body's lifetime; the other is that, just like the changes during reproductive life, the old-age syndrome and death have been designed by natural selection to be the last steps in an individual's quest for reproductive success. On the face of it, these look like two separate theories. But they may not be. They could in fact be two different ways of saying the same thing, as we shall see.

The mutation hypothesis is, in principle, very simple. Every time a cell in the body divides, the genes it contains, in the form of long strands of the chemical DNA, have to replicate themselves exactly so that after division copies will pass into each cell. Other structures made of DNA, the mitochondria which are a cell's power-house, also have to divide. More often than not, the cell's DNA replicates itself perfectly. In fact, the cell has genes whose job it is to correct mistakes, chopping out mutated DNA and replacing it with a faithful replica. Every so often, though, mistakes escape correction, and the cell mutates. Cell lineages have a built-in obsolescence. They are guided through their divisions by yet more DNA, called telomeres, located at both ends of each chromosome. Telomeres gradually deteriorate through mutation, with the result that cells can divide only a fixed number of times, until their telomeres are exhausted – then they give up. Only three types of cell escape this obsolescence, and these are rejuvenated by a special enzyme that mends the telomeres. These cell types are eggs, sperm, and cancer cells.

The result of all of this cellular activity is that, as people age, their bodies accumulate more and more mutations – of genes, mitochondria and telomeres. Gradually, an increasing number of cells – and hence the body itself – cease to function properly, with the inevitable result. People become senile and eventually die.

At first sight, this might seem to run counter to the evolutionary theory. We have discussed the strategies that natural selection has devised to permit both women and men to maximise their reproductive output. During the grandparental phase, the main contribution is help, advice, resources and experience. However, throughout most of human evolution, and even among today's hunter-gatherers and agriculturists, there has been one important cost to set against this benefit: grandparents take up space and require food. During early-grandparenthood, when grandchildren need more watching and carrying and require relatively little food, the grandparental contribution is considerable. But as the grandchildren grow, both in number and stature, and require more space and food, the advantage of grandparental care diminishes and their presence becomes more of a disadvantage. Eventually the balance tips, and the continued presence of the grandparents begins to reduce their reproductive success because they begin to compete for resources which are more useful to their own children and grandchildren.

One way in which the grandparents can reduce the drain on resources that they constitute and delay the moment when their contribution is outweighed by their cost is to require less space (by becoming less mobile) and less food (by shrinking in stature). Eventually, having reduced their needs to a minimum, they can only cease being a threat to their own reproductive success by removing themselves completely – by dying. If they retained the option of staying alive by not shrinking and not becoming frail then, like Pacific salmon, they would probably lessen their reproductive success. Natural selection, therefore, has programmed people first to become frail and then to die.

This evolutionary theory explains most of the changes that take place during old age. It also explains one of the main programmed differences between men and women: the fact that, on average, women live longer – usually several years – than men. On average, women today can expect to live over four years longer than men – 67.2 years as against 63. The female advantage is greatest in Europe – almost eight more years – and smallest in South-East Asia, where it is just one. Global variation probably reflects more the impact of medicine than the impact of evolution. All the same, the difference between the life expectancies of men and women almost certainly has an evolutionary basis. As a woman is more certain of her parenthood and grandparenthood, she contributes more to the care of grandchildren, and so has a greater opportunity to enhance her reproductive success during her grandparental years than has a man. She is also, on average, smaller and competes less for food than does a man. As her grandchildren grow, it will take longer for the positive influence she has on her reproductive success to be exceeded by her negative influence. In other words, she will be older before death becomes her final strategy for maximising her long-term reproductive success. According to this interpretation, those diseases such as some cancers and heart disease which are now known to have a genetic basis become tools by which the body kills itself when the time comes. We are back to the mutation hypothesis.

So which of the two theories of ageing is more likely to be correct – mutation or natural selection? The answer could be that they are both correct! They are not mutually exclusive. All of the consequences of cell division clearly happen, but they could simply be the mechanism by which natural selection has shaped the ageing process, not the actual cause of it. The sequence of mutation and repair could itself have been arranged by natural selection in order to achieve the process of senility and death that most enhances people's reproductive success.

There is nothing inevitable about the accumulation of mutations. Cells can repair both mutations and telomeres, when it suits them. Males die before females because they have a higher mutation rate than females, and females have a higher mutation repair rate. But it didn't have to be like that. More than likely, the reason that this difference exists is because females gain more from living longer, which is *why* they have evolved with a lower mutation rate and a higher repair rate. Presumably, if people could enhance their reproductive success by living for two hundred years, then that is how natural selection would have shaped them, as it has tortoises and trees. All it needed to do was adjust the rate of mutation and repair.

Whichever theory we accept – or the combination of the two – the difference between ancient and modern situations seems clear. The old-age syndrome will have evolved in our hunter-gatherer ancestors in the context of extended families with constraints on living space and availability of food. In such a context, we would expect natural selection to have produced a scenario for ageing and death that on the whole maximised people's reproductive success. In the modern environment, however, the erosion of grandparental influence due to rapid environmental change and the concomitant decline of the extended family have combined to reduce the contribution that people can make to their reproductive success during their years as grandparents. In addition, the impact of modern medicine has been to render people a drain on their family's resources for longer. The net result could well be an imbalance of costs and benefits which natural selection has had no time to correct.

It is not surprising, therefore, that more and more families in the modern environment see their ageing grandparents as more of a burden than an asset. Sadly, the plight of the woman in our scene is becoming increasingly common. Experiences and resources built up by grandparents in their lifetime would previously have cascaded down the generations, enhancing the grandparents' reproductive success by enhancing the lives and prospects of their descendants. Now such resources get eaten up in keeping them alive and comfortable in their extended old age. Many must now reach a point at which they become a drain on their children and grandchildren, to the detriment of their own reproductive success.

A discussion of death as a strategy for enhancing the reproductive prospects of a person's descendants seems an appropriate theme on which to end a book on parenthood. To many people, the most surprising – and to some, outrageous – idea linking all of the discussions in this book will be the central principle of evolutionary biology itself: that all aspects of human parenthood, death included, have been shaped by natural selection, and that they are therefore orchestrated by genes, mediated by body chemistry, and manifested as largely subconscious motivations and urges. (Just occasionally these innate strategies surface in our conscious minds, but most of the time we have no need to think about what we are doing – we just do it.)

The reason parental behaviour has been moulded so forcefully by natural selection is that it has a direct influence on the very crux of the selection process – reproductive success. Every aspect, from conception to death, has long-term repercussions on the individual's reproductive output. The details of these repercussions have been illustrated in the various scenes, while a few major themes have threaded their way through almost the whole range of parental experience and behaviour.

The first theme is that children are the stepping-stones to grandchildren and beyond. Natural selection will not award its prizes to those who simply produce the most children. It will wait to see how the quality and quantity of the children complement each other in their descendants. It is because of this delay in measuring success that mate choice, family planning and parental favouritism are all so important, and that there is more to raising children than simply keeping them safe. The way they are fed, educated, protected – and given rein – all make a big difference to the individual's long-term reproductive output, and this is why the accumulation of wealth and status is as important in the biology of parenthood as the more overtly biological phenomena such as health, fertility and behaviour.

The second theme is that of conflict – as we have seen, babies do mean wars. Conflicts arise at every stage – conception, pregnancy, labour, babyhood, childhood, adolescence, parenthood and grandparenthood – until the moment we take our last breath. All members of the family will compete with each other – parents, parents and offspring, siblings, grandparents and parents, and so on. In fact, so wide and varied are the clashes of interest between family members that it might almost seem surprising there are ever any quiet, tranquil moments within households – but yet there are, and these too owe their existence to natural selection. The more successfully a family can cooperate and acquire resources for the unit as a whole, the more everybody in the family benefits. Then, with the acquisition of those resources, the conflicts resurface in the form of sibling rivalry and parental favouritism. The result is the familiar tightrope that we have to tread between conflict and cooperation, love and hate, peace and bedlam that is family life for most people.

Then there is parental confidence, which emerged as one of the major factors influencing family conflicts. The concept is totally foreign to most women, who are almost incapable of identifying with male psychology over the matter. Fears that there may have been a mix-up of babies in hospital is perhaps the nearest a woman can get to empathising. Yet the possibility that a child, any child, may not be his is programmed deep in his psyche. Maybe some men never *consciously* accept it – or never voice it for fear of insulting their partner – but the possibility is ever-present and has far-reaching repercussions for the quality of paternal care. The fact that males can never be as certain of their genetic parenthood as can females explains many of the differences between the sexes in their treatment of children; and the less certain the man, the lower the quality of his parental and grandparental care. As has been shown by many studies, paternal confidence is as important a factor in the quality of paternal care in other species as it is for humans, which in itself demonstrates how subconscious are the urges that control that care.

The fourth theme is the confusion that can arise from the evolution of conditional strategies: in other words, from the instructions programmed into our bodies to check our circumstances before acting. The reaction to birth order is one such conditional strategy; how liberal to be in the sexual education of children, another. Superficially, such strategies may look like manifestations of nurture, not nature, of environment, not genes, but once it is understood that the instructions to check before acting are programmed by our genes we can see such behaviour in its true light. Conditional strategies are the main causes of differences in behaviour, not only between individuals but also between cultures. Different geographical regions, different periods of history, provide different environments with different opportunities and risks – such as variations in risk of disease – thus triggering different behaviour. As a result, cultures differ in what are considered to be societal norms for parenting. Natural selection was in fact the architect, but culture is a plagiarist and invariably claims to have thought of the rules for itself.

The fifth theme is the surprising range of behaviour that was first shaped and honed in ancestral environments but which has translated successfully to the completely different environment of modern industrial societies. An awareness of the ancient setting in which this or that piece of parental behaviour evolved has been an important factor in understanding that behaviour, whether it be the care of babies, the sexual education of children, grandparenthood, or old age and death. The advent of clothing, punitive legal systems and rapid environmental, including social, change have generated situations never anticipated by natural selection. Evolved responses were always happening, but did not always provide ideal solutions. From the minor, such as sore nipples and sleepless nights, to the devastating, such as the murder of children following sexual abuse – these are the prices that we have to pay for the modern way of life.

The last theme concerns the most far-reaching of modern developments: the demise of the extended family. Advances in medical science that allow people to live longer have combined with new social situations to sit uneasily within evolved urges and motivations. Casualties range from the unfulfilled urges of grandparents to the lack of outlet for the programmed urges of people with Down's syndrome. Given time, natural selection will do its best to reprogram people to behave in the way that is best suited to the modern environment. If that environment continues to change at its present rate, however, parenthood in the future could be a very different experience from anything yet encountered.

Further Reading

Books

Baker, R. R. (1982). *Migration: Paths through Time and Space.* Hodder & Stoughton, London.

Baker, R. R. (1996). *Sperm Wars: The Science of Sex.* Basic Books, New York.

Baker, R. R. and Bellis, M. A. (1995). *Human Sperm Competition: Copulation, Masturbation and Infidelity.* Chapman & Hall, London.

Bortolaia Silva, E. (1996). *Good Enough Mothering? Feminist Perspectives on Lone Motherhood.* Routledge, London.

Buss, D. M. (1994). *The Evolution of Desire: Strategies of Human Mating.* Basic Books, New York.

Dawkins, R. (1976). *The Selfish Gene.* Oxford University Press, Oxford.

Ford, C. S. and Beach, F. A. (1952). *Patterns of Sexual Behaviour.* Eyre & Spottiswoode, London.

Gibson, D. (1978). *Down's Syndrome: The Psychology of Mongolism.* Cambridge University Press, Cambridge.

Jones, S. (1996). *In the Blood: God, Genes and Destiny.* Flamingo, London.

Jones, S., Martin, R., Pilbeam, D. and Bunney, S. (1992). *The Cambridge Encyclopedia of Human Evolution*, p. 506. Cambridge University Press, Cambridge.

Krebs, J. R. and Davies, N. B. (1993). *An Introduction to Behavioural Ecology.* 3rd Edn. Blackwell Scientific Publications, Oxford.

McLanahan, S. and Sandefur, G. (1994). *Growing Up with a Single Parent: What Hurts, What Helps.* Harvard University Press, Cambridge, Mass.

Russell, D. E. (1984). *Sexual Exploitation*. Sage, Beverly Hills, Calif.

Sulloway, F. J. (1996). *Born to Rebel: Birth Order, Family Dynamics and Creative Lives*. Pantheon Books, New York.

Papers

Adler, N. A. and Schuts, J. (1995). Sibling incest offenders. *Child Abuse and Neglect* **19**, 811–19.

Bell, J. A. (1991). The epidemiology of Down's syndrome. *Medical Journal of Australia* **155**, 115–17.

Bereczkei, T. and Dunbar, R. I. M. (1997). Female-biased reproductive strategies in a Hungarian Gypsy population. *Proceedings of the Royal Society of London* **B 264**, 17–22.

Daly, M. and Wilson, M. I. (1985). Child abuse and other risks of not living with both parents. *Ethology and Sociobiology* **6**, 197–210.

Grammer, K., Dittami, J. and Fischmann, B. (1993). Changes in female sexual advertisement according to menstrual cycle. Paper read at the International Congress of Ethology, Torremolinos, Spain.

Grammer, K. and Thornhill, R. (1994). Human (*Homo sapiens*) facial attractiveness and sexual selection: the role of symmetry and averageness. *Journal of Comparative Psychology* **108**, 233–42.

Haig, D. (1996). Altercation of generations: genetic conflicts of pregnancy. *American Journal of Reproductive Immunology* **35**, 226–32.

Hartmann, P.E., Rattingan, S., Prosser, C.G., Saint, L. and Arthur, P. G. (1984). Human lactation: back to nature. *Symposium of the Zoological Society of London* **51**, 337–68.

Rogers, A. R. (1993). Why menopause? *Evolutionary Ecology* **7**, 406–20.

Russell, D. E. H. (1984). The prevalence and seriousness of incestuous abuse: stepfathers vs. biological fathers. *Child Abuse and Neglect* **8**, 15–22.

Singh, D. (1993). Body shape and women's attractiveness: the critical role of waist-to-hip ratio. *Human Nature* **4**, 297–321.

About the Authors

The authors have lived together since 1987 and have two children.

Dr. Robin Baker taught zoology in the School of Biological Sciences at the University of Manchester for twenty-two years. Since leaving academic life, he has concentrated on his career in writing, lecturing and broadcasting. He has published more than one hundred scientific papers and numerous books, including the international bestseller *Sperm Wars: The Science of Sex,* which was based on his own original research on human sexuality. His work and ideas on the evolution of human behavior have been featured on many television and radio programs around the world. In addition to his two children with Elizabeth, he has three from a previous relationship.

Elizabeth Oram is a graduate of the University of Manchester. She has published a number of articles in women's and wildlife magazines and is the author of five children's books. She also worked closely with her partner during his writing of *Sperm Wars.*